MONEY IN
ECONOMIC SYSTEMS

**Praeger Studies in
International Monetary Economics and Finance**

General Editors:
J. Richard Zecher, D. Sykes Wilford

MONEY IN
ECONOMIC SYSTEMS

George Macesich
and Hui-Liang Tsai

PRAEGER

PRAEGER SPECIAL STUDIES • PRAEGER SCIENTIFIC

Library of Congress Cataloging in Publication Data

Macesich, George, 1927-
    Money in economic systems.

    (Praeger studies in international monetary economics
and finance)
    Bibliography: p.
    Includes index.
    1. Money. 2. Finance. 3. Comparative economics.
I. Tsai, Hui-Liang. II. Title. III. Series.
HG221.M123   332.4   81-20977
ISBN 0-03-060428-1   AACR2

Published in 1982 by Praeger Publishers
CBS Educational and Professional Publishing
a Division of CBS Inc.
521 Fifth Avenue, New York, New York 10175 U.S.A.

Printed in the United States of America

FOREWORD
D. Sykes Wilford and J. Richard Zecher

Professors Macesich and Tsai have provided, in this book
on the role of money in various economic systems, an interesting
and detailed analysis of financial systems of several countries.
This is not unique in itself, but it is interesting that in examining
the role of money and monetary policy in various financial systems, a diverse group was chosen; i.e. the United States, Canada,
some EEC countries, as well as Sweden, the United Kingdom, and
Yugoslavia are examined. The theme as it is pointed out by
Professors Macesich and Tsai is that monetary policy is ideologically neutral and that monetary policy is relevant, no matter
what social system, economic system, or political system that
country may have. By the same token, it is certainly true that
the different "financial-political" structures will be important
in how the particular monetary policies in fact work. This is
a unique contribution to the study of money and monetary policies. There are very few books that provide such an exposition
on money across such societies. To attempt to pursue such an
undertaking is certainly, in itself, something to be congratulated.

Pursuing this goal of a better understanding of the general
nature and effects of money or monetary policy, no matter the
social system, has led Professors Macesich and Tsai to begin
where we all must begin in examination of monetary policy and
that's with the theory of money itself. Having established the
monetary framework that cuts across different socioeconomic,
legal, and political systems, one then can begin to develop a
general framework of analysis. In doing so we find as readers
of this volume, that many things that have been familiar to us
in the study of domestic money and monetary policy remain familiar, no matter the system. Indeed, the original message of
Macesich and Tsai comes back home to haunt us that money, in
itself, is neutral to the system within which it operates. The
financial environment however, plays an important role in how
monetary arrangements will affect monetary policy, and how
monetary policy, given these financial arrangements will impact
the economy. This leads Professors Macesich and Tsai to the
real world.

To obtain the real world implications of their research,
Professors Macesich and Tsai examined particular country cases
as individual institutional arrangements, and at the same time

in the context of a wider international financial system. The reader is provided with a better understanding of money and its role in economic organizations. And, money matters. It matters mainly in the sense, that whatever the form of the economy, money has a role. To analyze an economy without analyzing the importance of money in that economy is only partial analysis. One must analyze the whole system, including the effect of money and monetary policy, if one is to obtain a complete picture of the economic structure of any economy.

PREFACE

This book covers present-day monetary and financial systems in the United States, Canada, the six original European Economic Community countries, Sweden, the United Kingdom, and Yugoslavia. The theme is that monetary theory is ideologically neutral; it is relevant whatever a country's economic system. The comparative and analytical approach taken in the study is particularly useful in gathering the common threads of monetary experience in several countries. In some respects such an approach, by offering the formality of observational controls, comes closest to laboratory techniques available in most social sciences. It enables us to peek into the structure and functioning of several different monetary models.

The countries selected for inclusion in this comparative study have in common an experience of sustained, more-or-less successful economic, legal, political, and social development. Although they all share the cultural inheritance of Western civilization, their economic, political, and social systems differ in important respects. While having features in common, the countries selected represent a sufficient variety in the nature and character of their monetary and financial systems to enable us to draw meaningful conclusions about both their similarities and their differences.

The organization should be useful in teaching because comparisons between systems must integrate experience with research and theory if they are to be useful. For this reason we focus on the theoretical and empirical underpinnings derived from general monetary theory to the specific experience of individual and groups of countries. This approach recognizes that the role of money and monetary policy need not be the same in all countries, though the evidence tends to support the view that "money does matter—that any interpretation of short-term movements in economic activity is likely to be seriously at fault if it neglects monetary changes and repercussions."*

---

*Milton Friedman, "The Quantity Theory of Money—A Restatement," in Studies in the Quantity Theory of Money, ed. Milton Friedman (Chicago: University of Chicago Press, 1956), p. 3.

We are grateful to Professors Marshall R. Colberg, Dimitrije Dimitrijević, Anna J. Schwartz, Rikard Lang, Dragomir Vojnić, and Walter Macesich, Jr., for useful comments and suggestions. A note of thanks is owed to Grace Colberg, Mary Martha McWilliams, and Carol Bullock for their assistance in editing, proofreading, and typing the manuscript.

CONTENTS

Page

FOREWORD v
D. Sykes Wilford and J. Richard Zecher

PREFACE vii

LIST OF TABLES xii

Chapter

1 MONEY AND MONETARY THEORY IN
PERSPECTIVE 1

Role of Money 1
Implications 7
Notes 9

2 MONEY AND FINANCIAL FRAMEWORK 11

Financial Institutions and Economic Development 14
Demand and Supply of Financial Institutions 15
Money Market 16
Socioeconomic, Legal, and Political Systems
and Monetary Behavior 21
Problems of Independent Monetary Policy in
Common Market Countries 23
Notes 27

3 THEORETICAL FRAMEWORK 30

Framework 30
Money Demand Function 32
Money Supply Function 36
Notes 41

4 DEMAND FOR MONEY 45

Liquidity Preference Models 45
Wealth Models 54

Chapter   Page

       Permanent Income Models   62
       Notes   66

5   SUPPLY OF MONEY   70

       Friedman and Schwartz   73
       Cagan   74
       Brunner and Meltzer   75
       The Various Approaches: An Appraisal   78
       Summary   80
       Notes   82

6   MONETARY AND FINANCIAL ENVIRONMENT   85

       Canada: The Bank of Canada and Monetary
          Policy   85
       The United States   90
       Sweden, the United Kingdom, and Yugoslavia   93
       Monetary Arrangements within the European
          Economic Community   101
       Sovereignty, Money Creation, and a European
          Federal Reserve System   103
       Notes   111

7   MONEY DEMAND AND SUPPLY: EMPIRICAL
       RESULTS   115

       Statistical Tests   115
       Estimates of Money Demand Functions   117
       Estimates of Money Supply Functions   125
       The Income Velocity of Money   131
       Notes   132

8   GOALS OF MONETARY POLICY   134

       Stated Goals   134
       Limits to Monetary Policy   137
       Do Policy Goals Conflict? A Quantitative
          Analysis   139
       Notes   149

Chapter   Page

9   THE PROBLEM OF TIMING   150

     The U.S. and Canadian Experience   150
     The European Experience   159
     Notes   160

10   RULES VERSUS DISCRETIONARY AUTHORITY
     IN MONETARY POLICY   164

     The Merits   164
     Discretionary Authority and the Political-
       Administrative System   165
     Quantitative Tests for Rival Monetary Rules   166
     Quantitative Tests for Rival Monetary Rules:
       European and North American Experience
       1956–80   169
     Implications   182
     Notes   186

11   MONETARISM AND THE INTERNATIONAL
     ECONOMY: SOME OUTSTANDING ISSUES   188

     Monetarism and the Monetary Approach to
       the Balance of Payments   188
     Monetarism and Flexible Exchange Rates   190
     Notes   194

12   MONEY AND THE ECONOMIC ORGANIZATION:
     A SUMMARY VIEW   197

     Monetary Approach   197
     Money, Politics, and Ideology   208
     Notes   210

BIBLIOGRAPHY   213

INDEX   233

ABOUT THE AUTHORS   237

LIST OF TABLES

Table   Page

7.1   TSLS Estimates of Money Demand Function, 1951-80   118

7.2   Income Elasticities at Sample Mean Levels, 1951-80   120

7.3   Interest Elasticities at Sample Mean Levels, 1951-80   121

7.4 Z Elasticities at Sample Mean Levels, 1951-80   123

7.5   TSLS Estimates of Money Supply Function, 1951-80   126

7.6   Elasticities of M_1^S and M_2^S with Respect to U at Sample Mean Levels, 1951-80   128

7.7   Elasticities of M_1^S and M_2^S with Respect to r^d and r^s at Sample Mean Levels, 1951-80   130

7.8   Elasticities of M_1^S and M_2^S with Respect to v_{-1} at Sample Mean Levels, 1951-80   131

8.1   Estimates of Money Supply Function (Dewald-Johnson Model), 1956-80   144

8.2   Reaction Function of Money Supply (Dewald-Johnson Model), 1956-80   146

9.1   Specific Cycles in Canadian "Leading Monetary Indicator" and Its Relation to Canadian Cycles, 1867 to 1965   154

9.2   Monthly and Quarterly Turning Points in Rate of Change in the Canadian Money Stock, 1868 to 1908   156

10.1   Overall Tests: Average Deviation of dM/M from Ideal Values under Alternative Money Rules, Belgium, 1956-80   170

Table		Page
10.2	Overall Tests: Average Deviation of dM/M from Ideal Values under Alternative Money Rules, France, 1956–80	172
10.3	Overall Tests: Average Deviation of dM/M from Ideal Values under Alternative Money Rules, Germany, 1956–80	174
10.4	Overall Tests: Average Deviation of dM/M from Ideal Values under Alternative Money Rules, Italy, 1956–80	175
10.5	Overall Tests: Average Deviation of dM/M from Ideal Values under Alternative Money Rules, the Netherlands, 1956–80	177
10.6	Overall Tests: Average Deviation of dM/M from Ideal Values under Alternative Money Rules, the United Kingdom, 1956–80	178
10.7	Overall Tests: Average Deviation of dM/M from Ideal Values under Alternative Money Rules, Sweden, 1956–80	180
10.8	Overall Tests: Average Deviation of dM/M from Ideal Values under Alternative Money Rules, Yugoslavia, 1956–80	181
10.9	Overall Tests: Average Deviation of dM/M from Ideal Values under Alternative Money Rules, Canada, 1956–80	183
10.10	Overall Tests: Average Deviation of dM/M from Ideal Values under Alternative Money Rules, the United States, 1956–80	184
12.1	Target Practice: The United Kingdom, Canada, France, West Germany, Italy, and the United States	202
12.2	Monetary Targets and Outturns	205

MONEY IN
ECONOMIC SYSTEMS

1

MONEY AND MONETARY THEORY IN PERSPECTIVE

"Monetary theory," writes Nobel Prize winner Milton Friedman, "has no ideological content. It deals with a scientific question—how a particular social contrivance works . . . the same ideas guide monetary policy in Russia and Yugoslavia as those in Chile, Brazil and Argentina or in Germany, Great Britain and Japan."[1] In other words, monetary theory is relevant whatever a country's economic system. The issue of ideological neutrality of monetary theory is all the more important thanks, in part, to the surge of membership in the International Monetary Fund (IMF) and World Bank.[2] These organizations, and indeed the world as a whole, find themselves confronted with ideologically diverse and often highly critical member countries pushing from theory to practice ideas often at odds with received monetary theory. As a case in point, there are various proposals calling for "new" international monetary systems, many encumbered with heavy economic, political, and ideologic baggage.

Just how well received monetary theory can accommodate ideologically diverse economic systems is explored in our study of several countries during the turbulent post-World War II decades as we examine the demand and supply of money in the different economic systems of Canada, the United States, Great Britain, Sweden, Yugoslavia, and the six original member countries of the European Economic Community (EEC).[3]

ROLE OF MONEY

The role of the stock of money in determining the course of economic events has long been a source of controversy among economists. Some regard the stock of money as controlling

economic activity, while others believe that it has little consequence in determining the course of economic events.

Those economists who regard the stock of money as being
of little consequence do so for essentially two reasons: One is
that the quantity of money adapts itself to the "needs of trade"
so that it is a passive element in the economic system. Since
it is passive, some other variable must be the source of economic
disturbances. This is in fact a variation on the "real bills"
theme. The second reason is that even if it is granted that
independent changes in the stock of money can and in fact do
take place, the economic effects of such changes are unpredictable because the ratio of money to other assets is extremely
variable. In effect, income velocity behaves in an erratic manner.

Economists who regard the stock of money as an important
factor in the economy do so because of three reasons. First,
changes in the stock of money can produce substantial changes
in economic activity. Second, the ratio of money to other assets
is relatively stable and dependable so that changes in the stock
of money may have relatively predictable effects on the economy.
Third, the stock of money is capable of being controlled fairly
accurately by deliberate government policy.

These differences suggest that the issue dividing economists
according to the degree of importance they attach to the money
stock is empirical rather than theoretical. In Keynes' General
Theory, [4] to which is usually attributed the development of the
income expenditure theory, attempts are made to explain changes
in the level of economic activity by means of a limited number
of variables: the stock of money and liquidity preference determine the rate of interest; the rate of interest and the marginal
efficiency of capital determine the level of investment; and the
level of investment and the marginal propensity to consume
determine income, output, and employment. In this income
expenditure theory, the marginal propensity to consume and
the multiplier (which is equal to one divided by one minus the
propensity to consume) is considered to be a largely constant
factor. Such constancy permits us to say that when there is
an increment of aggregate investment, income will increase by
an amount that is equal to the multiplier times the increment in
investment. On the other hand, the quantity theorist would
argue that when there is an increase in the stock of money,
income will increase by an amount that is income velocity times
the increase in the money stock.

It is clear then that if the propensity to consume and thus
the multiplier were relatively stable, the income expenditure
theory would be correct in viewing investment as the key varia-

ble, just as the quantity theory would be correct in emphasizing the money stock if in fact velocity is stable. The appeal the income expenditure theory holds for some lies in the alleged stability of the multiplier. Once investment was given, the multiplier did the rest and savings, income, and employment could be easily determined.

The unfortunate aspect of the income expenditure theory is that it promoted the view that "money does not matter." This need not have been the case because the theory does assign to the stock of money an important role in determining the interest rate through the liquidity preference and so in determining investment. In practice, however, it was asserted that invest- ment was unresponsive to interest rates and emphasis was placed on the connection between two flows—investment and consumption—as the important aspects of income determination. This connection, as already noted, was the investment multiplier or the number of dollars of income associated with each dollar of investment.

The failure of the predictions of postwar income based on the stability of the multiplier provided a clue that the confidence in the stability of the multiplier was misplaced.[5] Perhaps even more important, the postwar inflations that have occurred in many countries brought about an agonizing reappraisal of the view that "money does not matter." In some countries that had innocently or otherwise adopted this view, the problem of infla- tion assumed critical proportions. Pressure on the price level in these countries was relieved only when some control over the stock of money was reestablished and after interest rates were allowed to have some degree of freedom.

Studies conducted under the general direction of Milton Friedman and David Meiselman at the University of Chicago and elsewhere shed considerable light on the empirical stability of the investment multiplier and income velocity. Briefly, these studies suggest that in the countries studied the quantity theory's income velocity is a more stable magnitude than the investment multiplier of the income expenditure theory. These results, moreover, are upheld under widely varying economic, social, and political conditions as well as for various years covered by the studies.

The methods involved in testing the empirical stability of velocity and the investment multiplier are too complicated for any extended discussion in this chapter. We shall describe as simply as possible the method of testing the results and some of their implications.

Basically the approach taken in these studies is to express the income expenditure theory and the quantity theory in their simplest forms and then to examine statistically which of the two theories is most consistent with available data. Thus the income expenditure theory is expressed in the following way: A country's income is a linear relationship of investment or, more generally, of autonomous expenditures. Similarly, the quantity theory in its simplified form states that a country's income is a linear relationship of the stock of money. As in any linear or straight-line relationship, however, two constants are required.[6] For our two theories these are a and V (income velocity) in the case of the quantity theory and α and K (multiplier) for the income expenditure theory.

From the results obtained in the United States, Canada, and other countries, it appears that the income velocity of money is empirically more stable than the investment multiplier in all periods for which the results are available, except during the early years of the Great Depression after 1929.[7] There is a consistently closer relationship between the stock of money and income than between autonomous expenditures and income, which is to say that income velocity is more stable than the investment multiplier. It is of considerable interest to note that the "Keynesian Revolution," with its deemphasis on the importance of the stock of money, occurred during the 1930s and almost precisely at the time when the income expenditure theory achieved its best historical performance.

It is true, of course, that statistical correlations by themselves tell us nothing about the direction of cause and effect. Close correlation between money and income does not necessarily mean that the direction of causality is from money to income. Indeed, such correlation may also mean that causality is from income to money or perhaps even the result of a common third factor. These and still other cases are clearly possibilities. Additional studies other than purely statistical in character are needed to judge the direction of causality. Some of these studies have already been made.[8] They suggest that on occasion changes in the supply of money can be separated from contemporary changes in income. For example, changes in the money supply brought about by currency reforms and gold discoveries are hardly associated with income changes.

What are the implications of the above results for economic theory and policy? It would seem that these implications are obvious. From the theoretical viewpoint, the quantity theory of money approach to income changes appears to be more relevant than the income expenditure theory approach. The viewpoint

of economic policy control over the stock of money is a more
effective way of influencing total money income than control
through investment or more broadly autonomous expenditures.
From the point of view of practical policy operations, this is a
fortunate result. It is far easier to predict or control the stock
of money than it is to predict or control autonomous expenditures. The stock of money is thus at one and the same time
the more potent and most easily controlled variable.

There are, however, qualifications to this conclusion that
must be taken into account. In the first place, the studies
reported on deal with relative and not absolute stability of the
investment multiplier and income velocity. In the second place,
the studies concerned themselves with average performance and
not with performance in the individual case. It is, however,
in the individual case and on the basis of absolute performance
that monetary policy must be determined. The fact that changes
in the money stock are more closely associated with subsequent
changes in income than are autonomous expenditures holds true
on the average, but may not be true in specific cases. It is
the specific case performance that is required if precise control
over the stock of money would have the desired effect of controlling aggregate money demand. Indeed, such evidence as is
available suggests that though changes in the money stock on
the average do lead to changes in economic activity, the lead
is variable. [9] Moreover, we do not have any way of knowing
beforehand what in fact it will be in any given circumstance.
Thus attempts to use changes in the money stock as a "leading
economic indicator" suggest that caution should be exercised.

Money's Effect on Output

Nominal money refers to the money stock—or the actual
dollar (dinar, pound, franc, and so on) amount of money
(currency and deposits) in the economy. Real cash balances,
on the other hand, can be thought of as the total dollar amount
of money adjusted for changes in the price levels. If, for
example, the nominal money stock stays constant but prices
double, then the amount of real cash balances in the system
can be thought of as declining by 50 percent. The quantity
theorist assumes that the nominal quantity of money can be
controlled by the monetary authorities but that the amount of
real cash balances is determined by activities within the economic
system.

The relationship between changes in nominal money and changes in real cash balances lies at the heart of the quantity theory. Increasing (decreasing) the rate of growth of the money supply is hypothesized to leave households and businesses with excess (deficient) cash balances. People have three options with which to dispose of these excess funds: They can use a portion of them to purchase credit instruments; they can use them to purchase goods and services; they can do both. Increasing the demand for goods and services will affect prices, however; this, in turn, will affect the level of real cash balances.

The extent to which an increase in nominal money leads to an increase in real cash balances depends on the extent to which prices change. Generally speaking, in periods of high unemployment—such as during a recession—increasing the amount of nominal money would be expected to increase aggregate demand and output of goods and services relatively more than prices. On the other hand, when the economy is fully employed—such as during a boom period—increases in the amount of nominal money would be expected to lead to an increase in prices.

Money's Effect on Interest Rates

The second major aspect of the quantity theory is the relationship between changes in the nominal quantity of money, prices, and interest rates. To explain this relationship, quantity theorists like to talk about three effects of changes in the rate of growth in the money supply on interest rates: the liquidity effect, the income effect, and the price anticipation effect. The magnitude of each of these effects and the time lag before they are felt depends, in part, on how fully employed the economy's resources are.

The first to be felt is the liquidity effect, which results from the fact that increasing (decreasing) the rate of growth of the money supply will leave households and businesses with more (less) money than they wish to hold. Increases cause them to shift some portion of these excess balances into credit instruments, increasing the price of these instruments and, therefore, decreasing interest rates. According to the quantity theorists, increasing the stock of money will also lead to an increase in the demand for goods and services. This, in turn, will tend to stimulate, after a three- to six-month lag, the demand for credit on the part of businesses and households. This increased demand for credit, called the income effect, leads to a decline in the price of credit instruments and to an increase in market interest rates.

In addition, the quantity theorists say the increased aggregate demand for goods and services will tend to increase prices. The amount of inflation, however, depends upon the extent to which resources are employed. More importantly, as households and businesses begin to feel the effect of inflation they tend to expect more of it. This, in turn, will add to the credit demand. If people expect prices to increase and if interest rates are low, it is logical that people will want to go into debt.

The increase in the demand for credit caused by inflationary price expectations leads to the price anticipation effect on interest rates. Lenders also come to expect inflation and, therefore, require a higher return to compensate for the expected loss in purchasing power.

As a result of this price anticipation effect, quantity theorists like to speak of interest rates as being made up of two parts. One portion of the interest rate relates to the "real" return on capital assets (assuming no expected inflation), while a second portion relates to changes in expected prices.

Let us assume that an individual anticipates no inflation and receives a 4 percent return on his investments. Now let events change and assume he anticipates 3 percent inflation to continue indefinitely. It is hard to expect this individual to be content with his 4 percent return. Instead, he will want the 4 percent he was receiving plus 3 percent additional to compensate for the expected inflation. Market interest rates thus reflect these price expectations.

This theory explains the often-heard contention of quantity theorists that increasing the money supply, while admittedly decreasing interest rates in the short run (the liquidity effect), will eventually lead to higher interest rates (the income and price effects). Because quantity theorists believe that the economy is inherently stable, they contend that the real rate of interest, as opposed to the market price of interest, does not change very much. Most of the changes, therefore, that are observed in the market rate of interest result from erratic historical changes in the money supply.

IMPLICATIONS

History, cultural patterns, ideologies, stage of development, political factors, and mutual relationships among countries all affect the monetary structure, stability, and policy formation. One cannot be sure which experience from which country is squarely applicable to another country. The evidence and analysis presented in this study, however, underscore the generality of our theoretical monetary apparatus. They suggest that money does indeed matter even within different socioeconomic and political environments.

Among the countries under study, some, such as Canada, Sweden, and Yugoslavia, are relatively small countries heavily dependent on foreign trade, with a high rate of labor force growth and capital inflow in the cases of Yugoslavia and Canada. These economies are sensitive to external disturbances. In contrast, the United States, with exports of goods and services only a small proportion of the gross national product, is less sensitive to external disturbances.

Yugoslavia is a socialist country with the financial institution being reconstructed to serve the very different functions required by a decentralized system based on individual decision making and a market mechanism. It combines the market mechanism with conceptions of property rights very different from those in the United States, Canada, Sweden, and the EEC countries. However, the concept of demand and supply of money and the experiences of advanced capitalistic countries apply almost directly to Yugoslavia. The analysis of the financial and monetary environment suggests the variety of banking systems in operation.

The definition of money also plays an important role in monetary policy formation. Since the decisions of a central bank affect the national economy by influencing the supply of money, central banks require a definition of money that is suited to their policy intentions.

Since the contribution of Friedman, most studies use "permanent income" defined as some type of average income for the income variable. In other studies, "real income" is used as the income variable. In our study real income satisfactorily plays the role of income variable. In an economy with rapid rates of growth and price inflation, the concept of "permanent income" may lose its meaningfulness in consumption decisions.

The important implication of Friedman's analysis is the nature of income that is relevant for monetary policy. Our evidence shows that monetary policy can be based largely upon real income. The fact that the income coefficients and income elasticities are so highly significant may mean that Friedman's contention in his Restatement of Quantity Theory that the quantity theory is "a theory of demand for money which is highly related to the broadly defined income" is a good theory as far as the economic situation in the countries under study during the period is concerned.[10] Our study shows that money supply, among other variables, depends on the government-controlled bank rate of interest and the short-term market interest rate. Since the latter is found to be inversely related to money demand, the stock of money becomes an endogenous variable. However, this evidence is by no means conclusive.

The economic evidence obtained suggests that: while broad as well as restricted definitions of money will yield a satisfactory demand for money function, the relevant arguments entering the function are different for the two definitions; it is the income constraint that has the stable coefficient and the high significance level; although our results are not entirely conclusive, they do nevertheless suggest the importance of the interest rate and expectations as to the future rate of change of prices on the demand for real cash balances; and money demand function is well-behaved as monetary economists suggest.

Finally, no consistent patterns are found in the monetary sector of different economic structures that would enable them to serve as a safe model for the others. This is in no way contrary to studies that have detected similarities among different economies. By judicious choice, such similarities can be observed. More basically, money is fundamentally a social phenomenon and, like all social phenomena, is subject to continuous change. What appears to be needed is not some final, excessive catalog of assets labeled money, but a flexible framework aimed at helping analysts and policy workers determine to what extent specific asset classes are functioning as money at particular points in time.[11]

NOTES

1. Milton Friedman, "Marx and Money," Newsweek, October 27, 1980, p. 95.

2. When the IMF opened its doors in 1947 it had only 39 members, the World Bank 45; by 1958 their members had risen to 67 each; by 1967 to 106; by 1980 membership stands at 140 for the IMF and 135 for the World Bank.

3. These six countries are France, the Federal Republic of Germany, Italy, Belgium, the Netherlands, and Luxembourg.

4. John Maynard Keynes, The General Theory of Employment, Interest and Money (New York: Harcourt, Brace, 1936).

5. See, for example, W. Woytinsky, "What Was Wrong in Forecasts of Postwar Depression," Journal of Political Economy 55 (April 1947):142-51, and the writings of Clark Warburton.

6. For a straight line they are a and b so that any straight line can be expressed by the relation: $Y = a + bX$. Our two theories in their simplest forms can thus be expressed: the income expenditure theory as $Y = \alpha + KA$, where Y is the country's income, α is the intercept, K is the multiplier, and A is taken as a symbol for autonomous expenditures; the quantity theory as $Y = a + VM$, where Y is the country's income, a is the intercept, V is income velocity, and M is the country's stock of money. These constants are determined arithmetically by the "method of least squares," commonly used in statistics.

7. See also George Macesich and F. A. Close, "Comparative Stability of Monetary Velocity and the Investment Multiplier for Austria and Yugoslavia," Florida State University Slavic Papers 3 (1969), and "Monetary Velocity and Investment Multiplier Stability Relativity for Norway and Sweden," Statsoknonmisk and Tidsskrift, 1969.

8. See, for example, George Macesich, "Sources of Monetary Disturbances in the United States, 1834-45," Journal of Economic History, September 1960, pp. 407-34, and The International Monetary Economy and the Third World (New York: Praeger, 1981).

9. See ibid., and George Macesich, "The Rate of Change in the Monetary Stock as a Leading Canadian Indicator," Canadian Journal of Economics and Political Science, August 1962, pp. 424-31.

10. Milton Friedman, ed., Studies in the Quantity Theory of Money (Chicago: University of Chicago Press, 1956), p. 4.

11. A. Broaddus, "Aggregating the Monetary Aggregates: Concepts and Issues," Economic Review, Federal Reserve Bank of Richmond, Virginia, November/December 1975, p. 7.

2
MONEY AND FINANCIAL FRAMEWORK

Money is only one among many kinds of financial assets that consumers, business firms, governments, and other economic units hold in their wealth portfolios, but the economist's emphasis on money per se is certainly not misplaced. Unlike other financial assets (savings deposits, savings and loan association shares, government securities, and corporate stocks and bonds, to name some of the more important monetary financial assets), money is the essential ingredient in carrying out most economic transactions. Both the supply of money and the demand for it as an asset have pervasive repercussions on economic activity.

It is not an accident that the most highly developed nations have the most completely organized monetary systems and institutions. Without a stable monetary system and without well-functioning monetary and financial institutions, trade and industry are not likely to develop and prosper.[1]

Consider the views of eighteenth- and nineteenth-century economists on the role of money in economic activity.[2] Conditions of economic instability at the beginning of the eighteenth century promoted examination of the connection between money and output. The most outstanding contributors were John Locke and John Law. In essence, they focused on the obvious fact that total monetary receipts must equal total monetary payments. Locke and Law contended that increases in the quantity of money and in the velocity of circulation not only raised prices but expanded output. Their policy prescription was to increase the quantity of money through policies designed to create a favorable balance of trade.

Richard Cantillon focused on the processes by which variations in quantity of money led to variations in prices and output—thereby providing useful insights into monetary dynamics. He also recognized what many would later point out: that nominal quantity of money is beneficial to trade only during the period in which money is <u>actually increasing</u>. Once a new equilibrium is reached, output would return to its original level only with a higher price level. This process of <u>increasing</u> the quantity of money, however, cannot last indefinitely for the reason that the process leads to an adverse balance of payments and so to an outflow of money. How to buy the benefits of the inflationary process without generating balance-of-payments problems is a monetary policy goal conflict all too familiar to contemporary society.

David Hume and Henry Thornton drew implications for monetary policy identical to those of Cantillon. Both had little confidence in a policy that would continuously increase the stock of money for any length of time. Ultimately, such a policy would lead to balance-of-payments problems. In effect, Cantillon dealt with money in transition periods, Hume with money in transition periods and comparative equilibria, and Thornton almost exclusively with the latter.

David Ricardo and John Stuart Mill focused attention on the role of money in "comparative statics" thanks largely to events in the nineteenth century. The Industrial Revolution— if one chooses to call the culmination of events and circumstances that occurred in the nineteenth century by this name—did indeed change the economic situation in the nineteenth century as compared to what went before. Cost reductions, innovations, transportation improvements, including financial, when coupled with inflation during the Napoleonic wars, underscored the importance of "real" forces. Unlike the eighteenth century when Cantillon's model appeared most applicable, Ricardo's model in which output is independent of money seemed most appropriate. In fact, Mill was straightforward in his argument that the quantity of money was unimportant provided that it was not allowed to get out of order. Economists, however, have been quick to add that money does indeed get out of order, especially during periods when its quantity undergoes rapid change. On this score both Keynes and Friedman have emphasized the importance of money.

To John Maynard Keynes, writing during the upheaval of the post-World War I period, the nineteenth-century model of Ricardo and Mill offered little in the way of guidance. Money, in fact, was out of order. The uncertainty generated by monetary disturbances affects expectations. Businessmen in turn are reluctant to undertake investment in the face of uncertainty generated by such disturbances. In effect, if rapid monetary changes have occurred in the past and are expected to be

repeated in the future—in which direction no one knows—
businessmen will refuse to bear the risk of investment.

Keynes concluded that a world of rapidly fluctuating prices
such as characterized the post-World War I era would create
uncertainty on the part of businessmen who as a consequence
would reduce investment so necessary to achievement of economic
stability. The only recourse, under the circumstances, was for
government to undertake the necessary investment. In view of
the Bank of England's preoccupation with restoring the prewar
gold parity of the pound and the willingness to accept and en-
force any price fluctuations necessary, Keynes became convinced
that Britain would have to place emphasis on means other than
monetary policy to stabilize output and prices.

Friedman also deplores the uncertainty generated by monetary disturbances, arguing that marked instability of money
accompanies instability of economic activity. They both desire
a stable growth rate in the money supply as a way of minimizing
fluctuations in prices, output, and employment. They differ,
however, in how to achieve the benefits of monetary stability.
Keynes thought that exclusive reliance on monetary policy was
unrealistic on political grounds and opted for fiscal policy.
Friedman has little confidence in the role political authorities
may play in providing monetary stability and opts from discretionary monetary and fiscal authorities to a fixed rule.

The vexing problem of unemployment combined with inflation
received an explicit and perhaps unique examination by Nobel
Prize winner F. A. Hayek.[3] His views on the possibility of a
simultaneous occurrence of unemployment and inflation were put
forward in the 1930s—not a propitious time for such views. The
times and events dominated by unemployment provided little
hearing to theories purporting to explain the simultaneous occurrence of both unemployment and inflation. The 1960s and 1970s,
however, are another matter. Keynes' views advanced for the
1930s provide little guidance to contemporary policy makers and
Hayek's view requires modification if it is to be used as an aid
to understanding the economic scene of the 1960s and 1970s.

Hayek's basic theory is that bank credit (or money supply)
expansion, by lowering the market role of interest below the
natural rate, benefits private investment at the expense of consumers, owing to a shift of resources for the production of more
producer goods. This shift reduces the supply of consumer
goods and so raises prices. Consumers are unwilling to pay
the new higher prices and are "freed" to save.

If the banking system cuts back on its credit advances to
producers, and additional savings are not forthcoming, the

market rate of interest rises to the natural rate, making additional investment unattractive. Consumer prices, however, continue to advance thanks to supply reductions and incomplete investment profits providing nothing to consumer supply. Since workers in the producer goods sector cannot readily shift to the consumer goods sector, the economy is faced with unemployment and rising prices.

Conditions have changed since the 1930s when Hayek presented his analysis. It is no longer private investment that benefits by bank credit or money supply increases at the expense of consumers, but government. For example, in the U.S. economy consumer expenditures as a percentage of GNP declined from 75 percent in 1929 to 63 percent in 1974, whereas government spending increased over the same period from 8 percent to 22 percent. On the other hand, investment that was at 16 percent of GNP in 1929 and about 15 percent in 1974 was almost the same.

FINANCIAL INSTITUTIONS AND ECONOMIC DEVELOPMENT

Historical data on most countries support the view that economic growth and development are closely associated with the growth and development of financial institutions.

The growth of an economy requires the proper allocation of resources to their most efficient uses. Resources flow from households to producers offering the highest relative price for their services. It is only with the use of money that these allocations can properly and effectively be carried out. While production is made possible by the use of money, the distribution of real income to the various segments of the economy is also accomplished with the use of money.

Though it may be possible to accomplish the task of allocation, utilization, and distribution of resources without money, the mechanism will not be as smooth as with the use of money when a society becomes more complex. The growing complexity of society requires the use of money on a very wide scale. This complexity introduces the exchange relation between one country and the rest of the world. It involves international trade with imports and exports becoming very essential to the economic life of society. This in turn requires a deepening of the use of money internally as well as externally.

Money and its concomitant financial institutions have developed gradually over a long period of time. Money in its many forms has been with us for a long time; and it has taken many forms before the present one, which cannot be regarded as final. The functions of money may be classified into two broad categories: static and dynamic. By its static function, money serves as a passive technical device ensuring a better operation of the economic system without actively influencing its trends. By its dynamic function money tends to exert a powerful influence on the trends of the price level, on the volume of production, trade, and consumption, and on the distribution of wealth. It is capable of stifling or stimulating economic and social progress.

One important question then is how does an economy become highly monetized? An answer is provided by examining the facilitating financial institutions and agencies that made the monetizing of an economy possible within a relatively short period of time. Such financial institutions and agencies are the following:

Commercial banks and their availability on a large scale
Cooperative activities of commercial banks as agents of modern economy
The existence and dynamic role of a central bank and its influence on the activities of commercial banks in providing credit
Establishment of agricultural credit and industrial development banks
Role of government in such activity as regulating financial institutions, providing minting operations, taxing and revenue collecting, and disbursing activities

DEMAND AND SUPPLY OF FINANCIAL INSTITUTIONS

One approach to the development of financial institutions places emphasis on the demand side for financial services. It is argued that as the economy grows it generates additional new demands for these services, which bring about a supply response in the growth of the financial system. Accordingly, the lack of financial institutions in a country is simply a lack of demand for their services. This approach, or "demand-following" approach as it is sometimes called, implies that finance is essentially passive and permissive. Various historical examples may be cited in support of this approach. Late eighteenth- and nineteenth-century England can be cited as an example. Un-

doubtedly strong barriers exist at times to an increased supply
of financial services in response to demand. Ready examples
are provided by the restrictive banking legislation in nineteenth-
century France and religious barriers against loans and interest
charges. Another example is provided by the abortive upswing
of Italian industrial development in the 1880s mainly because
the modern investment bank had not yet been established in
Italy. Other examples will be found in this study in the case
of U.S. banking and the restrictive influence of outmoded ideas
in the theory of money and banking. In effect, the lack of financial services inhibits effective growth patterns and processes.

Another approach emphasizes the supply side or, as it is
sometimes called, the "supply-leading" phenomenon. In essence,
this approach places emphasis on the creation of financial institutions and the supply of their financial assets, liabilities, and
related financial services in advance of the demand for them.
The supply-leading approach concentrates on the transfer of
resources from traditional sectors to the modern growth sectors
and on the promotion and stimulation of activity in the modern
sectors. Financial intermediation that transfers resources from
traditional sectors, whether by collecting wealth and saving
from those sectors in exchange for its deposits and other financial liabilities or by credit creation and forced saving, is akin
to the concept of "innovation financing." The use of the "demand-
leading" approach is a more moderate form of financial development. Its use may in fact slow economic development. It will
tend to discriminate against smaller industries and borrowers.
It lends itself, moreover, to the development of monopoly trade.

The supply-leading approach may be used to encourage
and stimulate rapid economic development by increasing monetiza-
tion of the economy. It may aid economic development and planning by channeling investible funds to certain agreed-upon
priority sectors.

MONEY MARKET

There is no standardized universally accepted definition
of the term "money market." In its broadest sense, the money
market denotes all the available facilities for borrowing and
lending money. In this sense the money market excludes the
market for long-term funds as the "capital market" and restricts
the term "money market" to the market for short-term funds.
It is in this narrow sense that money market will be used in
this study.

For an individual banker the money market provides a place where changing liquidity requirements can be accommodated; but it is much more than that. It also serves the liquidity needs of an endless variety of individuals, business, and government units, foreign as well as domestic. It is an invaluable agency for promoting the flexibility, mobility, and full utilization of a country's resources. In addition, it is the principal point of contact for actions of the central bank designed to improve the operation of the economic system.

The existence of a money market implies two essential conditions. The first is a significant volume of highly liquid assets, which in effect means assets that can be exchanged for cash quickly and without substantial loss. The second requirement is a relatively high degree of concentration, geographically speaking, in dealing in these assets. The market may and ordinarily does serve an extensive hinterland; and it is likely to have connections with other money markets. The transactions themselves, however, focus in a limited area.

In the more highly developed money markets a common characteristic is a wide variety of liquid assets, possessing different features and serving different purposes. A corresponding variety and degree of specialization is to be found among the organizations and affiliated businesses dealing in these assets. The result is likely to be a more efficient market as indicated by services performed, economy of operation, and uniformity of charges. Major money markets such as New York, London, and Paris have close connections with one another as well as with local money markets within their respective countries. They are closely integrated also with their central banks, which tend to assume the role of ultimate guarantor of liquidity or lender of last resort.

Accordingly, we may look on modern money markets as centers where highly liquid assets are bought and sold. This observation gives the key to what they are and to the basic functions they perform. It also provides the key to the institutional structure of the money market. The organization of the money market can be described in terms of three types of participants: suppliers and demanders of liquid assets, providers of ancillary services of a specialized character, and suppliers of routine mechanical services.

Suppliers and demanders of liquid assets are combined into one category, because the same participant may appear as supplier at one time and demander at another. There are, of course, exceptions to this statement. Nevertheless it is useful to view the institutional aspects of the money market in terms of demand

and supply for liquid assets. We may indicate briefly by way of illustration the major suppliers and demanders of funds in the New York money market:

	Suppliers	Demanders
Commercial banks	XX	X
Dealers and brokers		XX
Other financial corporations:		
Life insurance companies	X	
Finance companies		XX
Domestic business corporations	X	XX
Exporters and importers		XX
Foreign banks and others	XX	
Government		
Federal		XX
State and local	X	X
Federal reserve banks	XX	

The XX indicates a major role and X a minor role. The listings are not in order of importance in terms of volume. For example, the federal government is by far the largest demander of short-term funds. We have indicated whether a particular agency or business is to be regarded as supplier, demander, or both.

Commercial banks are considered primarily as suppliers of short-term credit. In the United States the so-called money market banks include the larger banks in New York City, a half-dozen in Chicago, plus perhaps 20 or so scattered throughout the country. The exact number included in this category varies inasmuch as shifts in prevailing money market conditions tend to make banks sometimes more and sometimes less money market conscious. Thus the number may rise when credit continues tight for some time and decline when it eases. By means of correspondent relations with the large city banks, the temporarily idle funds of a great number of small banks scattered all over the country are brought within the orbit of the New York money market. By the same token funds may move away from New York to the more local money markets under the attraction of yield differentials.

Of course, at the same time that some banks are supplying funds to the money market other banks may well be there as demanders of liquid assets. Thus, for example, a bank may borrow federal funds or sell Treasury or other types of assets for cash in order to replenish its reserves.

Another major category of participants in the money market consists of dealers and brokers. They require money for the purpose of carrying inventories of securities during the period when these are being distributed to the public. Government securities dealers are specialists who in fact make a market for government securities by continuously buying and selling all maturities. Of perhaps the most important dealers engaged in this business, five are banks (three in New York and two in Chicago). The role of dealers and brokers then is twofold: They are an important source of demand for short-term financing, and they themselves constitute a part of the market mechanism.

Life insurance companies are primarily suppliers of long-term funds and for that reason are more likely to participate in the capital market. At times they may also offer funds on a short-term basis while awaiting opportunity to dispose of such funds on a long-term basis.

Finance companies utilize large sums of money in connection with installment sales and personal loans. Since they find it necessary to supplement their own funds, their finance paper is offered on the market in substantial amounts.

Domestic business corporations have become important suppliers as well as demanders for short-term funds. Prior to the early 1950s there was little incentive for corporations to invest their idle funds on a short-term basis owing to the low rates that prevailed in the money market. This has changed thanks to the rise in interest rates. Many corporations now are quite alert in placing idle funds to work in the money market.

Exporters and importers have now achieved the prominence in the New York money market that they have in London, for example. Moreover, the development of other types of credit instruments in place of the trade acceptance often sent along with a bill of lading decreased further the importance of exporters and importers.

The post-World War II period witnessed a significant upsurge in the volume of short-term funds invested in the New York money market by foreign banks, international institutions, and others. A considerable part can be attributed to the expansion in the resources of the IMF with the resulting increase in its holdings in the United States.

The U.S. government, however, constitutes by far the largest net demander of short-term funds in the money market instrument in the post-World War II period and has played a significant role in this development. The Treasury bill market involves a continual turnover of maturing bills and their replacement with a new series.

The money market is entered from time to time by state and local governments in order to meet various requirements prior to receipt of tax revenues. The instrument typically used is the "tax anticipation note." They may also enter the market as suppliers of short-term funds by placing their excess cash funds in the market.

The major current and contingent supplier of funds to the money market, however, is the Federal Reserve Bank. The importance of Federal Reserve (central bank) credit operations to the money market is very significant indeed.

Suppliers of mechanical services to the money market include such routine services as telephone, telegraph, transfer, safe-keeping, maintenance of records, and printing. Mechanical and routine as they are, they are nonetheless very important and help to explain in part the concentration of money market activities in particular localities. Such concentration results in econ-omies whose effects are to lower the costs of conducting the operations of the money market.

The specialized services are those in such fields as statisti-cal bureaus, credit evaluating organizations, and securities analysis groups. These services also tend to be concentrated in large cities, partly because of the advantages of obtaining the latest detailed information by being on the scene. The New York Clearing House and similar institutions in other cities pro-vide both mechanical services and information to the money markets of which they are a part. Previously, Federal Reserve System clearinghouses provided emergency liquidity in periods of credit stringency by pooling resources and issuing highly negotiable certificates that at times even circulated as currency.

As in any market, the money market is a place where prices are determined. These prices establish the level and structure of short-term credit instruments.

A linkage exists within the structure of rates so that a major influence affecting one of the rates is likely to be felt all along the line. This means that the entire complex of interest rates tends to move more or less together, though the degree of movement may vary substantially, particularly over short periods of time.

The similar movement of interest rates may be attributed to several factors. Thus factors affecting one type of credit are likely also to influence others. There is, moreover, a high degree of substitutability among different types of credit instru-ments. The net effect is that any substantial distortion in the pattern of yields among the different types of credit may be expected to set forces in motion that will tend to correct the distortion.

The linkage of rates is, moreover, spatial in that a connection exists between rates in different parts of the country (and between countries) and among scattered money markets. Internal and international shifts in short-term funds occur if they are not prevented from doing so by various controls.

Indeed these linkages fairly well measure how developed and mature a money market is. In developed money market adjustments within the structure of rates and in relationship of rates throughout the economy, changes constantly will take place. However, they will take place rapidly and smoothly. For these reasons we would argue that in the United States and in some European countries, a developed and mature money market exists and in others it does not.

Treasury bills and federal funds provide a nearly perfect medium for adjusting the liquidity needs of commercial banks and in fact of the entire business community. Such other securities as banker's acceptance commercial paper and finance company paper contribute to the same end. Holders of idle funds can turn to the money market and there find instant employment for such funds. In effect, it is the money market that principally performs the function of facilitating the adjustment of liquidity requirements. The principal instruments for doing so are federal funds and Treasury bills.

In essence, the money market facilitates the management of earning assets. By contributing to the liquidity of assets held by the banking system it helps increase the amount of liquidity available to the entire economy.

SOCIOECONOMIC, LEGAL, AND POLITICAL SYSTEMS AND MONETARY BEHAVIOR

Those familiar with problems of comparative monetary and financial analysis are also aware of the influence a country's economic, legal, political, and social system has on the roles that money and financial institutions play. The role of money in an economy, and therefore the importance of monetary policies and institutions, depends upon the power of monetary decisions in the spending and saving decisions of households, firms, and the public or government sector to influence those real processes by which income and wealth are created and distributed. In all modern, contemporary economies this power of money to influence real processes is limited by the scope of direct administrative controls, whether they are exercised by individual decision units or by some other local or central authority. In contemporary economies these decisions concerning the real processes are implemented by some combination of monetary and administrative means.

It is necessary to distinguish between the degree of control central authorities in a country may have and the specific balance between monetary incentives and administrative controls by which these authorities need to implement their decisions. The evidence suggests that the degree of reliance that central authorities place on administrative measures as opposed to general monetary measures has tended to increase with the degree of centralized control over economic activity. Theoretically, of course, this need not be the case. Monetary incentives need not be replaced by direct administrative controls as the degree of centralization of economic decision increases. Thus central authorities with complete control over wages, prices, and the financial system, including the state budget, can so design the structure of money incentives and obligations as to force firms and households to produce any final bundle of goods and services within the productive capacity of the country's economy. The required degree of sophistication and precision on the part of monetary and financial institutions to achieve these results, however, is simply not available to any contemporary economy.

The comparative and analytical approach taken in this study is particularly useful in gathering the common threads of monetary experience in several countries. In some respects such an approach, by offering the possibility of observational controls, comes closest to laboratory techniques available in most social sciences. It enables us to peer into the structure and functioning of several different monetary models.

Few countries have elected to copy faithfully any given monetary model. In every case the monetary and financial organization is related to and has grown out of the distinctive economic, legal, political, and social traditions and the objective economic conditions of its specific environment. The Yugoslav case is an excellent illustration. Yugoslavia attempted to imitate the Soviet monetary and financial model, then, disillusioned with that, a mixed Soviet-Western model. What actually resulted is a model that in many respects is uniquely Yugoslav consonant with other Yugoslav institutions and traditions.[4] Another illustration is provided by the "Kemmerer missions" in the 1920s and their imposition of inappropriate and irrelevant central banks on countries of Latin America.

The countries selected for inclusion in this comparative study have in common an experience of sustained, more-or-less successful economic, legal, political, and social development.

While having these features in common, the countries selected
represent a sufficient variety in the nature and character of
their ideological background and in their monetary and financial
systems to enable us to draw meaningful conclusions respecting
both their similarities and their differences.

PROBLEMS OF INDEPENDENT MONETARY POLICY
IN COMMON MARKET COUNTRIES

Economic integration in a common market requires that
member nations coordinate their monetary policies to avoid
balance-of-payments difficulties, inflation, or less than maximum
employment. Indeed, monetary union is very likely the prime
requisite for a true economic union.[5] The coordination of national
monetary policies to achieve an overall program of optimum growth
for a common market community as a whole is a major problem.
Monetary measures instituted by one country have a singular
impact on other member countries and may even impede the
process of integration or harm the economic growth and stability
of member countries.

Nonmember countries can follow quite different monetary
policies, one country can pursue a contractive monetary policy
to avoid inflation while another pursues an easy monetary policy
to combat depression. Within a bona fide common market consisting of an integrated banking system it becomes difficult to
have a monetary policy that differs substantially from area to
area. It is likely that the common market would be undermined
if the monetary authorities discriminated against one of the
integrated countries.

The basic monetary problem in a common market arises
from the fact that there are two or more sovereign governments
while there can be only one source of money creation in an
effective common market. If the government of either Country
A or Country B, for example, lowers or raises expenditures,
borrowing the difference from its own banks or from central
banks, both countries may suffer inflationary consequences,
while only the first government gets what it buys with the
money. If one of the countries uses budgetary policy in a
conscious and responsible way to combat inflation, it may find
itself continually raising taxes and cutting its budget, while
the other country, which is causing the inflation by lowering
taxes and in general increasing its expenditures, is deriving
the benefits. The monetary system and the banking system,
in effect, constitute a pool of purchasing power available to

the governments of the several member countries. Understanding must be reached on how the members will share the available
purchasing power.

In essence, such an arrangement must be capable of coordinating monetary (and fiscal) policy so as to stimulate the
centralization of policy characteristic of national economies. At
the same time the operation of such a monetary system must not
prevent member countries from achieving what they view as
important domestic goals. If such goals were frustrated, secession from the monetary system and common market would very
likely occur on the part of those members who felt themselves
abused, or, at the very least, trade controls of one form or
another would be imposed, which is tantamount to secession and
disintegration. The balance between these requirements is a
very delicate one indeed, and it is particularly difficult to achieve
in the presence of nationalist aspirations on the part of culturally,
linguistically, and economically disparate member states.

Multiple Currencies under a Specie Standard and a Unified Currency System

A unified currency system or one with multiple currencies
provides possible solutions for the monetary problem created
by a common market. Interregional transactions within a single
country have much in common with international transactions
under the specie standard.[6]

In common with national currencies under a specie standard,
the currencies of the several regions of a country have a fixed
parity with one another. Interregional deficits on current
account have much the same effect on bank reserves and the
money supply as in the case of international deficits between
countries.

There is one significant difference, however. The leverage
effect of reserve changes in a region may be less within a single
country than between countries. One reason for this is the
existence of a regional central bank that may have an adequate
supply of government securities to liquidate and thus need not
reduce its deposit liabilities to member banks. In addition, the
existence of commercial banks within a country would enable
any branch to run a deficit with the main office as long as the
latter is willing to continue to make advances to the branch or
take over its earning assets.

Typically capital is assumed to be immobile internationally
and mobile between regions of a country.[7] As a consequence

the mobility of capital between regions is assumed to provide an additional equilibrating variable in the process of payments correction. This is in contrast to the standard theory of international trade, which argues that changes in price levels and changes in income are the only equilibrating variables employed in the process of payments correction.

There is reason, however, for being wary of the proposition that capital is necessarily more mobile regionally than internationally. During normal periods capital appears to be as mobile between principal financial centers as it is regionally. Indeed, funds may even move more easily in response to interest rate differentials between countries than between regions. Unlike regional centers where the range of liquid securities may be restricted, the large financial centers with highly developed securities markets may more easily attract funds owing to the existence of substantial liquid securities. This author has reported elsewhere on the problems experienced in such regional centers of the United States as Atlanta, Richmond, Kansas City, and Dallas in attracting funds.[8] In addition, the role of multinational companies in promoting international mobility of capital is often overlooked. They operate in much the same fashion as national companies with regional branches in allocating capital.

It is generally assumed that labor is more mobile between regions of a country than it is internationally. In a country in which labor is mobile a boom or depression tends to get transmitted over the whole country fairly rapidly. As a consequence economic conditions within a country tend not to be too divergent. This reduces the necessity for divergent monetary and credit policies within a country.

Labor mobility, in effect, sets limits to the extent of persistent divergencies of inflationary or deflationary pressures among different regions within a country.[9] This equalizing process is much less effective between countries to the extent that movement of labor between countries is more restricted than it is between regions of a given country. Of course the free movement of goods can transmit prosperity from area to area by its tendency to generate an import surplus. If exchange rates were adjusted between two areas for this purpose the entire process would be expedited. The movement of exchange rates, however, is precluded from our discussion. The currencies of the several regions of a given country are assumed to have a fixed parity with one another as in the case of national currencies under a specie standard. This is tantamount to fixed exchange rates.

Flexible Exchange Rates

Another possible solution to the monetary problem is to tie the common market together at the economic level with flexible exchange rates. Such an arrangement is especially suitable when a common market is to consist of culturally, linguistically, and economically disparate members. It would permit each member nation to develop its economy within the confines of its territory according to its own appraisal of possibilities. Flexible exchange rates provide an "automatic" trade-balancing mechanism, thereby eliminating the necessity for exchange and trade controls.[10] At the same time, the individual nations are freed from having to coordinate monetary (and fiscal) policies and economic development programs with other nations. Encroachment into the delicate area of national sovereignty is minimized. As a consequence, the chances for a successful common market arrangement are improved.

A system of flexible exchange rates would also help compensate for "stickiness" of wages and prices brought about by different stages of economic development among the member states of a common market. By promoting what would partially deputize for competitive price flexibility, flexible exchange rates would increase the effectiveness of the price mechanism and thus contribute to legitimate economic integration. Such an arrangement provides a means for combining interdependence among member countries through trade with the greatest possible amount of internal monetary and fiscal independence; no member country would be able to impose its mistakes of policy on others nor would it have their mistakes imposed on itself. Every country would be free to pursue policies for internal stability according to its own appraisal of possibilities. If all member countries succeeded in their internal policies, reasonably stable exchange rates would prevail. Effective intercountry coordination would be achieved without the risks of formal but ineffective coordination.

On the other hand, critics of a system of flexible exchange rates argue that an exchange rate left to find its own level will not necessarily trace out an optimum path through time. An optimum, however, is very difficult to define since its criteria hinge on the medium term and expectations that can never be guaranteed.[11] Nevertheless there is no necessity that the market per se will yield such a reasonably satisfactory rate. Moreover, in small undiversified and less developed countries, which may be members of the common market, a lack of sophisticated individuals with a heterogeneous outlook and sufficient capital may impair the working of a competitive market in foreign exchange.

Another criticism is that exchange rate adjustments will not necessarily insulate the level of domestic activity while correcting an internal balance.[12] Exchange rate adjustments are particularly desirable where price levels have moved out of line. The exchange rate correction will restore the terms of trade to their original position and leave the volume and balance of trade and real income in each country at their original levels. The units of measurement simply will be changed. This is no longer true where the sources of disturbance are structural changes in trading regions, different rates of full-employment growth in several regions joined in a common market, and cyclical income fluctuations. In effect, repercussions on domestic employment and output can be reduced but apparently they cannot be eliminated by flexible exchange rates.

The case for flexible exchange rates, however, appears to gather strength in a multinational common market where labor immobility owing to cultural differences exists or where a central government does not exist, or, if it exists, it is indifferent or incapable of assuming responsibility for easing a depressed or less developed region's adjustments. It may be just such a case that recent writers have in mind when they argue that if a common market is in effect divided into national regions, within each of which there is factor mobility and between which there is factor immobility, then each region can have a separate currency that fluctuates relative to all other currencies.[13] In this case the national region as an economic unit and currency domain coincide. Moreover, the stabilization argument for flexible exchange rates is valid when based on regional currency areas.

NOTES

1. See George Macesich, The International Monetary Economy and the Third World (New York: Praeger, 1981).

2. See, for example, J. H. Wood, in Business Review, Federal Reserve Bank of Philadelphia, September 1972. Wood argues that in fact there is but one monetary theory and it has been around for over 200 years.

3. F. A. Hayek, The Constitution of Liberty (Chicago: University of Chicago Press, 1960).

4. D. Dimitrijević and George Macesich, Money and Finance in Contemporary Yugoslavia (New York: Praeger, 1973).

5. George Macesich, Money in a European Common Market Setting (Baden-Baden: Nomos Verlagsgesellschaft, 1972).

6. Franz Gerhrels, "Monetary Systems for the Common Market," Journal of Finance, May 1959, pp. 312-21; and George Macesich, Commercial Banking and Regional Development in the United States, 1950-60 (Tallahassee: Florida State University Press, 1965).

7. J. C. Ingram argues that regions can borrow or sell securities in the national capital market more easily than countries can borrow abroad. See, for example, his contribution in Factors Affecting the United States Balance of Payments (Washington, D.C.: U.S. Government Printing Office, 1962). For a lucid discussion of these issues, see also Peter P. Kenen, "Toward a Supranational Monetary System," in Issues in Banking and Monetary Analysis, ed. G. Pontecorvo, R. P. Shay, and A. G. Hart (New York: Holt, Rinehart, and Winston, 1967).

8. See references in note 6. Macesich's observations would agree in part with those of Gerhrels, p. 313, when he writes:

National financial centers are well-developed markets
with plenty of highly liquid securities; regional
centers . . . are much less able to attract funds.
What they do instead is to liquidate government
securities or widely accepted private obligations
in the national center. An inflow of funds from
Paris to Frankfurt might normally be easier to bring
about than one from San Francisco to Kansas City.

Wilson E. Schmidt writes that before the Interest Equalization Tax a substantial portion, some guesses are as high as 50 percent, of foreign dollar public issues sold in New York were bought by foreigners. This was a way for foreigners to avoid their own inefficient markets and shift funds from low to high yields within their own areas. See his "Commentary" in I. O. Scott's paper in Pontecorvo et al., pp. 203-05.

9. See, for example, Robert A. Mundell, "A Theory of Optimum Currency Areas," American Economic Review, September 1961, pp. 657-64, and Ronald I. McKinnon, "Optimum Currency Areas," American Economic Review, September 1963, pp. 717-25. Kenen, pp. 218-20, on the other hand, argues that a diversification of output and internal labor mobility, geographic and occupational, may serve as effective substitutes for international or interregional labor mobility emphasized by recent writers. Such a diversification of output, moreover, may serve to avoid painful adjustments owing to insufficient averaging of trade-balance disturbances. In such cases significant changes in the

terms of trade may be needed to reestablish external and internal balance. See also L. B. Krause and W. S. Salant, eds., European Monetary Unification and Its Meaning for the United States (Washington, D.C.: Brookings Institution, 1973).

10. See, for example, L. B. Yeager, "Exchange Rates within a Common Market," Social Research, January 1959, pp. 415-38. George Macesich's published material relevant to the topic includes: Yugoslavia: Theory and Practice of Development Planning (Charlottesville: University Press of Virginia, 1964), "The Theory of Economic Integration and the Experience of the Balkan and Danubian Countries Before 1914," paper delivered before the First International Congress on Southeast European Studies, Sofia, Bulgaria, August-September 1966, Florida State University Slavic Papers 1 (1967), "Economic Theory and the Austro-Hungarian Ausgleich, paper prepared for the International Congress on the Austro-Hungarian Ausgleich of 1967, Proceedings of the Congress, "Inflation and the Common Market," Review of International Affairs, June 5, 1964, Money and the Canadian Economy (Belgrade: National Bank of Yugoslavia, 1967), and "Supply and Demand for Money in Canada," in Varieties of Monetary Experience, ed. David Meiselman (Chicago: University of Chicago Press, 1970).

11. See George Halm, "The Case for Greater Exchange-Rate Flexibility in an Interdependent World," and Albert G. Hart, "Commentary" in Pontecorvo et al., pp. 169-88.

12. See, for example, Gerhrels, p. 319.

13. See, for example, Mundell, pp. 663-64.

3

THEORETICAL FRAMEWORK

FRAMEWORK

The theoretical framework of this study—one that most economists would accept—is set forth by Milton Friedman in his "A Theoretical Framework for Monetary Analysis."[1] It is, moreover, a framework that suits the purpose of our study that monetary theory is ideologically neutral and thus useful in analyzing fluctuations in income and prices in a wide variety of institutional and sociopolitical arrangements.

Friedman's framework cast into a basic IS-LM apparatus can be described, briefly, as follows:

$$\frac{C}{P} = f(\frac{Y}{P}, i) \tag{1}$$

$$\frac{I}{P} = g(i) \tag{2}$$

$$\frac{Y}{P} = \frac{C}{P} + \frac{I}{P} \tag{3}$$

$$M_d = P1(\frac{Y}{P}, i) \tag{4}$$

$$M_s = h(i) \tag{5}$$

$$M_d = M_s \tag{6}$$

where C = consumption, P = price level, Y = income, i = interest rate, M_d = demand for money, and M_s = supply of money.

Friedman does not consider in dispute the demand for money equation, which is here written in a general version acceptable to most economists. At issue is the method of completing the system that has seven variables, but only six equations in it. According to Friedman the choice is either

$$P = P_0 \tag{7}$$

as in the income expenditure theory or

$$\frac{Y}{P} = y = y_0 \tag{8}$$

as in the quantity theory. The former (7) represents the case of rigid prices and the latter (8) is a statement that the economy is operational at the full employment level of real income. Equation (7), according to Friedman, does not square with available empirical evidence. The key differences between the Keynesian view and the Chicago (Monetarist) view, however, are that the Keynesian view argues that change in the quantity of money affects spending via the interest rate effect on spending, and the Monetarist view underscores wealth in portfolios and then on final spending.

Neither the quantity theory nor the income expenditure theory model is satisfactory as a framework for short-run analysis. According to Friedman this is so mainly because neither theory can explain

(a) the short-run division of a change in nominal income between prices and output, (b) the short-run adjustment of nominal income to change in autonomous variables, and (c) the transition between the short-run situation and a long-run equilibrium described essentially by the quantity-theory model.[2]

A third alternative way to determine the above system of equations is provided by Friedman in the monetary theory of nominal income.[3] This third method draws on Irving Fisher's ideas on the nominal and real interest rates and Keynes' view that the current long-term market rate of interest is expected to prevail over a long period. The Keynes and Fisher synthesis is then integrated into a quantity theory model together with the empirical assumption that the real income elasticity of the demand for money is unity and that a difference between the anticipated real interest rate and the anticipated growth of real income is determined outside the system. In effect, this is the counterpart assumption to equations (7) and (8) of income expenditure and quantity theory, respectively. The result is a monetary model in which current income is related to current and prior quantities of money.[4] This monetary model of nominal income, according to Friedman, corresponds to the broader framework implicit in much of the theoretical and empirical work that he and others have done in analyzing monetary experience in the short run and is consistent with many of the empirical findings produced in these studies.

The quantity theory of money is basically a theory of the demand for money. It is at its best when the demand for money is a stable function of a few key variables. For instance, its stability is important because it ensures that _mutatis mutandis,_ inflationary pressures from a change in the supply of money are transmitted to the general level of prices.

MONEY DEMAND FUNCTION

In the neoclassical analysis of money, the demand for money is functionally related to income, interest rates, and some types of wealth. The question of the nature of the income in the money demand function is still under debate: the current nominal income, real income, or Friedman's permanent income. The nature of the interest rate also commands attention: the short-term or long-term government bond rate, or the money market rate on private debt. In effect the arguments or variables that enter the demand function for money, and the definition of the quantity of money appropriate for the demand function, have received substantial attention in both the recent and distant past. A number of studies seem to suggest that in the long run the demand-for-money function may not be "stable." To judge from some of these studies the function shifts over different phases of the cycle, and no unique and stable function would therefore be obtained.[5]

Money is one of the forms in which an individual can hold his assets. In some economies, a small interest income is to be had from assets that are also used as money, but the desire to hold cash cannot be explained by this fact. There are many instances of money yielding no interest and being held neverthe-less. Two peculiar and interrelated characteristics of money have usually been emphasized in theories that set it apart from other assets. The first is that money is acceptable as a means of exchange for goods and services, and the second is that its market value is generally highly predictable. These two charac-teristics are not the exclusive property of money. Other assets also possess them in varying degrees. However, unlike other assets, money is universally accepted as a means of exchange, and its value is usually more predictable than that of other assets. It is argued that the three motives introduced by Keynes are the transactions, the precautionary, and the speculative motives. Keynes said, in developing in detail the motives to liquidity preference, that the subject was "substantially the same as that which has been sometimes discussed under the heading of the Demand for Money." Continuing, he may be quoted as follows:

> It [the analysis of the motives to liquidity preference] is also closely connected with what is called the income-velocity of money—for the income-velocity of money merely measures what proportion of their incomes the public chooses to hold in cash, so that an increased income-velocity of money may be a symptom of a decreased liquidity preference. It is not the same thing [as the analysis of the motives to liquidity preference], however, since it is in respect to his stock of accumulated savings rather than his income, that the individual can exercise the choice between liquidity and illiquidity.[6]

Keynes postulated that the level of transactions undertaken by an individual and also by the aggregate of individuals would be in a stable relationship to the level of income, and hence that the so-called transactions demand for money would be proportional to the level of income. The use of the term "transaction motive," however, was confined to describing the necessity of holding cash to bridge the gap between the receipt of payments and the disbursement of such proceeds, or to bridge the interval between purchase and realization.

The precautionary motive according to Keynes concerns the two aspects of the demand for balances: the demand for cash as a proportion of assets "to provide for contingencies requiring sudden expenditure and for unforseen opportunities of advantageous purchases . . .," and the demand for an asset whose "value is fixed in terms of money to meet a subsequent liability (for example, bank indebtedness) fixed in terms of money. . . ."[7] Keynes suggested that the demand for money arising from the precautionary motive would also depend largely on the level of income.

Marshall and Pigou had suggested that uncertainty about the future was one of the factors that might be expected to influence the demand for money, and Keynes' analysis of the speculative motive represents an attempt to formalize one aspect of this suggestion and to draw conclusions from it. Keynes said:

> The aggregate demand for money to satisfy the specu-
> lative motive usually shows a continuous response to
> gradual changes in the rate of interest, that is, there
> is a continuous curve relating changes in the demand
> for money to satisfy the speculative motive and
> changes in the rate of interest as given by changes
> in the price of bonds and debts of various maturities.[8]

Furthermore, he said, it is "important to distinguish between changes in the rate of interest . . . due to changes in the supply of money . . . and those which are primarily due to changes in expectations affecting the liquidity function itself."[9]

Accordingly, Keynesian theory of liquidity preference separates the demand for money into two parts:

$$M^D = L_1 (Y) + L_2 (r) \qquad (9)$$

The first part, $L_1 (Y)$, based on transactions and precautionary motives, is treated as a function of income and the second part, $L_2 (r)$, is based on speculative motives as a function of the interest rate. This analytical breakthrough by Keynes was significant in that it placed the demand for money in a behavioral framework consistent with the concept of utility maximization in an uncertain world and away from the restrictive notion of institutionally determined payments schedules. Later economists, however, have found that the demand for transactions balances was also interest elastic.[10] Since the alternative to holding cash for transactions purposes in short-run assets or time deposits, their rate of return should, therefore, influence the money demand and the short-term rate of interest should be treated as an argument in the demand function for money.

Moreover, people's behavior in holding cash balances is affected not only by the transactions, precautionary, and speculative motives as dictated by the Keynesian theory, but also by their expectation of changes in the price level.[11] An individual's alternative cost of carrying over his wealth from one period to the next in the form of cash balances is the profit that he could obtain by carrying over this wealth in the form of other assets such as commodities and bonds.

The profit that can be obtained by carrying over a bond is measured by the rate of interest. Similarly, the profit that can be obtained by carrying over commodities is measured by the anticipated rate of increase in prices. Hence just as we assume a negatively sloping demand curve for money as a function of the rate of interest, so can we assume one as a function of the rate of price increase. In both cases the negative slope expresses the fact that the higher the alternative cost of holding cash balances, the smaller the amount demanded.[12]

This symmetry between the rate of interest and the rate of price increase brings out the fact that even the existence of certain anticipations of a price increase will not cause an absolute flight from cash. Instead, just as in the case of the interest rate, it will simply cause the individual to adjust his holdings of real cash balances so that the marginal utility of the liquidity they provide compensates him for the opportunity costs of holding these balances.[13]

Therefore, the expected rate of change of the price level must be interpreted as an expected rate of return on money holding and, other things being equal, the higher is the expected rate of return to money holding the more of it will be held and the lower it is the less will be held. Thus the expected rate of change of the price level becomes a potentially important variable in the demand-for-money function. Since the actual rate of change in prices of the immediate past is probably the basic determinant of present expected change in prices, for simplicity, the former may be substituted as an argument explaining the demand for money. Thus, the demand for money may assume the basic form

$$\frac{M}{P} = f(r^s, \frac{Y}{P}, Z) \qquad (10)$$

where M^D is nominal money stock, P is the price level, r^s is the short-term market rate of interest, Y/P is the real income, and $Z = (P - P_{-1})/P_{-1}$ is the rate of changes in the price level. In equation (1) partial derivatives of M^D/P with respect to r^s and Z are expected to be negative, and with respect to Y/P to be positive.

MONEY SUPPLY FUNCTION

The pure theory of the demand for money assumes that the nominal supply of money is given and is varied at the discretion of the monetary authorities and government. Demand theory sets out to analyze the effects on general equilibrium of a change in the nominal quantity of money or of a change in demand for money arising from an exogenous change in tastes. This also explicitly assumes that the monetary authorities and government can control the nominal quantity of money. In contrast to this view there is a school that sees the money supply responding to demand; it therefore concludes that there is no point in attempting to control the economy by monetary policy. Hence, a theory of money, if it is to be consistent, requires that supply be determined independently of the money demand, and if the theory is to be of use, it must allow that the central bank can control the quantity of money in the hands of the public. [14]

Early theories of money supply developed a mechanistic approach that did not allow for the possibility of ratios being behavioral functions of economic variables. This stage of the theory's development is evocative of early quantity theory and Keynesian multiplier analysis. There is now considerable evidence showing that the supply of money can be expressed as a function of a few variables. [15] Basically, these functions are two types: Brunner and Brunner and Meltzer consider money supply as a function of the monetary base, currency-deposit ratio, and reserve-deposit ratio. [16] They contend that, with the monetary base given, the current rate of interest can have very little effect on the supply of money. In contrast, Teigen, Goldfeld, Smith, Modigliani, Rasche, and Cooper, and Bhattacharya attach importance to the interest rates. [17] The ability of banks to vary the level of excess and borrowed reserves they wish to hold provides an important reason for treating the money supply as an endogenous variable. The interest responsiveness of excess and borrowed reserves implies a supply function of money that is similarly responsive. To allow for this dependence Teigen has estimated a relationship in which the money supply is made a function of certain Federal Reserve parameters and of interest rates. While the study by Goldfeld is "a slightly high-order approach" in that he derives the money supply from bank behavior, a function of the Teigen-type is implicit in his model. In particular,

> when studies of money-supply determination are reviewed, two main theories emerge. One is that in

general there is a stable relationship between the
money supply by controlling total reserves of the
banking and monetary system. The other main theory
is that in the United States the volume of member-
bank borrowing from the Federal Reserve System and
the volume of excess reserves of the member banks
(or the net of these two in "free" reserves) influence
bank behavior in such a way that the rate of change
of bank deposits and money supply can be predicted
from these variables. An implication of the second
main theory for the operation of a central bank is
that attention should be focused on excess reserves
and borrowings, or on free reserves, rather than on
total reserves in attempting to control the money
supply.[18]

The two main theories are not so clearly alternative to one
another as they might at first seem to be. Each contains useful
insights regarding the behavior of the monetary system. If
they are combined, each of them may contribute an essential
element of a more satisfactory explanation of changes in money
supply than can be obtained from either of them separately.

In this section, we develop a way to incorporate variation
in excess reserves and borrowings, or in the two as combined
in free reserves, in a theory of money supply determination.
By so doing, we attempt to synthesize the two basic approaches
described above.

The derivation of the money supply model proceeds as
follows: monetary base, H, or high-powered money as it is
frequently referred to, is defined to include all monetary assets
capable of being used as banking reserves, and it is represented
by

$$H = C + R \tag{11}$$

where R = high-powered money inside the banks, that is, banking reserves, and C = high-powered money outside the banks,
that is, currency supplied by government. C is defined as

$$C = C_p + C_b \tag{12}$$

where C_p = currency held by the nonbank public and C_b =
currency held by commercial banks. Similarly, total bank
reserves, R, are defined as[19]

$$R = R_r + R_e \tag{15}$$

where R_r = required reserves of member banks, and R_e = excess reserves of member banks. Money supply, M_q^W, is defined as

$$M_1^S = C_p + DD \tag{16}$$

or

$$M_2^S = C_p + D \tag{16^1}$$

where DD refers to demand deposits and D the sum of demand and time deposits.

Whether the definition of money supply (16) or (16^1) is used, the arguments will remain the same; but the data on R_r will be different for demand deposits and aggregate deposits. Without loss of generality, we further assume that the public desires to hold a fixed proportion $g(0 < g < 1)$ of money supply in currency, and that the banking system maintains a fixed cash-deposit ratio $n(0 < n < 1)$, then we get

$$C_p = g_1 M_1^S \tag{17}$$

or

$$C_p = g_2 M_2^S \tag{17^1}$$

and

$$C_b = n_1 DD = n_1(M_1^S - C_p) \tag{18}$$
$$= n_1(1 - g)M_1^S$$

or

$$C_b = n_2 D = n_2(M_2^S - C_p) \tag{18^1}$$
$$= n_2(1 - g)M_2^S$$

If k is the required reserve ratio $(0 < k < 1)$, then we can write

$$R_r = k_1 DD = k_1(M_1^S - Cp) \tag{19}$$

or

$$R_r = k_2 D = k_2(M_2^S - C_p) \tag{19^1}$$

Here we note that if k, g, and n are constant, the authorities can control the money supply by fixing monetary base, H. However, if H is held constant and k, or g, or n changes, then the money supply does not remain constant. The reserve-deposit ratio rises as commercial banks keep larger reserves to ensure solvency in the face of increased uncertainty.

Thus, the money supply at any moment in time is the result of a portfolio decision by the central bank, by the commercial banks, and by the public. Whether the central banks, by controlling the monetary base, can actually achieve fairly precise control over the money supply depends on whether the link between the monetary base and bank reserves and between bank reserves and the money supply (the monetary base-bank reserves-money supply linkage) is fairly tight and therefore predictable. If there is a tight linkage the monetary authorities can formulate their policies and achieve any particular target for the money supply; on the other hand, if there is significant and unpredictable slippage, and the central bank control over the money supply is not sufficiently precise to achieve a given target, it will necessarily have to formulate its policies in terms of other variables that it can control. The variable used to define the central bank's objective, or to implement its policy decisions, must therefore be one that it can control within reasonable limits. [20]

Let U be the unborrowed monetary base, defined as

$$U = H - R_b \tag{20}$$

where R_b refers to the borrowings by commercial banks from the central bank. Then, from (2) through (9), we obtain

$$U_1 = C_p = C_b + R_b + (R_e - R_b) \tag{21}$$

$$= (g + n - ng + k - kg)M_2^S + R_f$$

where $R_f = R_e - R_b$ is free reserves.

Free reserves are used in this discussion rather than the component excess reserves and borrowings in part for convenience in exposition and in part because there are plausible theoretical grounds for this procedure. The question will be kept open as to whether excess reserves and borrowings should be treated separately or combined in free reserves.

Member banks hold excess reserves because they want to be able to meet the cash demands of their depositors without drawing down their legal reserves and hence incurring a penalty cost on reserve deficiencies. Excess reserves, however, are nonearning assets. The opportunity cost to the banks is the yield they must give up by not acquiring an earning asset such as government securities.

Banks are supposedly discouraged from borrowing from the central bank except to meet unexpected short-term contingencies. Nevertheless, there is some interest elasticity with respect to the discount rate.[21] If the discount rate is substantially below the yield that can be earned on short-term government securities, commercial banks will prefer to borrow from the central bank instead of selling these securities. Thus the lower the discount rate relative to short-term market interest rates, the lower will be the level of free reserves if the central bank does not take offsetting measures. That is, the level of the discount rate determines to some extent whether banks sell short-term securities or draw down their excess reserves.

> Banks will prefer to decrease their reserves by a greater amount the larger the (positive) spread between short-term interest rates and the discount rate, and they will sell more bills the smaller this spread. Because there is often considerable hesitancy about continued borrowing from the Fed, one would not expect the effects of changes in each interest rate to be symmetrical. A change of 1 percent in the short-term rate should have a greater effect on banks' reserve position than a change of 1 percent in the discount rate. . . . But changes in both rates exert an influence on bank behavior.[22]

Without specifying the direction of causality between the discount rate and the short-term interest rate, the free reserves function can be treated as a function of the discount rate (r^d) and the short-term market rate of interest (r^s).[23] Free reserves will also vary with the lagged reserve ratio of commercial banks, v_{-1}, defined as the ratio of the holdings of reserves by banks to their deposit at the beginning of each year. v_{-1} is a lagged endogenous variable as its components are all determined within system.[24] These considerations suggest that the free reserves function may assume the basic form

$$R_f = h^*(r^d,\ r^s,\ v_{-1}) \tag{22}$$

In equation (22) partial derivatives of R_f with respect to r^d and v_{-1} are expected to be positive, and with respect to r^s to be negative Combining equations (21) and (22) and solving for M_q^S, $q = 1$, 2 we obtain the basic form of money supply function

$$M_q^S = h(U, r^d, r^s, v_{-1})\tag{23}$$

In equation (23) partial derivatives of M_q^S with respect to U and r^s are expected to be positive, and those with respect to r^d and v_{-1} to be negative.

If free reserves are assumed to be linear of the basic form

$$R_f = a_0 + a_2 r^d - a_3 r^s + a_4 v_{-1}\tag{24}$$

then we get the money supply function as

$$M_q^S = 1/m(-a_0 + a_1 U - a_2 r^d + a_3 r^s - a_4 f_{-1})\tag{25}$$

where $q = 1$, 2, and $m = (g + n - ng + k - kg)$.

The money supply function postulated in equation (25) differs from the money supply functions derived by Teigen and others. Teigen has distinguished the actual from the potential money supply; but this is not the case of equation (25). It also differs from that of Bhattacharya, who has introduced the differential between the discount rate and a short-term market interest rate as an explicit variable.

NOTES

1. Journal of Political Economy 78 (April/May 1970):193–238; "A Monetary Theory of National Income," Journal of Political Economy 79 (April/May 1971):323-37.

2. Friedman, "A Theoretical Framework for Monetary Analysis."

3. Friedman, "A Monetary Theory of National Income."

4. Ibid.

5. H. P. Minsky argues in his paper entitled "Central Banking and Money Market Changes," Quarterly Journal of Economics 71 (May 1957) that innovation in the money market may be responsible for such shifts. On the other hand, see Scott E. Hein, "Dynamic Forecasting and the Demand for Money," Review, Federal Reserve Bank of St. Louis, June-July 1980, pp. 13-23. Hein rejects the notion of a constantly shifting

money demand relationship and concludes that money is a useful policy instrument. Innovation has had little effect on the demand for money over the past decade.

6. John Maynard Keynes, The General Theory of Employment, Interest and Money (New York: Harcourt, Brace, 1936), p. 194.

7. Ibid., pp. 170-71 and 195-97.

8. Ibid., p. 197.

9. Ibid.

10. In his later writings Keynes did permit the rates of interest to affect L_1 () as well as L_2 (); see his "Theory of the Rate of Interest" (1937), as reprinted in the Readings in the Theory of Income Distribution, ed. W. Feller and B. F. Healey (Philadelphia, 1946), p. 422.

11. Milton Friedman, "The Demand for Money—Some Theoretical and Empirical Results," Journal of Political Economy 67 (June 1959):327-51; R. Selden, "Monetary Velocity in the United States," in Studies in the Quantity Theory of Money, ed. Milton Friedman (Chicago: University of Chicago Press, 1956); D. Laidler, The Demand for Money: Theories and Evidence (Scranton, Pa: International Textbook Co., 1969), pp. 106-97; and Lawrence B. Smith and John W. L. Winder, "Price and Interest Rate Expectations and the Demand for Money in Canada," Journal of Finance, June 1971, pp. 671-82.

12. Don Patinkin, Money, Interest, and Prices, 2d ed. (New York: Harper & Row, 1965), pp. 144-45.

13. Ibid., p. 145.

14. Harry G. Johnson, Macroeconomics and Monetary Theory (London: Gray-Mills Publishing, 1971), p. 135.

15. For a survey of this evidence, refer to A. J. Meigs, Free Reserves and the Money Supply (Chicago: The University of Chicago Press, 1962), and P. H. Hendershoot and F. De Leeuw, "Free Reserves, Interest Rates and Deposits: A Synthesis," Journal of Finance 25 (June 1970):599-614.

16. Karl Brunner, "A Schema for the Supply Theory of Money," International Economic Review, January 1961, pp. 79-109; Karl Brunner and Allan Meltzer, "Predicting Velocity: Implications for Theory and Policy," Journal of Finance, May 1963, pp. 319-54.

17. Ronald L. Teigen, "Demand and Supply Functions for Money in the United States: Some Structural Estimates," Econometrica, October 1964, pp. 476-509; Stephen M. Goldfeld, Commercial Banking Behavior and Economic Activity: A Structural Study of Monetary Policy in the Post-war United States (Amsterdam: North-Holland, 1966); P. E. Smith, "Money Supply

and Demand: A Cobweb?" International Economic Review, February 1967, pp. 1-11; F. Modigliani, R. H. Rasche, and J. P. Cooper, "Central Bank Policy: The Money Supply and the Short Term Rate of Interest," Journal of Money, Credit and Banking, May 1970, pp. 168-218; and B. B. Bhattacharya, "Demand and Supply of Money in a Developing Economy: A Structural Analysis for India," Review of Economics and Statistics 56 (1974):502-10.

18. Meigs, p. 1.

19. In the United States, currency held by commercial banks (vault cash) can also be counted as required reserves. It can also be used for excess reserves. In this case, high-powered money is defined as

$$H = C_p + R \tag{13}$$

where total bank reserves, R, are then defined as

$$R = R_r + R_e + C_b \tag{14}$$

In either case, the definition of high-powered money is not changed.

20. David I. Fand, "Some Issues in Monetary Economics," Review, Federal Reserve Bank of St. Louis, January 1970. It is for this reason that we have treated the unborrowed monetary base as the policy variable.

21. Goldfeld, pp. 43-50.

22. Michael K. Evans, Macroeconomic Activity (New York: Harper & Row, 1969), pp. 314-15.

23. The relationship between free reserves and the interest rates and discount rates developed here is analogous to that by Meigs, Goldfeld, Teigen, and Bhattacharya. Based on his empirical evidence, Meigs concludes that the free reserves ratio is functionally related to market rate of interest and the discount rate. Bhattacharya assumes free reserves to be an increasing function of the differential between the discount rate and a short-term market rate of interest. If anything, borrowing is sometimes held to be a function of that differential. If that differential widens, banks may borrow additional funds, but they do not necessarily retain those funds as resources.

24. The studies that have related quantities of reserves supplied to the banking system to changes in volume of earning assets or deposits of the banks are: George Horwich, "Elements of Timing and Response in the Balance Sheet of Banking, 1953-55," Journal of Finance, May 1957, pp. 238-55; Allan H. Meltzer, "The Behavior of the French Money Supply: 1938-54," Journal

of Political Economy, June 1959, pp. 275-96; and Stephen L. McDonald, "The Internal Drain and Bank Credit Expansion," Journal of Finance, December 1953, pp. 407-21. An extensive discussion bearing on the reserve ratio and free reserves is given by Albert E. Burger, The Money Supply Process (Belmont, Calif.: Wadsworth, 1971), pp. 24-72. Reference should also be made to Meigs' discussion on free reserves and the money supply.

4

DEMAND FOR MONEY

LIQUIDITY PREFERENCE MODELS

Empirical studies of the demand for money are a succession of attempts to evaluate competing theories' correspondence to date. Each different theory will imply a different form of the demand-for-money function. They differ either by postulating different explanatory variables or by postulating different values for the parameters. The competing theories may be classified into three broad groups: "Keynesian" liquidity-preference models, "wealth" models, and "permanent income" models of the demand for money.

The degree of emphasis placed on the demand functions for money has depended to a large extent on the theoretical inclination of the model builder. In an attempt to determine empirically the importance of money's influence on key economic variables, monetary economists have conducted a number of econometric studies of the demand for money during the past decades.

In the early studies by A. Kisselgoff and James Tobin and in somewhat later work by M. Bronfenbrenner and T. Mayer, attempts were made to test a very faithful version of the Keynesian theory by estimating a relationship between "idle balances" and interest rates.[1] It was assumed that only the demand for the idle balances was responsive to the rate of interest; the problem tackled was to measure the degree of responsiveness involved here. By constructing data on idle balances, these writers were successful in finding an empirical liquidity-preference relationship much like that postulated by Keynes.

More significant and more in line with modern liquidity preference theory[2] are those studies by C. F. Christ and H. A. Latane,[3] which are concerned with the hypotheses that total

45

money balances rather than idle balances are interest-elastic.
These studies estimate functions relating velocity of circulation
to interest rates, and they have obtained results that give
strong support to the liquidity-preference hypothesis. In his
two articles appearing in the Review of Economics and Statistics
in 1954 and in 1960, Latane attempted to isolate a stable relationship between M/Y, proportionate cash balances, and r, the
long-term rate of interest. The period covered in the first
study was 1919-52. Latane began with the following demand-
for-money function.

$$M^D/P = aY + bY \cdot r^{-1} \tag{1}$$

from which the function

$$M^D/PY = a + b(1/r) \tag{2}$$

was derived. Using regression analysis, Latane found that the
parameter, b, was significantly positive, indicating that the
demand for money is negatively related to the interest rate.
The equation fitted seemed to have some predictive power over
data generated outside the time period to which it was initially
fitted.

The two demand-for-money functions that Latane actually
tested statistically were:

$$M/Y = c/r + d \tag{3}$$

and

$$1/r = g(M/Y) + h \tag{4}$$

where M is demand deposits adjusted plus currency in circulation,
Y is gross national product, r is the interest rate on high-grade
long-term corporate obligations, and c, d, g, and h are parameters. Equation (3) states that the proportion of income that is
held in the form of currency and demand deposits is a linear
inverse function of the interest rate. The demand for money
is considered to be constrained by money income, and it is
implied that the equation is homogeneous of first degree in
income. Latane bases the latter assumption on statistical data.
He does not, however, test the homogeneity assumption explicitly.

Equation (4) reverses the direction of causality and makes
the rate of interest depend upon proportionate cash balances.
By the least-squares method, Latane derives the following
regression equations:

$$M/Y = .0074328/r + .108874 \qquad (3^1)$$

and

$$1/r = 111.775(M/Y) - 7.233 \qquad (4^1)$$

These equations exclude the years 1932, 1933, 1942, 1946, and 1947, because they were not considered representative. The coefficient of correlation is .87173.

In his later article Latane extended his analysis forward by more than six years (through 1958) and back to 1909.[4] In this study, Latane estimated a log-linear demand-for-money function of proportionate cash balances and the long-term rate of interest. The variables were defined as in the earlier study. He found some consistency of his regression equations with the hypothesis that there existed a relatively constant interest elasticity of the demand for cash balances of about .85, with the correlation coefficient of .88. Latane was thus able to find a stable long-run demand relationship defining money as currency plus demand deposits.

A drawback to these tests is that

> they each assume that the demand for money is pro-
> portional to the level of income, a postulate that
> would be challenged by those that regard wealth as
> a more appropriate variable to include in the demand-
> for-money function as well as by those who suspect
> that there may be economies of scale in money hold-
> ing.[5]

Apart from generally applicable criticisms, these studies have the special weakness of constraining the income elasticity of demand for money to be unity.[6] This assumption of unitary income elasticity would lead one to expect equal percentage changes in the demand for money and income and should have been tested explicitly. Even so, the consistency with which they point to the significance of the interest rate as a deter-minant of the demand for money is impressive. Two particularly advanced studies by A. M. Khusro and R. J. Ball have estimated equations that are more sophisticated developments of Keynes' hypothesis.[7]

A major theoretical development of liquidity preference in the post-Keynesian era was to recognize that wealth should be an argument of the demand functions.[8] Bronfenbrenner and Mayer extended a Keynesian liquidity preference equation to

include a wealth variable.[9] Their results, however, fail to
support any strong conclusions. In their joint study of the
demand function for money in the U.S. economy during the
period 1919-56, Bronfenbrenner and Mayer, by modifying Tobin's
method,[10] first analyze aggregate liquidity functions using total
money balances and idle balances as alternative dependent variables, and once using interest rate and wealth as independent
variables and once using last year's idle balances as a third
independent variable. They further disaggregate the demand
function for money by major holders, with major emphasis on
year-to-year changes. By so doing, they attempt to provide
answers to five fundamental questions concerning the demand-
for-money function:

> (1) Is there a definite observable liquidity function,
> i.e., a relation between money holdings and interest
> rates? (2) Assuming this function to exist, what is
> its interest-elasticity? (3) Assuming this interest
> to exist, what is its stability over time? (4) If shifts
> over time are observed, what are their causes, i.e.,
> what other variables are important? (5) Does the
> liquidity function appear to impose an observable
> floor to interest rates?[11]

In their empirical testings, Bronfenbrenner and Mayer use
the four-six month commercial paper rate to represent the yield
on alternative assets, because "beside being available readily,
this rate is nearly free of risk and appreciation factors, and it
is also more sensitive to economic changes than are longer term
rates."[12] The second independent variable used is the logarithm
of national wealth. For this variable, the authors use Goldsmith's
series on total national wealth in 1929 prices. Government-
owned assets wealth was not excluded, but rather used as a
proxy for the government securities omitted from the wealth
of the private sector. The third independent variable used
is the logarithm of prior year idle balances.

Bronfenbrenner and Mayer made three separate statistical
estimates of the demand-for-money functions. The first two
were estimates of the demand for idle balances and employed
the modified Tobin technique. Income was not one of the independent variables. The third was an estimate of the demand
for all private cash balances, and income was one of the independent variables. The first two estimates differ in that the
first includes the years 1926 and 1927, while the second excludes
them.

Using the ordinary least-squares method, Bronfenbrenner and Mayer obtained the following results:

$$\ln M_t^i = -4.2066 - 0.5304 \ln r_t + 1.6849 \ln W_t \qquad (5)$$
$$+ 0.5416 \ln M_{t-1}^i$$

$$\ln M_t^i = -1.9552 - 0.2772 \ln r_t + 0.8269 \ln W_t \qquad (6)$$
$$+ 0.7158 \ln M_{t-1}^i$$

$$\ln M_t^T = 0.1065 - 0.0928 \ln r_t - 0.1158 \ln W_t \qquad (7)$$
$$+ 0.7217 \ln M_{t-1}^T + 0.3440 \ln Y_t$$

where M_t^i and M_{t-1}^i are current and lagged idle balances, M_t^T and M_{t-1}^T are current and lagged total money balances, respectively, r_t is the current short-term interest rate, W_t is current national wealth, and Y_t is current GNP. Equation (6) omits the years 1926 and 1927. The multiple coefficients of correlation are .901, .978, and .997, respectively.

The statistical fits are obviously close. All variables except the wealth variable, W, are statistically significant at the 1 percent level. All elasticity coefficients except that of wealth in equation (7) have the signs suggested by theoretical considerations. The negative wealth-elasticity in equation (7) represents the extreme opposite of Friedman's conclusion that money is a luxury. While not statistically significant, according to Bronfenbrenner and Mayer, it suggests that "money may be an 'inferior asset,' of which people hold less as their wealth (and credit worthiness) increases."[13]

A more plausible explanation of the unexpected result of the negative elasticity for wealth is that the use of wealth and income simultaneously in the money demand function results in a high degree of multicollinearity, such that little significance should be attached to these particular income and wealth coefficients. It is curious that Bronfenbrenner and Mayer did not mention this possibility.

The interest rate plays a relatively small role in the demand functions for money in the Bronfenbrenner-Mayer study presented above, particularly in the total-balances function. They report that

the interest elasticity . . . the nub of liquidity
theory, is estimated at between 0.3 and 0.5 for
idle balances. . . . There is no evidence for the
proposition that any of these elasticities goes to
zero for high rates of interest or for the proposition
that some 'floor' or 'bottom stop' exists for interest
rates at which the elasticity goes to infinity.[14]

That the interest elasticity is lower for total balances than for
idle balances is to be expected from traditional economic theory
as "transactions" or "working" balances have usually been considered to be quite interest inelastic. The relatively low interest
elasticity of the Bronfenbrenner-Mayer functions, however, is
at variance with the results obtained by Latane. This divergence
may be due, in part, to the fact that Latane used a long-term
rate of interest in his analysis, whereas Bronfenbrenner and
Mayer employed a short-term rate. Bronfenbrenner and Mayer
are criticized on this issue by Robert Eisner, who argued that
a long-term rate is more appropriate because "the Keynesian
theory about the demand for money tending to become 'absolute'
at low rates of interest applies to long-term rates," and the
efficacy of monetary policy in influencing economic activity can
better be ascertained with reference to long-term rates.[15] Eisner
provides empirical evidence to show that the Bronfenbrenner-
Mayer idle balances are considerably more interest elastic with
respect to the long-term interest rate than they are with respect
to the short-term rate,[16] which is not surprising since the long-
term rate is less volatile than the short-term rate.

Utilizing additional data for the same 1916-56 period along
with the original series that Bronfenbrenner and Mayer used
in their study, Eisner refutes the Bronfenbrenner-Mayer conclusion that their data do not provide evidence for the existence
of a liquidity trap. Eisner points out that "measurement of
appropriate elasticities and slopes does in fact give strong support to the Keynesian proposition 'that some "floor" or "bottom
stop" exists for interest rates.'"[17] Eisner's particular criticism
serves to bring out the fact that the definition of "liquidity
trap" is not unequivocal. He points out that constant elasticity
of demand, such as is given by the relation

$$\ln M^D = a + b \ln r \tag{8}$$

where b is assumed to be less than zero, is consistent with the
liquidity trap, for in arithmetic form this would appear as

$$M^D = A/\alpha^{-b} \qquad\qquad (9)$$

and clearly as r goes to zero, M^D goes to infinity.
Eisner further argues that

> evidence that the elasticity goes to infinity or even
> gets larger at lower interest rates is quite unnecessary
> for the proposition that the money demanded goes to
> infinity as the interest rate is lowered. Findings that
> the elasticity does not get smaller in absolute amount
> as the interest rates get smaller would be sufficient—
> but not necessary—evidence for the liquidity traps.[18]

In view of the implication of a "floor" or "bottom stop" from
any constant interest elasticity, Eisner believes that in an actual
trap situation (both the elasticity of demand and the demand itself are infinite, that is, the slope of the function is zero), to
measure the responsiveness of the demand for money to changes
in interest rates, it is more useful to measure the money-interest
relationship in terms of arithmetic slope rather than elasticity,
since the demand for money can approach infinity as the rate of
interest falls, even though the elasticity of demand is constant.
"For the Keynesian theory would require the slope of the demand
curve to be closer to horizontal for low interest rates or high
amounts of idle balances."[19] Eisner provides empirical evidence
to show that the demand curve for idle balances became flatter
as the rate of interest fell during the period 1919-56.[20]

Bronfenbrenner and Mayer rejoin that in the General Theory
and in the standard expositions of Keynesian economics, the
concept of the liquidity trap is referred to in terms of elasticity
rather than of slope of the liquidity preference function; hence,
they are not breaking with tradition. They maintain that their
difference with Keynesian theory lies only "in considering the
elasticity of the liquidity preference function as a constant
rather than as shifting inversely with interest rates and eventually approaching infinity at some interest rate significantly
greater than zero." Furthermore, they believe that elasticity
is a more convenient measure than the slope, because of its
greater independence of units of measurement.

Allan Meltzer participated in the above discussion. He
asserts that "evidence for or against the liquidity trap must
rest on a demand function for money which explains more than
the period surrounding the supposed trap. The post-1920 data
alone are inadequate to support or reject the trap hypothesis."[21]

After estimating a money-demand function using a long-term interest rate and total assets as independent variables, he concluded that the long-term interest elasticity of the demand for total money balances was constant over the period 1900-58, and there appeared to be no kink in the function. Meltzer uses these results to assert that a liquidity trap did not exist during the 1930s.[22]

There are good arguments for using slope and for using elasticity as measures of the responsiveness of the demand for money to changes in interest rates; but no decisive argument has been advanced.

In the Bronfenbrenner-Mayer study, since single-equation models rather than complete systems of equations were used, they were forced, at least implicitly, to make some assumptions about the supply function of money. In effect, they assume that the demand-for-money function is independent of the supply function; that is, the supply of money is unaffected by any of the independent variables in the demand function. This assumption is questionable, particularly with regard to interest rates and lagged money balances. Bronfenbrenner and Mayer partially tested their assumption by supposing that lagged money balances reflect "supply relationships rather than demand inertia." The "supply relationship" is in this view the unwillingness of the monetary authority to permit sharp year-to-year changes in the money supply.[23] Bronfenbrenner and Mayer reestimated their aggregate functions excluding the lagged-balance variable and found that the multiple correlation coefficients are lower and significant autocorrelation in the residuals existed. They further showed that negative slopes predominated in their scatter diagrams, hence shifts in supply appeared to predominate over shifts in demand.[24] They thus concluded that they apparently had estimated demand functions.

Finally, Eisner makes a criticism of Bronfenbrenner and Mayer that is applicable to most empirical studies of the demand for money employing single-equation models. Implicit in the estimation of the demand for money by Bronfenbrenner and Mayer is the assumption that the rate of interest can be taken as an exogenous variable. More complete macroeconomic models generally assume that the quantity of money varies exogenously and that the rate of interest responds to it in accordance with the structural relation defined by the demand curve. Keynesian liquidity preference theory, for example, was developed in the first instance as a theory of the rate of interest. Therefore, if the interest rate is influenced by the quantity of money, then specifying a one-directional causal relation in a single-equation model causes bias in the estimates of the parameters. Eisner maintains that

> the effect of this kind of misspecification of the error
> is to cause underestimates of the elasticity of money
> with respect to the rate of interest or, perhaps more
> appropriately, to lead one to infer greater than true
> elasticities of the rate of interest with respect to the
> quantity of money.[25]

Eisner inverts the money-interest relation and makes interest rates a function of idle balances. Regression of short- and long-term interest rates on idle balances was performed and elasticity estimates of -0.69 and -0.2, respectively, over the entire 1919-56 period were obtained. Since other variables are included in these functions, it is impossible to specify the direction in which the coefficients are biased in the single-equation fits. The multiple coefficients of determination of the functions using idle balances as the dependent variable are significantly higher than those of the functions using interest rates as the dependent variable, suggesting that the former specification of the relation fits the data more closely.

However, since economic theory tells us that the rate of interest influences the demand for money, and that interaction between the supply of and demand for money influences the rate of interest, the only satisfactory way to analyze the money relations is within the context of a structural model of the monetary sector. This appears to be the only way to avoid specification error and simultaneous equations bias in single-equation estimates of parameters.

A somewhat similar test to that of Bronfenbrenner and Mayer was carried out by Laidler for the time period 1892-1960.[26] Laidler divided the whole time period between those years when the interest rate was above its average value for the period and those when it was below it. Such a division was made both for the long-term and the short-term rate of interest, and regressions of the money stock on the level of permanent income and the interest rate were performed for these two sets of data separately. He employed both definitions of money, including and excluding time deposits. He failed to discover any tendency for the interest elasticity of demand for money to be higher for low-interest observations than for high; nor did he find any evidence that "the function was any less stable at low rates of interest." However, permanent income and the interest rate were found to be the best explanatory variables for both definitions of money, with the broader definition of money providing the more satisfactory results. Time deposits alone were better explained by nonhuman wealth and the interest rate.

On the basis of these results, Laidler argues that any empirical definition of money must be an approximation, rather than a direct counterpart, of the theoretical concept; that the definition that includes time deposits is the more appropriate; that the demand for money is dominated by different motives from those that dominate the demand for other financial assets; and that money is most approximately viewed as a consumer durable, rather than as an inventory of transactions balances or a risk-offsetting asset in the nonhuman wealth portfolio.

WEALTH MODELS

More significant contributions to our knowledge of the role of wealth in the demand for money have been made by Brunner and Meltzer. Meltzer started with a general demand function for money similar to that in Friedman's restatement article, [27] and with some simplifying assumptions derived an equation showing that money demanded is a product of wealth and a certain function of the interest rate. That is, Meltzer formulates a money demand function containing variables that reflect wealth and substitution effects on the amount of money demanded. The general demand function for money as formulated by Meltzer is

$$M = f(r^*, z, d^*, W_n) \tag{10}$$

where M represents the nominal value of the quantity of money demanded; r^*, the yield on financial assets; z, the yield on physical assets; d^*, the yield on human wealth; W_n, nonhuman wealth; and f_i specifies the signs of the derivatives for each argument of the function. Meltzer hypothesizes that the demand function is homogenous of first degree in the money value W_n; thus the function becomes

$$M = f^*(r^*, z, d^*, 1)W_n \tag{11}$$

Meltzer assumes that d^* can be divided into two components, Yh/Y_h^*, where Y_h is actual human income, Y_h^* is expected human income, and W_h is human wealth. That is, the yield on human wealth is now viewed as the product of two components. The first term, Y_h/Y_h^*, measures short-run deviations of actual from expected human income; it is an index of the transitory component of human income. In the short run, wealth holders may adjust the composition of their portfolios in response to changes in this index, but in the long run actual income is assumed to be equal to expected income. Since Meltzer is primarily concerned with the long-run demand function for money, Y_h/Y_h^* is assumed to be constant. The second term, Y_h^*/W_h, the ratio of expected human income to its decapitalized value, is assumed to be stable in the long run and therefore is taken as a constant. The assumption that $d^* = Y_h/Y_h^* \times Y_h^*/W_h$ is a constant eliminates the direct effects of human income from the long-run money demand function.

Another assumption that Meltzer makes is that r^* and z have sufficiently high covariance and they can be combined in a single long-term interest rate, r. Thus, with this assumption and those mentioned above, the demand function is shortened to

$$M = g(r)W_n \tag{12}$$

In this form, the equation reflects the wealth constraint and substitution effect on the demand for money. Meltzer further hypothesized that $g(r) = r^b$. A linear logarithmic demand function

$$\ln M = a + b \ln r + c \ln W_n \tag{13}$$

was estimated for the period 1900-58.

To test his hypothesis, Meltzer uses three definitions of money in the empirical study: the sum of currency plus demand deposits, M_1; M_1 plus time deposits at commercial banks, M_2; and M_2 plus savings deposits at mutual savings banks and the postal savings system, M_3. For the interest rate the author has used Durand's basic yield on 20-year corporate bonds. In the first estimates, wealth is defined as total wealth from Goldsmith's Table W-1[28] plus monetary and nonmonetary government debt minus government assets.[29] The regression estimates obtained are as follows:[30]

$$\ln M_1 = -1.65 - 0.781 \ln r + 1.01 \ln W_n + u_1 \quad \bar{R} = .994$$
$$ (13.5) (66.8) \tag{14}$$

$$\ln \frac{M_1}{p} = -1.48 - 0.949 \ln 4 + 1.11 \ln \frac{W_n}{p} + u_2 \quad \bar{R} = .992$$
$$\phantom{\ln \frac{M_1}{p} = -1.48 -} (21.8) (42.0) \tag{15}$$

$$\ln \frac{M_2}{p} = \underset{(10.8)}{-1.98 - 0.500 \ln r} + \underset{(53.2)}{1.32 \ln \frac{W_n}{p}} + u_3 \quad \bar{R} = .994$$

$$(16)$$

In Equations (9) and (10), p is the implicit price deflator for net national product.

Meltzer's findings suggest that a stable demand function of money is consistent with more than a single definition of money balances, and that nonhuman wealth and interest rates explain almost all of the variances in money balances whether money is defined inclusive or exclusive of time deposits at commercial banks. They also suggest that the definition of money is relatively important for a "proper appraisal of issues in monetary theory." A further result is that the interest rate and wealth elasticities differ substantially with different definitions of money—the more inclusive the definition of money, the lower the interest elasticity and the higher the wealth elasticity.

Meltzer's explanation of the lower interest elasticity is that when interest-bearing assets are included in the definition of money, part of the substitution effect of interest-rate changes occurs within the money variable itself. The estimates of the wealth elasticity shed some light on two issues raised by Gurley and Shaw. First, Gurley and Shaw maintain that the liabilities of financial intermediaries are very close substitutes for currency plus demand deposits, and that a stable demand function for money requires a broader definition of money. Second, the Gurley-Shaw analysis presupposes that the demand for M_1 has declined relative to other assets.[31]

Meltzer's estimates suggest that the growth of financial intermediaries is a wealth effect and not primarily a substitution effect, and that, for a given percentage increase in real wealth, the community has chosen to increase its time deposits by a greater percentage than its demand deposits and currency. "In short, the public has chosen to hold a larger proportion of its wealth in the form of income-yielding assets."[32]

Finally, Meltzer's results strongly indicate that the demand to hold currency plus demand deposits is at least as stable as other alternative demand functions. Thus there appears to be no compelling reason for broadening the definition of money to include time deposits at commercial banks (Friedman), or liabilities of financial intermediaries (Gurley-Shaw). The results further suggest that the measurements of yields on a variety of alternative assets by a single financial rate provide a reasonable approximation for the long-run function.

To distinguish between the income and wealth models, Meltzer experimented with a money demand function by incorporating real net national product as an argument. In some of the functions the interest rate and real income are the only independent variables; in others real wealth is added. The functions are tested over three periods: 1900-58, 1900-29, and 1930-58. For the demand equation using only the interest rate and real income as explanatory variables, the interest elasticity for the long period (1900-58) was -0.79, for 1900-29 it was -0.05, and for 1930-58, -0.69. Meltzer concludes that "those who argue that the demand for money depends on real income must deny the importance of the interest rate during much of the time period we have considered."[33]

Meltzer, however, fails to point out that one of his earlier results for the period 1900-29, using nominal wealth and the interest rate as arguments, yielded an interest elasticity of only -0.15. The long-run interest elasticity for the same function was -0.78. When real wealth was used with the interest rate, the interest elasticity for the period 1900-29 was only -0.32, whereas the long-run interest elasticity for the same function was -0.95.

Indeed, most of the functions tested over the two periods yielded very low interest elasticities for the earlier period. This would lead to the conclusion that the demand for money was relatively unresponsive to changes in interest rates during the period 1900-29.

The estimates of the functions using both real wealth and real income along with the interest rate suggest that "real income has no significant effect on the demand for real money balances when real nonhuman wealth appears in the equation." Substantial multicollinearity because of the high correlation income and real wealth impedes interpretation of this finding; however, the interest rate and wealth coefficients are generally quite similar to those estimated in other regressions, while those for the real income coefficients are quite different. Thus Meltzer concludes that "the addition of real income to the money demand equation does little to improve the explanatory ability of the demand function for money."[34]

Meltzer's wealth model of the demand for money was tested on the assumption that the effects of human wealth could be excluded from the empirical wealth measure without biasing the results. The yield on human wealth, $Y = Y_h/Y_h^* \times Y_h^*/W_h$, was assumed to be constant in the long run. Although he was unable to measure human wealth, Meltzer was convinced that the evidence suggested that the omission of human wealth (or the income received as wages and salaries) did not introduce a substantial bias to his wealth elasticities, and the elasticity of the demand for money with respect to human wealth is approximately the same as the elasticity with respect to nonhuman wealth.

In summary, Meltzer's findings suggest that a relatively stable long-run demand function for money can be isolated and its principal arguments are interest rates and nonhuman wealth. They are of almost equal importance in explaining the demand for real cash balances. Interest rates have played the predominant role in determining the level of velocity. The demand-for-money functions defined inclusive of time deposits or time plus savings deposits are no more stable in the long run than the demand-for-money function defined exclusive of these financial assets. The use of broader definitions of money avoids the problem of mixing the effects of general and relative changes in interest rates on desired money holdings. Meltzer further suggests that "the observed growth of financial intermediaries relative to commercial banks reflects the effect of increased wealth on the desired allocation of wealth rather than a substitution effect as Gurley and Shaw have suggested."[35] Thus, Meltzer maintains that money need not be defined more broadly than currency plus demand deposits. He also concludes that the demand function is more stable when a wealth rather than an income constraint is used.

The salient feature of the work of Meltzer is to place emphasis on wealth rather than income as an explanatory variable. The result obtained by Meltzer is supported by a different test published by Brunner and Meltzer (1963).[36] In their study, Brunner and Meltzer tested theoretical explanations of velocity rather than money balances. They attempted to determine the short-run stability of the demand function for money based on the wealth-adjustment process. It differs, however, because it is concerned with the problem of predicting velocity in the short run. The criterion by which the theories were evaluated was not how well the regression equation fitted past data, but how well the regression equation with parameters estimated from past data predicted future velocity. The predictive performance of the wealth model is compared with the performance of a number of alternative theories of the demand for money to obtain both relative and absolute measures of the power of the various demand-for-money or velocity relations in the short run.

The various demand functions were used to predict velocity for each of the years in the 1910-40 and 1951-58 periods. Data for 1941-50, however, were excluded from both the computations

and the predictions since bond prices were pegged by the
Federal Reserve during these ten years. Predictions were
obtained by regressing each money-demand function or velocity
equation for a moving ten-year period. The parameters thus
obtained were used with the value of the independent variable
in the "eleventh" year to predict the dependent variable for
that year.[37] The mean absolute percent error and the root-
mean square, or standard deviation, were then calculated and
used as criteria to determine the predictive ability of the alternative equations.

Brunner and Meltzer tested six equations based upon the
money-demand hypothesis of Keynes' General Theory. The first
three were used to predict the demand for idle balances, the
latter being computed by the same procedure used by Tobin
and Bronfenbrenner and Mayer. The only independent variable
in these equations was the long-term rate of interest. Two of
the equations were tested in linear form, and the other was in
the log-linear form. The statistical results for these equations
led Brunner and Meltzer to conclude that "the predictions from
the . . . hypotheses are extremely poor for the period as a
whole and for each of the subperiods. . . . The model is virtually
useless as a guide to predicting "speculative" balances, a result
which casts doubts on the usefulness of the 1947 Tobin form of
the Keynesian hypothesis. . . ."[38]

The other three Keynesian money-demand functions tested
were based on Latane's studies. Two of these equations, with
money defined as currency plus demand deposits, were used to
predict velocity, and the third was used to predict the demand
for real balances. In the first velocity equation

$$\ln V_1 = a + b \ln r \tag{17}$$

the demand for money was assumed to be homogeneous of first
degree in money income (NNP), the independent variable was
the long-term rate of interest, and the function was assumed
to be in the log-linear form. In the second velocity equation

$$\ln V_2 = a + b \ln r + c \ln y \tag{18}$$

Brunner and Meltzer tested the homogeneity assumption explicitly
by including income as an independent variable. This function
also was assumed to be linear in the logarithms. Using the
demand for real balances they further test the linear Keynesian
equation

$$M/p = a - br + cy \tag{19}$$

which includes both the interest rate and real income as independent variables. The results suggest that this equation predicts with smaller percent absolute error and root mean square (RMS) than any of the other Keynesian-type hypotheses.

Brunner and Meltzer also tested three velocity equations based upon Friedman's permanent-income hypothesis. The first velocity equation hypothesized that permanent velocity (the money measure includes time deposits at commercial banks) depends upon real per capita permanent income. The velocity equation is used to test the predictive power of the demand-for-money model that Friedman has proposed. The result shows that it has a smaller mean and root-mean square absolute percent error than any of the previously tested money demand functions. The question arises as to whether this improvement results from the definition of money balances, from a more appropriate specification of the demand function for money, or from both. The other two velocity equations, which include variables representing transitory income and prices to account for short-run influence on income velocity, are used to predict measured velocity. Two definitions of money, M_1 and M_2, are used in the testings.

From the empirical results obtained, Brunner and Meltzer conclude that the Friedman-type equations are better predictors of velocity than both the naive and the Keynesian models, but that "the error in predicting velocity . . . is sufficiently large that it would fail to distinguish between predictions of prosperity or recession in a given year."[39]

Brunner and Meltzer further develop the wealth model of the demand for money. The long-run wealth model of the demand for money in ratio form,

$$\ln M_1/W_n = a - b \ln r \tag{20}$$

where money is defined as the sum of demand deposits and currency, and the long-run velocity function

$$\ln rW_n/M_1 = -a + (1 + b) \ln r \tag{21}$$

where the income from nonhuman wealth is used as the numerator of the velocity relation in the long run, were tested.

Most emphasis, however, was placed on two short-run functions. In the short run, actual and expected human income need not be equal; thus, an index of transitory income is required in the short-run function to measure this ratio of actual and expected human income. Since there were no adequate measures of human income available back to 1900, Brunner and Meltzer used the ratio of measured to permanent income (NNP), Y/Y_p, as a measure of transitory income. The short-run demand function

$$M_1/W_n = h^*(r, Y/Y_p) \tag{22}$$

was assumed to be log-linear and was tested in ratio form. This function predicted with smaller average error for the period as a whole and for two of the subperiods than any other demand or velocity function tested.

To predict measured velocity or measured income rather than the short- or long-run demand for money the above equation was modified. The short-run velocity function was presented in the following form:

$$Y/M_1 = Y/W_n \times W_n/M_1 = U(r, Y_p/Y)(Y/W_n)$$
$$= U(r, Y_p/y, P_p/P_y)(Y/W_n) \tag{23}$$

The wealth model views measured velocity as composed of two principal elements. The first is "permanent velocity" expressed in equation (21). It reflects the long-run desire to hold part of wealth in the form of money. The second is the response to essentially short-run events that affect the short-run demand for money through Y_h/Y_h^* (or Y/Y_p) in equation (22) and affect measured velocity through Y_h^*/Y_h (or Y_p/Y) and Y/W_n in equation (23). Thus, short-run influences enter the velocity function via inverted indexes of real transitory income and transitory prices. It is assumed that an increase in the index of transitory income will lower the demand for money and increase velocity in the short run. This reflects the idea that money is not a shock absorber in the portfolios of economic units. Another short-run influence on the velocity function is shown by Y/W_n, the ratio of net national product to net nonhuman wealth of households and business. This ratio is a crude measure of the rate at which the stock results of the test show that "the predictions obtained from this equation are substantially closer to the actual values of measured velocity and are much less variable" than any of the Keynesian, Friedman, or "naive" equations.[40]

Both definitions of money, M_1 and M_2, are used in the wealth model to predict velocity; but the wealth model predicts velocity less accurately when M_2 is used.

In summary, the major conclusions of the Brunner-Meltzer study are the following:

The wealth model is a better predictor of short-run velocity than the Keynesian, Friedman, or "naive" models.

Interest rates play an important, independent role in the prediction of short-run measured velocity and income; and the short-run wealth model includes as variables the rate of interest, transitory income and prices, and nonhuman wealth.

A comparatively stable demand function for money is observed when wealth rather than measured or permanent income is used as the constraint.

The more appropriate definition of money is currency plus demand deposits, M_1.

The measure of wealth that is used successfully by Brunner and Meltzer in their study is a measure of private-sector non-human wealth. Theory suggests, however, that several alternative measures of wealth may be important influences in the demand for money. Of major importance in recent monetary controversies have been Friedman's arguments in favor of including human wealth as an influence on the demand for money, in opposition to the Keynesian liquidity preference theory. In its general form, wealth, both human and nonhuman, is regarded as the constraint on money demand, and the fundamentals of capital theory are applied to the problem of assets equilibrium. Friedman's empirical work is aimed at offering a theoretical explanation of the discrepancy between the secular and cyclical behavior of income velocity. [41] He finds that the stock of money generally rises secularly at a considerably higher rate than does money income. Thus, income velocity tends to fall over long periods as real income rises. During cycles, on the other hand, the money stock usually increases during expansions at a lower rate than money income and either continues to rise during contractions or falls at a lower rate than money income. Over the cycle, therefore, income velocity rises and falls with income, that is, it moves procyclically. The issue, then, is: In the long run the income elasticity of the demand for money is considerably above unity, whereas in the short run it is less than unity (occasionally even negative).

PERMANENT INCOME MODELS

In an attempt to explain economic behavior of this cyclical phenomenon and to examine the relationship between the stock of money and money income, Friedman has hypothesized that the demand for money, defined as currency plus demand and time deposits at commercial banks, is a function of permanent income rather than measured income. Permanent income is measured as an exponentially weighted average of prior measured income and is considered to fluctuate less over the cycle than the corresponding measured magnitudes. If permanent income rather than measured income is used to compute cyclical velocity, then the latter would fluctuate countercyclically, and the conflict between secular and cyclical velocity would be resolved. As Friedman states: "If money holdings were adapted to permanent income, they might rise and fall more than in proportion to permanent income, as is required by our secular results, yet less than in proportion to measured income, as is required by our cyclical results."[42] The particular money demand function formulated by Friedman is

$$M/NP_p = a(Y_p/NP_p)^b \qquad (24)$$

where M is currency plus demand and time deposits at commercial banks, P_p is the permanent price level, Y_p is permanent nominal aggregate income, N is population, and a and b are parameters. This equation states that permanent real balances per capita are a function of permanent real income per capita. Friedman concludes that money is a luxury with a per capita income elasticity of 1.8. However, the rate of interest is shown to have negligible effect. In fact, of the many experiments that have been performed, only one, which was carried out by Friedman for the period 1869–1957, failed to find a relationship between the demand for money and the interest rate. Friedman reasoned that, since the greater part of variations in the rate of interest take place within the business cycle, a demand-for-money function fitted to data that abstract from the cycle, if it is used to predict cyclical fluctuations in the demand for money, should yield errors in prediction related to the rate of interest. He therefore took data on the average values of the variables concerned over each business cycle. The variable used was money defined to include time deposits and permanent income and to them was fitted a log-linear regression whose parameters were then used to predict annual variations in the velocity of circulation. He found no close relationship between the errors of prediction and the rate of interest.

However, we observe closely that if interest rates on time deposits are positively correlated with other interest rates, then demand for time deposits being directly related to their interest rates is also often positively related to other interest rates. This is why the inclusion of time deposits in the definition of money often leads to the rejection of Keynesian liquidity preference hypothesis in empirical analysis. It may also be the reason why Friedman and many others have found no significant inverse relationship between money demand and interest rate.

The findings of a relationship between money balances and "permanent income" data have been corroborated by other studies. Meltzer finds that Friedman's equation fits 1900-58 data well, but he finds that the wealth hypothesis fits the data even better. Discovering that the explanatory power of Friedman's equation is improved by including interest rate as an independent variable, Meltzer rejects Friedman's findings on the unimportance of interest rates. He obtained a significant negative relationship between the demand for money, however defined, and the rate of interest, regardless of the other variables included in the equation. Meltzer's result also indicates that the wealth elasticity of the demand for real money balances does not support the view that money is a luxury. However, Meltzer points out that most of the empirical differences between his wealth model and Friedman's permanent income hypothesis can be accounted for by "differences in specification of the variables rather than by inherently conflicting implications."[43]

Using successively a short-term and a long-term rate of interest and using permanent income as the "other" variables, Laidler finds, for the period 1892-1960, regardless of whether the definition of money used included time deposits or excluded them, that "permanent income" is a better explanatory variable for the demand for money than is either measured income (NNP) or nonhuman wealth.[44] Interest elasticities of the demand for money of about -0.7 for the long-term rate of interest and of about -0.15 for the short-term rate were found.

Meltzer's result was criticized by T. J. Courchene and H. T. Shapiro for its deficiency in the statistical treatment of neglecting autocorrelation in the random disturbances.[45] Using income rather than wealth as a determinant, they gave the estimates showing that the relevant parameters were stable for different time periods.

In his 1965 study, H. R. Heller used the interest rate as well as GNP and wealth for different definitions of money. The evidence led him to conclude that: wealth is more important as a determinant for time deposits, while income is the appropriate determinant for cash and demand deposits, which reflects the respective motives for holding these balances; the short-term interest rate is more significant than the long-term interest rate, supporting the argument that the closest available substitute for money should be used as an indicator of the opportunity cost of holding money; and the relevant elasticities are slightly higher in the downswing than in the upswing. [46]

Furthermore, for the years 1951-64, T. H. Lee used data on the interest differentials between demand deposits and various other assets including time deposits at commercial banks and savings and loan association shares to explain the demand for money. [47] The model employed for the analysis is a variety of Friedman's permanent income formulation of the demand for money. The demand function is specified as

$$M = f(Y_p, r) \qquad (25)$$

where Y_p is per capita real permanent income, M denotes per capita money stock in real terms for the traditional concept of money, and represents a vector of interest rate differentials between yields on other assets and the yield on money. The yield on traditionally defined money is derived as the weighted average of rates of return on demand deposits and currency. The price deflator employed for real variables is current price rather than permanent price. This static model was then cast into a dynamic stock adjustment model of Chow and Teigen varieties [48] by introducing a lagged dependent variable, M_{-1}, as

$$M = g(Y_p, r, M_{-1}) \qquad (26)$$

Log-linear forms of the above two equations for both the traditional and Friedman's concept of money were fitted to the data by the least-squares method, using single interest rate differentials of alternative rates, two interest rate differentials using both the yield on savings and loan shares and the yield on other assets, and three interest rate differentials utilizing the yield on savings and loan shares, the yield on time deposits, and the yield on the rest of other assets. The empirical evidence shows that the yield on nonbank intermediary liabilities is the most significant interest rate variable in affecting the demand for money. It also shows that distributed lags of the demand for money in response to interest-rate changes are negligible when the yields on close cash substitutes are incorporated into the demand function. Thus, Lee concludes that his empirical results do not support the rationale used by Friedman et al. for the broad definition of money. Unlike M. J. Hamburger, however, he did not find the yield on corporate equities a potentially important determinant of the demand for money. [49]

Another important contribution to the study of demand-for-money function is G. C. Chow's article on the long-run and short-run demand for money.[50] Based on his statistically suggestive hypotheses on the demand for automobiles,[51] Chow formulated an equilibrium demand function for money with the long-term interest rate and the variable of the relevant constraint, such as permanent income, private wealth, and current income. His short-run demand for money is composed of two components: the long-run or equilibrium component, which reflects the effect of permanent income, and the short-run component, which shows the effect of the allocation of savings and hence the effect of current income. It also serves as a mechanism for the adjustment of the actual money stock to the desired stock. The rather long time series of annual data covering 1897-1957 are used for statistical tests of these two sets of equations, both in logarithmic and linear forms. Chow concludes that in an equation to explain the equilibrium money stock, "permanent income" is a better explanatory variable than either nonhuman wealth or net national product. The long-run interest and income elasticities of the demand for money are estimated to be -0.75 and 1, respectively. Current income, through its influence on savings, is a better variable than permanent income when the money stock of the previous year is introduced according to his short-run formulations of the demand-for-money equation.

As to other variables that might be important in the function, it is useful to note that Lerner's study of the inflation in the Confederacy, Cagan's study of European hyperinflations, and Harberger's study of Chilean inflationary experience all provide strong evidence of the importance of the expected rate of change of prices as a determinant of the demand for money.[52] Both Friedman and Selden have looked for the influence of this variable on the demand for money in the United States without success, perhaps because during the periods studied prices did not change as dramatically as in other countries.[53]

This survey of the literature dealing with the statistical estimation of the demand for money is by no means exhaustive. It does, however, contain a fairly representative sample of contributions in this field.

NOTES

1. A. Kisselgoff, "Liquidity Preference of Large Manufacturing Corporations," Econometrica, October 1945; James Tobin,

"Liquidity Preference and Monetary Policy," Review of Economics and Statistics, February 1947; and M. Bronfenbrenner and T. Mayer, "Liquidity Functions in the American Economy," Econometrica, October 1960.

2. See H. G. Johnson, "Monetary Theory and Policy," American Economic Review, June 1962, p. 345.

3. C. F. Christ, "Interest Rates and 'Portfolio Selection' among Liquid Assets in the United States," in C. F. Christ et al., Measurement in Economics: Studies in Mathematical Economics and Econometrics in Memory of Yehuda Grunfeld (Stanford, Calif.: Stanford University Press, 1963); and H. A. Latane, "Cash Balances and the Interest Rate—A Pragmatic Approach," Review of Economics and Statistics, November 1954.

4. H. A. Latane, "Income Velocity and Interest Rates: A Pragmatic Approach," Review of Economics and Statistics, November 1960.

5. David E. Laidler, The Demand for Money: Theories and Evidence (Scranton, Pa.: International Textbook Co., 1969), p. 93.

6. R. L. Teigen, "The Demand for and Supply of Money," in W. L. Smith and R. L. Teigen, Readings in Money, National Income, and Stabilization Policy (Homewood, Ill.: Richard Irwin, 1965), p. 54.

This renders the models different from Keynes' hypothesis and W. Baumol's and J. Tobin's hypotheses of transaction, which are the theoretical basis of a relationship between total balances and interest rates. See W. J. Baumol, "The Transactions Demand for Cash: An Inventory Theoretical Approach," Quarterly Journal of Economics, November 1952.

7. A. M. Khusro, "Investigation of Liquidity Preference," Yorkshire Bulletin of Economic and Social Research, January 1952; and R. J. Ball, "Some Econometric Analysis of the Long-Term Rate of Interest in the United Kingdom, 1921-1961," Manchester School of Economic and Social Studies, January 1965.

8. Johnson, p. 346. See also J. Tobin, "Liquidity-Preference as Behavior Toward Risk," Review of Economic Studies, February 1958; and R. Turvey, Interest Rates and Assets Prices (London: George Allen and Unwin, 1960).

9. Bronfenbrenner and Mayer, pp. 813-21.

10. Building on a formulation ascribed by Tobin, Bronfenbrenner and Mayer in effect define idle balances as

$$L_t = M_t - Y_t \, (M/Y)_{min}$$

where L represents idle balances, M represents the quantity of money (demand deposits plus currency), and Y represents private GNP, all in billions of dollars, and $(M/Y)_{min}$ represents the minimum ratio of the quantity of money to private GNP in the period under consideration, which was achieved in 1926.

11. Bronfenbrenner and Mayer, p. 811.

12. Ibid., p. 815.

13. Ibid., p. 818.

14. Ibid.

15. Robert Eisner, "Another Look at Liquidity Preference," Econometrica 31 (July 1963):532-33.

16. Ibid., pp. 534-36.

17. Ibid., p. 531.

18. Ibid., p. 532.

19. Ibid.

20. Ibid., pp. 535-37.

21. Allan Meltzer, "Yet Another Look at the Low Level Liquidity Trap," Econometrica 31 (July 1963):545.

22. Ibid., pp. 545-49.

23. Bronfenbrenner and Mayer, p. 820.

24. Ibid., p. 823.

25. Eisner, p. 534.

26. David E. Laidler, "Some Evidence on the Demand for Money," Journal of Political Economy 74 (February 1966):55-68, and "The Rate of Interest and the Demand for Money—Some Empirical Evidence," Journal of Political Economy 74 (December 1966):545-55.

27. Milton Friedman, "The Quantity Theory of Money— A Restatement," in Studies in the Quantity Theory of Money, ed. Milton Friedman (Chicago: University of Chicago Press, 1956).

28. R. W. Goldsmith, A Study of Savings in the United States (Princeton, N.J.: Princeton University Press, 1956).

29. A. Meltzer, "The Demand for Money: The Evidence from the Time Series," Journal of Political Economy 71 (June 1963):224.

30. Ibid., p. 225.

31. J. Gurley and E. S. Shaw, Liquidity and Financial Institutions in the Post-War Economy, Study Paper 14, Joint Economic Committee, 86th Congress, 2d Session, Washington, D.C., 1960.

32. Meltzer, "The Demand for Money," pp. 219-46.

33. Ibid., p. 233.

34. Ibid.

35. Ibid.

36. K. Brunner and A. H. Meltzer, "Predicting Velocity: Implications for Theory and Policy," Journal of Finance, May 1963, pp. 319-54.

37. Ibid., p. 324.

38. Ibid., p. 328.

39. Brunner and Meltzer, p. 333.

40. Ibid., p. 337.

41. See Friedman.

42. Ibid., p. 8.

43. Meltzer, "The Demand for Money," p. 234.

44. Laidler, "Some Evidence," pp. 55-68.

45. T. Courchene and H. Shapiro, "The Demand for Money: A Note from the Time Series," The Journal of Political Economy 72 (October 1964):498-503.

46. H. R. Heller, "The Demand for Money: The Evidence from the Short Run Data," Quarterly Journal of Economics 79 (May 1965):291-303.

47. T. H. Lee, "Alternative Interest Rates and the Demand for Money: The Empirical Evidence," American Economic Review 57 (December 1967):1168-81.

48. G. C. Chow, "On the Long-Run and Short-Run Demand for Money," Journal of Political Economy 74 (April 1966): 111-31; and Teigen, p. 54.

49. M. J. Hamburger, "The Demand for Money by Households, Money Substitutes, and Monetary Policy," Journal of Political Economy 74 (December 1966):600-23.

50. Chow, pp. 112-31.

51. G. C. Chow, Demand for Automobiles in the United States: A Study in Consumer Behavior (Amsterdam: North-Holland, 1964).

52. Eugene Lerner, "Inflation in the Confederacy 1861-65," in Studies in the Quantity Theory of Money, ed. Milton Friedman (Chicago: University of Chicago Press, 1956); Phillip Cagan, "The Monetary Dynamics of Hyperinflation," in ibid.; and Arnold G. Harberger, "The Dynamics of Inflation in Chile," in Christ et al., Measurement in Economics.

53. Milton Friedman, "The Demand for Money—Some Theoretical and Empirical Results," Journal of Political Economy 67 (June 1959):327-51; and Richard Selden, "Monetary Velocity in the United States," in Friedman, Studies in the Quantity Theory of Money.

5

SUPPLY OF MONEY

Compared to the amount of literature investigating money demand functions, studies concerning the supply of money are few. In particular, there were very few studies conducted on the functional specification of supply-of-money relationships before 1960. The almost universal practice is to assume that the supply of money is exogenously controlled by the monetary authorities. The supply studies typically consider the relationship among free reserves of the commercial banking system, the Federal Reserve discount rate (in the case of the United States), and the various interest rates. There have been several attempts to remedy this situation.

J. J. Polak and W. H. White were among the first economists to analyze the elasticity of the banking system's supply of money.[1] They assume that banks want to balance the convenience of a high reserve ratio against a low rate of interest and the inconvenience and risk of a lower ratio against a higher rate of interest. Using a simple aggregative formulation, Polak and White postulated an inverse relationship between the ratio of member-bank net free reserves (defined as excess reserves less borrowing) to their total deposit liabilities and the Treasury bill rate. Their empirical tests led to the important conclusion that a functional specification of supply-of-money relationship can be shown to exist.

A. James Meigs, using the theoretical background provided by the Polak-White study, developed a money supply theory based on free reserves variation.[2] Member banks' responses to changes in free reserves, reserve requirements, market interest rates, and the discount rate were examined. Meigs' major hypothesis is that banks seek to maintain desired ratios of free reserves to total deposits and that these ratios are functionally related to market interest rates and the discount rate

and that the influence of open-market operations on the free
reserves ratio is small and affects the ratio with a time lag.

Another earlier attempt was made by Karl Brunner.[3] He
obtained aggregate relationships of the money supply by summing
over a set of microeconomic equations describing the supply
behavior of individual banks. No extensive empirical results
have been reported for the rather complicated relationships
that result.

One of the most sophisticated studies of the supply of
money was conducted by Ronald Teigen.[4] Based on the work
by Polak and White, Teigen presented a money supply hypothesis,
which is "more general and broader in coverage." His study
jointly estimated money supply and demand functions and an
income function. An attempt was also made to segregate the
exogenous and endogenous aspects of the money stock. As
Teigen states:

> The level of total reserves in the Federal Reserve
> System (R^T), the underlying investigations and
> rules (such as the legal reserve requirements in
> effect at any given time for member banks), and
> certain regular behavioral relationships (between
> currency in circulation and the total money stock,
> deposits in nonmember banks and the money stock,
> etc.) determine a maximum attainable money stock
> at any given time.[5]

Teigen further suggests that the maximum attainable money
stock can be considered to be the sum of two parts. The first
part of this is considered to be exogenous and is "based upon
the reserves supplied by the Federal Reserve System." The
second part is "based upon reserves created by member-banks
borrowing" and is considered to be endogenous. Teigen then
attempts to explain the ratio of the observed money supply to
the exogenous segment of the total potential money supply by
a measure of the profitability of commercial bank lending.[6]
The supply function hypothesis is written as follows: $M/M^* =
X(r, r_c)$, where M denotes the observed money supply, M^* the
exogenous portion of the money stock based on reserves provided by the central bank (that is, a policy variable of the
Federal Reserve System), r the four to six-month rate on prime
commercial paper, representing the return to commercial banks
from making loans, r_c a weighted average of the 12 regional
Federal Reserve Banks' discount rates, based on deposits at
each bank. The structural demand function for money is based

on a generalization of Tobin's work, with some modifications.
The structural income function, specifying that income is a
linear function of current exogenous expenditure, net worth,
and lagged income, is based on a simple open Keynesian
consumption-investment model in which private domestic investment, exports of goods and services, and government expenditures at all levels are taken to be exogenous.

Using quarterly data, Teigen obtained two-stage least-
squares estimates of the supply functions for the period 1946-59.
He concludes that the hypothesis that the supply of money
should be treated endogenously, instead of as an exogenously
determined quantity, receives further support from his structural estimates. The supply ratio is shown to be a function of
the short-term interest rate, along with other variables; it is
this short-term rate that links the supply function to the rest
of the model. No evidence of a time lag was found in the supply
functions.

Another approach to the supply side of monetary analysis
can be found in Phillip Cagan's article, "The Monetary Dynamics
of Hyperinflation."[7] In order to relate desired real cash balances
to observable phenomena, Cagan assumes that these desired
balances are "equal to actual real cash balances at all times";[8]
and actual and desired cash balances are almost always synony-
mous. No identity problems should arise.

·   In his study, David Fand assumes that "the demand for
money is a demand for real balances but that the dependent
variable in the supply function is the supply of nominal money
balances."[9] It implies that an estimate of a supply function of
money is possible without incorporating the influence of demand
parameters in the analysis. A similar view can also be found in
a paper presented by George Morrison at the meeting of the
Econometric Society in 1966.[10] Morrison found that the results
obtained tended to "confirm suppositions that the demand for
nominal balances is homogeneous of first degree in money income
and prices and that the demand for real balances is homogeneous
of first degree in real income and population."[11]

The works by Cagan, Fand, and Morrison deal primarily
with the problems of identification on the supply side of monetary
analysis. Other approaches to this problem can also be found
in works by Smith, Liu, Modigliani, Rasche, and Cooper, and
Bhattacharya.[12] The general method of handling the problem
of identification in these studies is to specify the supply function
as one element of a system of simultaneous equations that form
a model of the monetary sector. This is the approach taken
by Brunner and Meltzer and Teigen in their supply hypotheses.

Before we go further into the discussion of these studies, the major contributions to the analysis of determinants of the money supply and money supply hypotheses attributed to the studies by Friedman and Schwartz, Cagan, and Brunner and Meltzer should be mentioned.[13] They will be summarized in the following sections.

FRIEDMAN AND SCHWARTZ

A useful analytical apparatus for dealing with the supply of money is in the monumental work, A Monetary History of the United States 1867-1960, by Milton Friedman and Anna J. Schwartz. In this work, Friedman and Schwartz analyze the proximate determinants of the nominal stock of money. Three determinants are discussed. The first is high-powered money (H), or the kinds of money that can be used for currency or as reserves,[14] defined as the sum of specie and obligations of monetary authorities.

The second determinant of the money stock is the amount of reserves, which banks wish to hold relative to their deposit liabilities.[15] This depends upon legal reserve requirements, if any, and the precautionary reserves that banks desire to hold. The ratio D/R is used to denote the amount of reserves banks wish to hold relative to deposits "in order to have the determinant in a form that is positively rather than inversely related to the money stock."[16]

The third determinant is the proportion of deposits and currency that the public chooses to hold. This proportion, denoted by the ratio D/C, "depends on the related usefulness of the two media, on the cost of holding them, and perhaps on income."[17]

Based on this notion, Friedman and Schwartz derive the relationship of the money stock with the three determinants in the following manner:[18]

$$M = C + D \tag{1}$$

$$H = C + R \tag{2}$$

$$M = \frac{C + D}{C + R} = \frac{\dfrac{D}{R}\left(1 + \dfrac{D}{C}\right)}{\dfrac{D}{R} + \dfrac{D}{C}} \tag{3}$$

or

$$M = H \frac{\frac{D}{R}\left(1 + \frac{D}{C}\right)}{\frac{D}{R} + \frac{D}{C}} \tag{4}$$

where C = currency held by the public, D = savings, time, and demand deposits held by the public, M = money supply, R = bank reserves, and H = high-powered money.

The findings of Friedman and Schwartz in their study for the period 1867-1960 in the United States suggested that, in the long run, changes in the broadly defined money stock were due primarily to changes in high-powered money, but that changes in the two other determinants proportioned a large share of the changes in the cycles, with the currency ratio being more relevant for mild cycles and the deposit ratio for critical situations.

CAGAN

Based on the work of Friedman and Schwartz, Phillip Cagan attempts to clarify the source of covariation between money and business activity by examining the factors affecting the amount of money supplied.[19] He places greater emphasis on the behavior of the three sectors of economy that affect the amount of money supplied: the government, the public, and the commercial banks. The behavior of the government sector is reflected in high-powered money. The public holds currency in circulation that is a part of high-powered money and affects the distribution of high-powered money between itself and commercial banks by changing the ratio of currency outside commercial banks to the total money stock. Commercial banks affect the money stock by their decisions on the level at which to maintain the ratio of high-powered money reserves to deposits held by the public. Based on the above, Cagan derives the following identities:[20]

$$H = C + R \tag{5}$$

$$\frac{H}{M} = \frac{C}{M} + \frac{R}{D} - \frac{C}{M} \times \frac{R}{D} \tag{6}$$

or

$$M = \frac{H}{\frac{C}{M} + \frac{R}{D} - \frac{C}{M} \times \frac{R}{D}} \tag{7}$$

where H = high-powered money, C = currency in circulation, D = commercial bank deposits held by the public, M = the money stock, defined as $M = C + D$, and R = high-powered money reserves. The identity (3) expresses the total money stock in terms of the quantity of high-powered money, the currency-money ratio, and the reserve-deposit ratio. Cagan referred to these three variables as the determinants of the money stock.

Cagan's findings confirmed Friedman's results on the secular movements, but they did not attribute significance to the deposit ratio, considering the currency ratio as the relevant factor in determining cyclical movements. Cagan went one step further to conclude that the movements in the currency ratio were the result of changes in economic activity.

It is interesting to note that none of the studies conducted by Friedman and Schwartz and Cagan found interest rates as having a large influence in movements of money stock.

BRUNNER AND MELTZER

Karl Brunner and Allan Meltzer have suggested several money supply hypotheses based upon their works.[21]

Linear Hypothesis

The first of their hypotheses, a linear hypothesis, is based upon banks' response to surplus reserves and grew out of the Phillips tradition.[22] Two mechanisms are presented. One specifies the portfolio response of banks to surplus reserves; the other characterizes the processes generating or absorbing surplus reserves independent of the banks' induced portfolio responses.[23]

Brunner and Meltzer define surplus reserves as the difference between actual and desired reserves.[24] They suggest that banks, in response to surplus reserves, adjust portfolios until the surplus is eliminated. In the case of a positive surplus, a bank is induced to acquire earning assets. "This usually generates a loss of reserves to other banks, an outflow of currency, and an increase in required reserves."[25] Thus, according to Brunner and Meltzer,

the magnitude of any particular bank's response to surplus reserves, involving a re-adjustment of its asset portfolio . . . depends on the average loss of

surplus reserves associated with portfolio adjustments. The larger this loss per dollar of portfolio
adjustment (the larger the average loss coefficient),
the smaller the response to a given volume of surplus reserves.[26]

Brunner and Meltzer maintain that the magnitude of new surplus
reserves emerging at other banks in the system, as a result of
portfolio adjustments of a bank, depends upon the fate of the
deposits generated by the expanding banks. "These deposits
may be converted into currency at the receiving banks or reallo-
cated in different ways between checking and time accounts."[27]

They further suggest that the secondary responses "induce
other banks to readjust their portfolios, etc., until the repetitive
redistribution of surplus reserves over the system and associated
portfolio adjustments absorb the initially available surplus reserves."[28]

Based on these assumptions, Brunner and Meltzer derive
a function for the money stock, including time deposits in the
definition. This function takes the form

$$dM = m_1 s + q dB \qquad (8)$$

where M = the money stock, B = the monetary base or the amount
of money issued by the government sector, q = the "proportion
of base money injected that affects simultaneously the banks'
reserve position and deposit liabilities," and m_1 = the money
multiplier. The supply function of money obtained is of the
form

$$M = m_0 + m_1(B + L) - m_1 a_1 c_0 + m_1 a_2 t_0 - m_1 v_0^d(i) \qquad (9)$$

where m_0 = constant; i = the rate of interest; L = the "cumulative
sum of changes in required reserves attributable to changes
in existing requirement ratios, and the distribution of demand
deposits between classes of banks with different requirement
ratios";[29] and v_0^d, c_0, t represent the underlying theories of
a demand function for available cash assets, or cash assets in
excess of required reserves, by the banks, a demand function
for currency by the public, and a demand function for time
deposits by the public. The magnitude $B + L$ in (9) is referred
to as the extended base and it reflects the assumption that "the
response in M to changes in B coincides with the response to
changes in L"[30] while the expression $v_0^d(i)$ "introduces the
dependence of the money stock on interest rates i operating
via the banks' desired cash asset position."[31]

Nonlinear Hypothesis

A second hypothesis, a nonlinear hypothesis, suggested by Brunner and Meltzer represents "a specific view of the credit market on which banks operate."[32] The emphasis of this hypothesis is placed on the difference between actual reserves (R) and desired reserves (R^d). Desired reserves are in turn a function of demand deposits (D), time deposits (T), a vector of interest rates (i), and the discount rate (ρ).[33]

The basic theory is completed with four equations:

$$A = [b(D + T) - A] \tag{10}$$

$$B = A + B^a \tag{11}$$

$$B = R + C^\rho \tag{12}$$

$$R + E = D + T + A \tag{13}$$

where A is composed of discounts and advances of the Federal Reserve.

Equation (10) pertains to the banks' borrowing behavior and describes "the banks' adjustment of their indebtedness to Federal Reserve Banks."[34] The term b indicates "the banks' desired borrowing ratio so that $b(D + T)$ yields the desired volume of outstanding indebtedness." In the remaining three equations, the base (B) specifies "the sum composed of discounts and advances plus the adjusted (relatively exogenous) base."[35]

To empirically explore this system, Brunner and Meltzer postulate that "all adjustment processes are relatively rapid."[36] This enables them to approximate all the dynamic relations of the system with static relations, and to obtain two equations: one for the money supply (14) and one for the bank-oriented credit market (15):

$$M = m^2 B^a \tag{14}$$

$$(m^2 - 1) B^a = E(i, W) \tag{15}$$

where m^2 denotes the monetary multiplier appropriate for the second hypothesis, and B^a and W are specified as relatively exogenous variables. Thus, the money supply and an interest rate are determined jointly by the two equations (14) and (15). The money supply analysis is extended to include responses not only in the real sector but also in the financial sector. As a consequence of this extension, some of the variables that are exogenous in the other formulations are determined by the nonlinear model.

THE VARIOUS APPROACHES: AN APPRAISAL

The discussion so far has clearly dictated two different basic approaches to the analysis of the supply of money. One is the Friedman-Schwartz and Cagan type of analysis; the other is the Brunner-Meltzer and Teigen form of analysis. [37] The studies by Friedman and Schwartz and Cagan provide a framework within which ex-post changes or rates of change in the money stock can be allocated to several determinants, with a view, in the Friedman-Schwartz case, toward extracting "influences about the role of money from an examination of successive historical periods," [38] or in the Cagan case, toward isolating and measuring "the factors responsible for changes in the stock of money." [39] The Brunner-Meltzer and Teigen form of analysis, on the other hand, may be described as the application of regression analysis, both ordinary and two-stage least squares, to money stock data, with a view, in the case of Brunner and Meltzer, toward "providing a theory of money incorporating policy actions and the behavior of banks and the public," [40] or, in the Teigen case, toward testing "a structural model of the monetary sector of the United States economy . . . [and investigating] the validity of the usual exogenous assumptions concerning the supply of money. [41] Thus, while the Friedman-Schwartz and Cagan approaches view the crucial monetary variables as exogenous and attempt to attribute to them part or all of the change in the money stock, the Brunner-Meltzer and Teigen approaches construct simultaneous models of the monetary sector, thereby assuming that the crucial variables are mutually determined and view the money supply within the context of the model.

Aside from the general differences emanating from the views of the two basic approaches, there are several other important differences. While the Friedman-Schwartz and Cagan approach attributes part of the rate of change in the money stock to the currency ratio (deposit-currency or currency-money), Teigen, in his analysis, holds the currency-money ratio constant. Another difference between the two approaches stems from their views of money multipliers. The Brunner-Meltzer and Teigen approach views multipliers as empirical relationships estimated by statistical procedures while the Friedman-Schwartz and Cagan approach views these as definitional relationships. [42]

While there are distinctive differences between these two approaches, there are also similarities between them. One common element is the attempt by all to use a broadly defined concept. An example is the relationship between high-powered money in the Friedman-Schwartz and Cagan case and the monetary base in the Brunner-Meltzer and Teigen case. The adjusted monetary base of the latter approach is equivalent to unborrowed high-powered money in the former approach. Another example is the attempt by all to include some types of relationship between currency and money. [43] A more important similarity among the various hypotheses of the money supply is to accept the independent existence of the money stock as "an economic variable determined by behavior and subject to analysis,"[44] rather than accept the simple mechanical and arithmetic concept of the determination of the money supply by the monetary authority in a system where "banks use all their reserves, where there are no free reserves, and where both the banks and the public do not undertake portfolio changes."[45]

The discussion of major hypotheses of the money supply summarizes the theoretical aspect of the supply side of monetary theory. There are several recent empirical studies that must be mentioned.

In his paper entitled "Money Supply and Demand: A Cobweb?" Smith examines briefly the dynamic consequences of adding a money supply equation to a simple IS-LM model and to specify and statistically estimate the parameters of a pair of small exploratory quarterly models of the U.S. economy in such a manner that: the models can be used for forecasting purposes, and some insights are gained into the implications of a simple money supply function for the stability of the economy. [46]

The money supply equation formulated is

$$M^S = h_0 + h_1 r_{-1} \qquad\qquad (16)$$

where r denotes the rate of interest.

In their paper, Modigliani, Rasche, and Cooper present a theory of the supply of demand deposits based on the demand of the banking sector for earning assets. [47] The supply of currency in their framework is entirely controlled by the demand for currency. They hypothesize that, in the face of an upsurge in commercial loan demand, banks will endeavor to accommodate the demand for earning assets because of the importance of their commercial loan customers as a source of deposits as well as other business. On the other hand, in the face of a decline in demand, there is rather little they can do to prevent borrowers from reducing their indebtedness.

Modigliani, Rasche, and Cooper formulate, estimate, and test a structural model of the money supply and short-term rate of interest in the U.S. economy. These variables are seen as resulting from the interaction of the demand for money by the public and the supply of money that reflects the behavior of the Federal Reserve setting certain policy variables, the behavior of the commercial banks in managing their assets and liabilities in response to fluctuations in their reserves and the demand for commercial loans, and the behavior of the U.S. Treasury cash balances reflecting fiscal and debt management operations. Both ordinary least-squares and two-stage least-squares regression methods are used in estimating the coefficients. The results obtained provide support for their model in that the estimated coefficients are in agreement with the a priori specifications, and the model accounts rather well for the behavior of the variables it purports to explain.

In studies by Smith and Modigliani, Rasche, and Cooper, the findings suggest that money supply, like money demand, is sensitive to the interest rate. This has two important implications: the supply of money may not be an exogenous variable in a monetary system; and the ordinary least-squares estimates of the money demand function with the interest rate as an explanatory variable may suffer from simultaneous equation bias.

In his case study of India, Bhattacharya investigates some of these familiar issues in monetary economics as well as some monetary issues peculiar to developing economies. By formulating the money supply and the money demand functions for the Indian economy within the framework of a Hicks-Hansen-Modigliani-type model, with the money supply function being a broad synthesis of the approaches used by Brunner-Meltzer, Teigen, Goldfeld, and Modigliani, Rasche, and Cooper, Bhattarcharya concludes that money supply is not an exogenous variable in a monetary system. Money supply, among other variables, depends on the interest rate differential between the central bank discount rate and the short-term rate of interest of the organized money market. Since the latter is found to be inversely related to money demand, the money stock becomes an endogenous variable.

SUMMARY

Despite voluminous literature on the demand for money, opinions vary widely as to which explanatory variable is a relevant determinant of the demand for money, and much still remains to be done on establishing its exact nature. In the neoclassical analysis of money, the demand for money is functionally related to income, interest rates, and some types of wealth. The question of the nature of income in the money demand function remains under debate: current nominal income, real income, or the permanent income à la Friedman. The nature of the interest rate also commands attention: short-term or long-term government bond rate, and/or the money market rate on private debt. In effect, the arguments or variables that enter the demand function for money, and the definition of money appropriate for the demand function, have received substantial attention. Although we have come a long way, on the demand side three empirical issues remain outstanding: the definition of money to be used, the relevant constraint on the money balances, and the importance of interest rates.

On the supply side, debate has been centered on money supply determination. Two main theories have emerged. One is that in general there is a stable relationship between the money supply and the reserve base. Accordingly, a central bank can control the money supply by controlling total reserves of the banking and monetary system. The other theory is that the volume of bank borrowing from the central bank and the volume of excess reserves of banks influence bank behavior in such a way that the rate of change of bank deposits and money supply can be predicted from these variables. Therefore, a central bank should focus its attention on excess reserves and borrowings, or on free reserves, rather than on total reserves in attempting to control the money supply.

It is common to treat the money stock as exogenously determined in empirical investigations of the demand-for-money functions. However, there is now evidence showing that the money supply can be expressed as a function of a few variables. Two basic types of supply function have been empirically investigated: Brunner and Brunner and Meltzer consider money supply as a function of high-powered money, reserve-deposits ratio, and currency-deposit ratio. The empirical evidence has led them to conclude that with the high-powered money given, the rate of interest can have little effect on the money supply. In contrast, Teigen, Goldfeld, Modigliani, Rasche, and Cooper, and Bhattacharya attach prime importance to the interest rates. They suggest that money supply like money demand is sensitive to the rate of interest. Therefore, the supply of money may not be an exogenous variable; and the ordinary least-squares estimates of the money demand function with the interest rate as an explanatory variable may suffer from simultaneous equation bias.[48]

Thus, neither theoretical nor empirical analysis has produced a consensus among economists as to precisely what the money supply is or how the money supply should be measured. This lack of agreement is not very surprising. For one thing, a given financial asset can serve its holder in more than one fashion. There is no particular reason for insisting that the definition of money either include or exclude the entire stock of one particular financial asset. More precisely, this state of affairs reflects the fact that money is simply not as concrete and unambiguous a concept as is commonly believed. It is fundamentally a social phenomenon, and, like all social phenomena, is subject to continuous change. "What appears to be needed is not some final, exclusive catalog of assets labeled money, but a flexible framework aimed at helping analysts and policy-makers determine to what extent specific asset classes are functioning as money at particular points in time."[49]

This study draws on the money demand and money supply hypotheses presented above and the main institutional features and operating characteristics of different types of economic and banking systems to gain insights into the general workings of the money supply mechanism so as to enhance our understanding of general monetary behavior.

NOTES

1. J. J. Polak and W. H. White, "The Effects of Income Expansion on the Quantity of Money," IMF Staff Papers 4 (August 1955).

2. James A. Meigs, Free Reserves and the Money Supply (Chicago: University of Chicago Press, 1962).

3. Karl Brunner, "A Schema for the Supply Theory of Money," International Economic Review 2 (January 1961):79-109.

4. Ronald L. Teigen, "Demand and Supply Functions for Money in the United States: Some Structural Estimates," Econometrica 32 (October 1964):476-509.

5. Ibid., p. 478.

6. Ibid.

7. Phillip Cagan, "The Monetary Dynamics of Hyperinflation," in Studies in the Quantity Theory of Money, ed. Milton Friedman (Chicago: University of Chicago Press, 1956), pp. 27-35.

8. Ibid., p. 33.

9. David Fand, "Some Implications of Money Supply Analysis," Papers and Proceedings of the American Economic Association 57 (May 1967):380.

10. George Morrison, "Transitional Elements in the Demand for Money," Econometrica 35 (Supplementary Issue, 1967):136.

11. Ibid.

12. P. E. Smith, "Money Supply and Demand: A Cobweb?" International Economic Review 8 (February 1967):1-11; Fu-Chi Liu, Essays on Monetary Development in Taiwan (Taipei: China Committee for Publication Aid and Prize Awards, 1970); F. Modigliani, R. H. Rasche, and J. P. Cooper, "Central Bank Policy, the Money Supply and the Short Term of Interest," Journal of Money, Credit and Banking 2 (May 1970); and B. B. Bhattacharya, "Demand and Supply of Money in a Developing Economy: A Structural Analysis for India," Review of Economics and Statistics 56 (1974);502-10.

13. Milton Friedman and Anna J. Schwartz, A Monetary History of the United States 1867-1960 (Princeton, N.J.: Princeton University Press, 1963); Phillip Cagan, Determinants and Effects of Changes in the Stock of Money 1875-1960 (New York: Columbia University Press, 1965); and Karl Brunner and Allan Meltzer, "Some Further Investigations of Demand and Supply Functions of Money," Journal of Finance 19 (May 1964).

14. Friedman and Schwartz, p. 790.

15. Ibid., p. 785.

16. Ibid., p. 786.

17. Ibid., p. 787.

18. Ibid., p. 791.

19. Cagan, Determinants and Effects.

20. Ibid., p. 12.

21. See Karl Brunner, "A Case Study of U.S. Monetary Policy: The Inflationary Gold Flows of the Middle Thirties," Schweizerische Zeitschrift fuer Volkswirtschaft und Statistik 44 (June 1958); Allan Meltzer, "The French Money Supply 1938-1954," Journal of Political Economy 67 (June 1959); Karl Brunner and Allan Meltzer, "Predicting Velocity: Implications for Theory and Policy," Journal of Finance 18 (May 1963); Brunner and Meltzer, "Some Further Investigations"; Brunner, "A Schema for the Supply Theory of Money"; Karl Brunner, "The Structure of the Monetary System and the Supply Function of Money" (unpublished paper, 1961); Federal Reserve Bank of St. Louis, Working Paper No. 7, "A Summary of the Brunner-Meltzer Non-Linear Money Supply Hypotheses," 1968; and Federal Reserve Bank of St. Louis, Working Paper No. 1, "The Three Approaches to Money Stock Analysis," 1967.

22. C. A. Phillips, Bank Credit (New York: Macmillan, 1921).

23. Brunner and Meltzer, "Some Further Investigations," p. 244.

24. Ibid.

25. Ibid.

26. Ibid.

27. Ibid.

28. Ibid.

29. Ibid., p. 245. The secondary responses must be differentiated from the primary responses summarized by the loss coefficients of the expanding bank.

30. Ibid., p. 248.

31. Ibid.

32. Ibid., p. 249.

33. Ibid.

34. Ibid. $\dot{A}$ is the desired volume of outstanding indebtedness.

35. Ibid., p. 251. The ratio b is a function of interest rate and the discount rate with a negative derivative with respect to the discount rate and a positive derivative with respect to the interest rate.

36. Ibid., pp. 251-52.

37. Clyde Austin Haulman, "Determinants of the Money Supply in Canada, 1875-1964," Ph.D. dissertation, Florida State University, 1969.

38. Cagan, Determinants and Effects, p. xxvii.

39. Ibid.

40. Brunner and Meltzer, "Some Further Investigations," p. 242.

41. Teigen, p. 476.

42. Haulman, p. 87.

43. The comparisons of major money-supply hypotheses presented above are obtained from Haulman.

44. Fand, p. 380.

45. Ibid.

46. Smith, pp. 1-11.

47. Modigliani, Rasche, and Cooper, pp. 168-218.

48. Bhattacharya, pp. 502-03.

49. Alfred Broaddus, "Aggregating the Monetary Aggregates: Concepts and Issues," Economic Review, Federal Reserve Bank of Richmond, Virginia, November/December 1975, p. 7.

6

MONETARY AND FINANCIAL ENVIRONMENT

A country's monetary and financial system is the product of its economic, legal, social, and political system. No two central banks, for example, conduct monetary policy in precisely the same way nor with identical instruments. Even if they are identical, the exercise is conducted under dissimilar economic conditions and against a different historic background. Much the same is true of the other monetary and financial institutions in a country.

The concept of monetary and financial organization involves several ideas: behavior of economic units, financial intermediaries, methods of extending credit, money and capital markets, and monetary controls. The term "monetary policy" as it is usually understood by economists focuses on the objectives, tools, and processes involved in the regulation of the supply of money and credit. Underlying this view is the idea that the supply of money (currency and bank deposits adjusted) should be related secularly, if not cyclically, to the rate of growth in the economy and the level of economic activity.

Consider the monetary and financial environment of Canada, the United States, Sweden, the United Kingdom, Yugoslavia, and the six original European Economic Community countries that provide the background for our analysis. [1]

CANADA: THE BANK OF CANADA AND MONETARY POLICY

In Canada the government's assumption of responsibility for conscious monetary management dates only from the establishment of the Bank of Canada in 1935, although the theory and practice of monetary control has enjoyed a much longer development in many countries. This was because the strong opposition from almost all of the chartered banks had effectively discouraged an earlier effort to introduce a central bank and a consciously formulated Canadian monetary policy at the end of World War I. From its very beginning the development of chartered banking in Canada had been closely related to the financing of export staples, and the relative scarcity of capital characteristic of the pioneer economy had dictated a high degree of banking centralization. The branch banking system was admirably suited to this purpose and to providing banking facilities in the frontier areas of the economy that otherwise would have been either not forthcoming or long delayed.[2] Much of the strength and social usefulness of present-day Canadian banking is attributed to the institution of the branch banking system in early times. Many Canadians tend to take the system for granted, but it is nevertheless fundamentally different from that of the unit banking system that operates in much of the United States and in some other countries where banks are completely prohibited from operating branches or are able to do so only to a limited extent.

To meet growing needs, the number of branches operating in Canada has increased over the years. There were more than 6,500 banking offices across the country at the time of writing. The branch system has played a vital role in the development of Canada and has helped to overcome the difficulties of immense geographic spread and scattered population. It enables the Canadians to put the resources of the whole nation to work where they are most needed for the common good.

The commercial banking system forms part of the general banking system that, in turn, is part of the overall financial framework of Canada. The banking system as a whole comprises the Bank of Canada, which is the government-owned central bank, and ten commercial or chartered banks owned by shareholders. In addition, the Bank of Canada controls the subsidiary Industrial Development Bank and there is one Quebec-based savings bank that accepts deposits but does not carry out the normal lending business of a chartered bank. By law, only these 13 institutions are designated as "banks." No other institutions are permitted to use this terminology. The function and responsibility of these banks are summarized in this section.

The provisions of the Bank Act of 1934 enable the central bank to determine the total amount of cash reserve available to the chartered banks as a group and in that way to control the rate of expansion of the total assets and deposits liabilities of the banking system as a whole. The Bank of Canada also has the responsibility for regulating credit and currency in the

interest of the economic life of the nation and the power of
determining the combined total of the most common forms of
Canadian money held by the community chartered bank deposits
and currency.

Under the Bank Act of 1934 each bank in allocating resources
must maintain a primary reserve consisting of a deposit with the
Bank of Canada that, along with its holdings of Bank of Canada
notes, must be at least equivalent to fixed ratios of its Canadian
deposits. The minimum cash reserve requirements that came
into effect under the legislation beginning February 1, 1968,
is 12 percent for demand deposits or current accounts and 4
percent for other deposits such as Canadian notice deposits.
The ability of the chartered banks as a group to expand their
total assets and deposits liabilities is therefore limited by the
total amount of cash reserve available. It is also noted that
the Canadian branch banking system, with its large banks and
method of calculating reserve requirements, maintains a much
lower excess reserve position than does the U.S. banking system. This, together with the reluctance of Canadian banks to
borrow from the Bank of Canada, suggests that the interest
sensitivity of the money supply is much below that found in the
United States.

The banks' deposits with the Bank of Canada are essential
to the central bank in exercising its function of influencing
monetary policy either to relax or restrict credit conditions in
the banking system and, through it, the rest of the economy.
In using the powers at its disposal, the Bank of Canada attempts
to bring about credit conditions appropriate to both domestic
and external conditions. In a technical sense, these powers
allow the central bank to exert a strong influence over economic
activity but, in practice, the range through which credit conditions can be permitted to vary is necessarily limited. Changes
in credit conditions in Canada affect the position of some groups
in the economy much more than that of others, and this uneven
impact is bound to inhibit the central banks' operations. Furthermore, the change of interest rates in Canada in relation to those
abroad cannot be made without producing large capital movements
that might complicate Canada's international payments position.
These consideration suggest that monetary policy must be used
in appropriate combination with other public economic policies
in order to help achieve national economic goals.

Although the cash reserve system in Canada enables the
Bank of Canada to determine within broad limits the total amount
of chartered bank assets and deposit liabilities, it leaves the
allocation of bank and other forms of credit to the private sector

of the economy. The influence of the central bank—based on
its power to expand or contract chartered bank cash reserves
through its market purchases or sales of securities—is thus
both indirect and impersonal. It is brought to bear on financial
conditions generally through the chartered banks and the numerous interconnected channels of the capital market.

The Bank of Canada, in addition to its role as Canada's
central bank, acts as the fiscal agent for the government of
Canada in the payment of interest and principal and generally
in respect of the management of the public debt of Canada.
The sole right to issue paper money for circulation in Canada
is vested in the Bank of Canada.

The Bank of Canada was also given the power, by the
Bank Act of 1970, to impose a secondary reserve, which is
made up of cash, Treasury bills, and day-to-day loans. The
secondary reserve cannot be more than 6 percent of total deposits
when first introduced nor can it exceed 12 percent; effective
January 1972, the required level was 8 percent.

The exact relationship between the central bank and the
government, as provided and clarified by the Bank Act revision
in 1967, involves regular consultations between the governor
of the Bank and the minister of finance. In the event of a disagreement between the government and the Bank that cannot
be resolved, the government may, after further consultation
has taken place, issue a directive to the Bank as to the monetary
policy that it is to follow. Any such directive must be in writing,
in specific terms, and must be applicable for a specific period.
It must be published immediately in the Canada Gazette and
tabled in Parliament. Thus, it is clear that the government
must take the ultimate responsibility for monetary policy, but
it is also clear that the central bank is in no way relieved of
its responsibility for monetary policy and its execution.

The Industrial Development Bank

The Industrial Development Bank (IDB), a federal crown
corporation and a subsidiary of the Bank of Canada, was established by an act of Parliament in 1944 to provide capital assistance
to develop new businesses and to finance the expansion programs
of existing small and medium-sized businesses that are unable
to obtain financing elsewhere in Canada under reasonable conditions and terms. The purpose is to promote the economic welfare
of Canada by ensuring the availability of credit to industrial
enterprises that may reasonably be expected to prove successful,

by supplementing the activities of other lenders and by providing financial assistance to industry, with particular emphasis in meeting the needs of small enterprises.

The Chartered Banks

Canada's commercial banking system consists of ten privately owned banks. By the early 1980s there were over 6,500 banking offices in Canada and 270 abroad.

Under the Canadian system, a chartered bank is both a savings and a commercial institution. It has a head office as its administrative center, regional offices where necessary, and a network of branches. These chartered banks engage in a very wide range of activities; they accept various types of deposits from the public including accounts payable on demand, both checking and nonchecking, notice deposits, and fixed-term deposits. The banks, in addition to holding a portfolio of securities, make loans under a wide variety of conditions for commercial, industrial, agricultural, and consumer purposes. These two functions are conducted by and through the branch system.

In addition to the two basic functions of accepting deposits and making loans, the chartered banks provide many other financial services. Indeed, a branch of a chartered bank can be regarded as a "financial department store" where almost every service is available to do with money, its safeguarding, transfer, and conversion into other currencies, as well as the money lending services that are a fundamental part of modern banking.

Nonbank Financial Intermediaries

The closest competitors to chartered banks among nonbank financial intermediaries are the trust and mortgage loan companies. Trust companies closely resemble mutual savings banks and mortgage loan companies closely resemble savings and loan associations in the United States. In Canada the combined assets of these organizations are about 30 percent of those of chartered banks, though their impact on monetary policy may be even greater than this percentage implies because they administer large holdings of estate, trust, and agency funds. Moreover, they have grown much faster than the chartered banks in the post-World War II period.

THE UNITED STATES

Over large areas of the United States, bank organization is still passing through a phase of structural development that many other countries went through some decades ago. This is not to deny that there has been much experimentation in the evolution of the U.S. banking system, but its development has been subject to constraints that have certainly influenced the path that was chosen.

The Federal Reserve System and Banking Organization

The national banks[3] that existed in 1913 were made the core of the membership of banks in the Federal Reserve System when the Federal Reserve Act was passed by Congress, as an outgrowth of the financial panic of 1907. All national banks were required, and state banks were permitted, to become members of the Federal Reserve System, subject to specified reserve requirements and to certain limitations upon their operations. State banks were brought under federal regulation, but only if they voluntarily submitted to regulation by joining the system. Such regulation was entrusted to a new federal agency, the Federal Reserve Board (now the Board of Governors of the Federal Reserve System). Twenty years later, a nationwide banking crisis led to action that made federal deposit insurance available to all member banks, national and state, and to state nonmember banks that elected to obtain such insurance. As a result, federal regulation of state banks was further extended, but again only to state banks that voluntarily submitted to such regulation, and a third federal banking agency, the Federal Deposit Insurance Corporation (FDIC), was vested with certain regulatory functions with respect to nonmember noninsured state banks in the Federal Reserve System.

As a result of these developments, the United States has four classes of banks: national banks, which are chartered and regulated by the Comptroller of the Currency but regulated in some respect by the Federal Reserve; state member banks, which are chartered and regulated by the requirements of federal law and regulations of the Federal Reserve; nonmember insured state banks, which are chartered and regulated by the states but voluntarily subject to certain requirements of federal law and requirements of the FDIC; and nonmember noninsured state banks, which are chartered and regulated, with a few exceptions,

only by the states. Consequently, the U.S. banking system
is one of almost unbelievable complexity. The banking laws of
the 50 states are marked by countless differences. The powers
of state banks and the limitations under which they operate are
different in numerous respects from the powers of national banks
and the limitations imposed on their operations by federal law.
Restrictions of federal law on the operations of national banks,
state member banks, and nonmember insured state banks are
not entirely uniform. Without reason, some restrictions apply
only to national banks, some apply only to national and state
member banks. Even the different interpretation of the same
or similar provision of federal law applied to different classes
of federally regulated banks sometimes arises. Such a system
has given rise, not only to great confusion but, more important,
to competitive inequalities among different classes of banks.

The Federal Reserve System, a joint product of legislation
and practice, is charged with the formulation and execution of
monetary policy.

> The system has a regulated private base, a mixed
> middle component, and a controlling public apex.
> The mixture of public and private elements is unique
> among the closely regulated sectors of [American]
> national economy, and unique too among central
> banking systems around the world. It reflects in
> part the changing conceptions of the role of central
> banking over a half-century and in part the shift
> in interests and influences that has attended the
> System's evolution.[4]

At present, there are 12 Federal Reserve banks, each
located in an economically important region of the country,
which are coordinated by a Board of Governors. In effect,
they are really one central bank. The Board of Governors
consists of seven members appointed by the president with the
advice and consent of the Senate for 14-year terms. Aside from
the power to appoint these governors, the president of the
United States cannot exert legal influence over Federal Reserve
officialdom. Even that power is constrained in the sense that
rarely is the majority of the board likely to be appointees of a
single president—the 14-year tenure of governors being responsible for that. In fact, most new appointments are to fill vacan-
cies in unexpired terms because of the length of the term. In
making appointments the president must give due regard to
"fair representation of financial, agricultural, industrial, and

commercial interests, and geographical divisions of the country,"
and not more than one member can be appointed from any one
Federal Reserve District. Thus, the status that board members
enjoy vis-a-vis the chief executive is analogous to the Supreme
Court-executive relationship.

Congressional control over the Federal Reserve System is
stronger since the system is a child of Congress; but the power
of the purse, that major weapon for ensuring that agencies
comply with congressional directives, is absent since the Federal
Reserve is self-financing. The Federal Reserve Board operating
funds come from semiannual assessments on the 12 Federal Reserve Banks. Thus, the independence invited by long, staggered
terms is reinforced by the system's complete exemption from the
controls of the budget and congressional appropriations.

Instruments of Monetary Policy

In the United States, the Federal Reserve authorities
("the Fed") are charged with the responsibility of executing
monetary policy. This is particularly true since 1951 and the
now famous "accord" reached by the U.S. Treasury and the
Federal Reserve Board that provided, at least tacitly, as a
matter of public policy that in case any open differences should
arise between them, the Treasury would be expected to accommodate its policies, insofar as possible, to those of the monetary
authorities.

In discharging its responsibilities the Fed has relied almost
exclusively on three policy techniques: open market operations,
changes in the rediscount rate, and changes in the minimum
reserve requirements of the member banks. All three instruments operate on the same basic principle of managing total
spending by regulating the availability and cost of credit and
the growth of the country's money stock.

In addition, the Fed has selective controls at its disposal.
A case in point is that of the securities markets. As a result
of the financial reforms of the 1930s, responsibility for regulating
margin requirements in connection with trading in and carrying
securities was delegated to the Federal Reserve Board.

Selective controls are considered by some as enjoying
special merits because they are brought to bear on a particular
sector of the economy, presumably without prejudice to the
economy as a whole, quite conceivably including other "particular"
areas where the situation might have called for exactly the opposite treatment. Others consider such controls as needless

meddling in economic affairs. They are, so the argument runs, discriminatory, personal, and contrary to the principles of the "free market."

SWEDEN, THE UNITED KINGDOM, AND YUGOSLAVIA

Sweden

The imposition in Sweden in 1952 of effective liquidity ratios on the commercial banks signaled a more active role for monetary policy in the country. Such a role has also brought about ingenious combinations of tax and fiscal policy measures and labor measures (including relocation measures) capable of rapid implementation to changing economic conditions. A case in point is the Swedish system of investment reserves. The idea is to spread private investment activity more evenly over the business cycle. Thus, during expansionary phases business is encouraged by tax incentives to deposit portions of its gross profits with the Bank of Sweden. If the economy should require stimulus, these deposits may be released to finance certain given types of investment.

The use of more traditional monetary instruments such as open market operations has suffered, owing to government bond market pegging by the bank. This was considered necessary in order to permit flotation of the large volume of bond issues necessary to finance the budget deficits and housing program. This practice continued until 1955.

In Sweden, commercial banks, savings banks, and mortgage institutions have been in operation for over 100 years. Other types of institutions have also developed; among these the Post Office Bank, various agricultural credit associations, the National Pension Insurance Fund, the National Housing Board, and insurance companies the most important in terms of resources.

Commercial banks are, in effect, "universal" or "all-purpose" banks, competing with almost every other type of financial institution. In 1969 various amendments to the Banking Acts enabled commercial banks, savings banks, and agricultural credit associations to operate on the same footing in regard to the types of financial services they provide. Nonetheless, differences among the institutions will very likely continue into the future. These differences are in tradition, present stock of assets and liabilities, and the fact that a narrow capital base of savings banks and agricultural credit associations will limit their possibilities for expanding lending into the business sector, since such lending according to law must be backed by a comparatively high degree of own capital.

Concentration in Swedish banking is indicated by the fact that the four largest banks that operate throughout the entire country account for about 80 percent, and the two largest for about 60 percent, of total banking resources. The remaining six regional banks, nevertheless, play an increasingly important role in their areas of activity. Banks in Sweden are under very tight control with regard to their financial activity. Moreover, bank charters are renewable every ten years. Branches cannot be opened without prior consent of the Board of Establishment. The Bank Inspection Board has a representative among the auditors of each bank. In 1971 the government obtained direct representation by the right to appoint three directors to the board of each bank, one of whom may participate in preparatory discussions of the management committee on matters later to be submitted to the board for final discussion.

Of growing importance is the National Pension Insurance Fund (NPIF), established in 1959. It was organized in connection with the introduction of a National Supplementary Pension Scheme. Owing to the fact that the Pension Scheme is based on the principle of the so-called assessment method of insurance, considerable loss of savings would have been inevitable until the system was fully built up. To compensate for that loss, higher premiums than required for current pension payments are charged. Indeed the premiums are set so high that within a decade of its establishment the fund almost outgrew the commercial banks to become the largest institution in the Swedish credit and capital market. There is every likelihood that the NPIF will continue to grow.

The NPIF funds, according to current law, must be invested in bonds and debentures publicly tendered by a Swedish bank, in loans to premium payers, or in other securities or notes issued by the government, local authorities, or credit institutions. To date about one-half of the total investments have been made up of housing loans and one-third of loans to the private business sector.

In the Swedish monetary and financial organization there is a combination of private, cooperative, semiofficial, and official institutions. These institutions have tended, to date, to preserve the desired degree of competition whereby private and public interest are well served.

The United Kingdom

British monetary policy is implemented by a combination
of discount policy and open market operations. Unlike the
situation in the United States, for example, the Bank of England
does not lend directly to commercial banks but only to discount
houses whose main operations are to underwrite weekly Treasury
bill issues with call loans secured mostly in the London clearing
banks. The Bank of England restricts credit by selling Treasury
bills or government bonds through its "special buyer" (a discount house) or the "government broker" (a securities dealer),
thus absorbing cash from the banking system. To restore their
cash and liquidity positions, the banks can withdraw their call
loans from the discount houses; the discount houses in turn
may be forced to borrow from the Bank of England at the bank
rate that, in contrast to the Fed's discount rate, is a penalty
rate.
   The London clearing banks together with smaller Scottish
and Northern Irish banks dominate the domestic commercial
banking system. Other important elements in the monetary
and financial structure are the discount houses, hire purchase
(rental) companies, insurance companies, superannuation and
pension funds, the Post Office Savings Bank, building societies,
and investment trusts.
   In contrast to the United States there are only about 20
banks in the United Kingdom but with 12,000 branches. The
11 members of the London Clearing House account for about 80
percent of these branches and about 85 percent of all deposits.
They in turn are dominated by a "Big Five."
   Though not required, British banks customarily hold balances at the Bank of England and vault cash equal to about 8
percent of their deposit liability. This figure is in addition to
special deposits at the Bank that banks might have to hold from
time to time under directives. Moreover, banks have come to
be expected to maintain a liquidity ratio of at least 30 percent:
Bank holdings of liquid reserves comprise vault cash, balance
at the Bank of England, money at call and short notice (usually
seven days), and commercial and Treasury bills and are expected
to be equal in value to at least 30 percent of their net deposit
obligations.
   One very important British practice is the "overdraft"
facilities that permit bank customers to write checks over and
above current accounts. The facility plays the same role as
the U.S. "line of credit." It confers to potential deficit spending

units the power to incur indebtedness. This is in contrast with
another source of liquidity, cash, permitting a deficit spending
unit to avoid further indebtedness. Overdraft facility and cash
are clearly imperfect substitutes.

In sum, the British central banking system differs from
that of the United States. British banks do not have a direct
access to the Bank of England; Bank rate always is penal;
liquidity ratios are very important; and, partly because British
banking is so concentrated, full Bank rate policy is plausible.
As in the United States, the British monetary base increased
significantly during World War II when the central bank purchased
government debt leading to a multiple expansion of bank assets.
The huge increment of government debt, together with the bank's
practice of maintaining at least a 30 percent liquidity ratio, has
opened up new possibilities for monetary control.

Yugoslavia

The influence of money in the economies of the socialist
countries of Europe has increased, and Yugoslavia is the pace-
setter for these countries.[5] When it abandoned the Soviet type
of planning apparatus, money began to play an important role
in economic activity. The former concept of the money supply,
defined in such a way as to include only coin and paper money,
was inadequate in a country that considered decentralization
seriously. By the beginning of 1952 a new definition more consistent with the new economic system was agreed upon. Since
1952 the money supply has been defined to include all monetary
means that can be used directly as a means of payment, such
as coin, paper money, transfer account of enterprises, liquid
assets in investment funds, and other monetary assets, such
as savings deposits, that can be readily converted. Such a
definition, however, does not establish a clear-cut division between liquid and nonliquid assets. The vast middle ground
between these types of assets is a growing source of concern
for the country's money managers.

The characteristic that distinguishes the Yugoslav economy
from other economies that place emphasis on a relatively free
market or economic planning is that it maintains economic planning
together with a considerable degree of freedom on the part of
individual economic units. Consequently, its economy can best
be described as a mixture of two apparently opposite elements.
The far-reaching and liberalizing economic reforms of July 1965
served to continue this mixture, even though greater freedom

was given individual economic units at the expense of the central authorities.

The institutional adjustments in the 1965 reform have had fundamental consequences in the financial field. Further decentralization of economic decision-making power, an increase in the role of autonomous economic processes, and particularly the substantial increase in the share of voluntary saving and financial saving formation have resulted in a significant increase in the role of financial variables.

In the monetary field, the institutional changes made monetary processes more complex and effective. Demand and supply functions of money involved new and important behavior variables. As a result, the adjustment processes of demand to the supply of money have become more complicated. Moreover, stabilization goals have become at least as important as production and development goals. This requires an efficient monetary equilibrium policy and involves the entire complicated body of problems related to monetary policy formation and implementation. Thus, the institutional changes of the reform have brought about a substantial increase in monetary effects. Monetary policy has not become one of the strategic economic policy instruments.

The consequences of these changes in the field of financial intermediation are even more important. The changes in saving formation and investment decision-making required comprehensive adjustments of financial institutions, instruments, and operations, including organization of efficient financial markets. Under the new conditions brought about by the reform, the financial structure has become responsible for a significant part of saving and financial saving formation on the one hand and economic allocation of the essential part of saving on the other. The efficiency of the financial mechanism has become the essential precondition for smooth functioning of economic processes and promotion of a high rate of economic growth. Failure of the financial mechanism would hamper the efficient functioning of the economic system and in effect require a backward readjustment of infrainstitutional structure.

Before the 1965 reform the structure of financial institutions involved a central bank, deposit banks, and investment loan funds. It was recognized very early that this structure of financial institutions and their operations had many deficiencies and that plans for the reform would have to include significant institutional adjustments in this area.

The principal deficiencies in the financial institutions came from their administrative character and the strong government influence. Investment funds were, in fact, government institu-

tions. Their resources came mainly from taxes, and the allocation of these resources was under tight government control,
although effected through granting credits and usually involving
competitive bidding. [6]

Banks also were under comprehensive government control.
They were established by government bodies. These bodies
appointed the management and had strong influence on bank
policy formation. Banks were authorized to operate only within
the territory of the government that had established them.
There was little room for economic reasoning and free decision
making. Such a structure for financial institutions was obviously
inappropriate for a system where autonomous economic processes
play a strategic role, especially in saving and investment. These
shortcomings are reinforced in the new system, where monetary
processes and financial intermediation now are based on a large
body of behavior variables and where financial institutions have
to perform a significant degree of economic calculation. This
structure was inappropriate even before the reform period, so
that plans for its readjustment became urgent relatively early.
It is for this reason that institutional changes in the financial
field were begun even before the reform, partly to make urgent
corrections and partly as preparation for the reform. As a
result, two groups of institutional adjustments were implemented
before the reform of 1965.

First, nearly all investment loan funds were abolished,
beginning with the Federal Investment Loan Fund in 1964. [7]
Second, new banking legislation was passed in March 1965, [8]
introducing fundamental changes in organization, management,
and functions of banks. Both of these groups of changes have
significantly adjusted the financial structure to the new needs
of financing. It will be seen, however, that institutional adjustment does not necessarily mean functional adjustment, and that
the above measures have only created a suitable institutional
basis for a long-run process of adjustment of functioning of
financial institutions to the new financing needs.

The banking structure introduced in 1965-66, after a
relatively long period of investigation, gave banks far more
responsibility for saving formation, stimulation of supply of
financial resources, and economic allocation of saving. In effect,
changes introduced by the new legislation included both organiza-
tional and conceptual modifications to decrease the influence of
government and increase the influence of enterprises on bank
policy formation.

The reorganization of banking involved the National Bank
of Yugoslavia as a central bank, commercial banks, investment
banks, and savings banks.

The role, organization, and operations of the National Bank of Yugoslavia[9] have not been changed significantly.[10] It remains the central bank of Yugoslavia, performing regular central banking operations, including monetary regulations, issue of bank notes and coins, holding of foreign exchange reserves, and so on.

The National Bank of Yugoslavia is an independent federal institution, established by federal law. The bank is managed by the governor, who is appointed by the Federal Assembly on the recommendation of the Federal Executive Council. He is responsible to both of these institutions for the implementation of bank operations and targets. There is another managing body in the bank: the Council of the Working Community. Its organization and election are similar to those of the Worker's Councils in socialist enterprises. Its responsibility, however, is rather limited, and it involves labor relations, working conditions, decision making in the field of personal income and investment, fixing fees for bank services, and establishment of bank bylaws. The council is not responsible for monetary regulations or performance of other bank operations.

The bank's head office is in Belgrade. In addition, there are six central offices in the capitals of the six republics.

One of the significant questions in interpreting a central bank's position is its relation to the government. As has been stated, the National Bank is an independent institution. It is not, however, independent in monetary policy formation. The Federal Assembly and the Federal Executive Council decide monetary policy targets, and the National Bank plays a significant role by preparing proposals and furnishing policy makers with the appropriate analysis for relevant economic developments and forecasts. The National Bank's monetary planning is particularly significant in this connection. Proposals by the National Bank are usually accepted by policy makers without significant corrections. As a consequence the National Bank's influence is considerable in monetary policy formation.

The role of the federal secretary of finance is reduced to supervision of the legal conformity of bank operations and regulations.

The balance sheet of the National Bank gives a useful indication of its operation. The assets side of this balance sheet is characterized by three peculiarities. First, there are no securities (because of the negligible amount of bonds issued). Second, the main part of the bank's assets consists of discount credits, showing that these credits are the strategic instrument of monetary policy. Third, there is no item relating to a gold (or foreign exchange) cover of bank liabilities. On the liability side there are no specific elements, except the existence of the item related to monetary float.[11]

The banking structure in operation since 1966 has been hampered by many obstacles. First, the existing structure of investments, which were made during a period when economic calculations played a minor role, proved resistant to attempts to readjust them to the new banking principles. Important external barriers existed that hampered improvement in the efficiency of banking—for example, the still-important influence of governments; an inadequate interest rate policy, which insisted on relatively low interest rates; a demand for financial resources that outpaced the supply because of relatively low risk elasticity, a low interest rate, and requirements for a high rate of economic growth; and a relatively undifferentiated financial structure that overloaded banks. Their net effect was to hamper stronger economic determination of bank behavior, to induce regional confinement of financial flows (under the influence of government bodies), and to weaken bank stimulation of saving and supply of financial resources and economic allocation of these resources. These facts suggest that the main cause of deficiencies in the banking structure come from external sources. This is a significant observation regarding future developments of banking structure, indicating that further improvement is needed on the external conditions of its functioning, rather than on new institutional adjustments. This is also consistent with the old rule that the banking system shares the advancement of efficiency of the whole economy.

In summary, the structure of financial institutions in Yugoslavia is relatively simple. More of its deficiencies can be traced to its functioning than to its institutional pattern. The fact that there are only two of six possible types of financial institutions does not mean very much. There are many economies more developed than Yugoslavia's whose financial structure does not include all types of financial institutions.

The above analysis of the structure of financial institutions in Yugoslavia shows that its deficiencies stem from both internal and external causes, though the external tend to dominate. Further development of the structure of financial institutions may be expected to take place. In this connection, the main improvements may come from a more realistic interest rate policy, reduction in government influence on bank policy, more energetic participation of socialist enterprises in bank policy formation, and a surmounting of the historical barrier of the administrative approach to the banking business and the structure of bank investments related to this approach, which have been inherited from the previous periods of rigid central planning. Some of these problems will very likely be resolved by provisions of the new Constitution approved and adopted in 1974. Among other things, the new Constitution envisions a dominant role for self-management of workers in associated labor in the management and use of the monetary accumulation.

MONETARY ARRANGEMENTS WITHIN THE EUROPEAN ECONOMIC COMMUNITY

The outstanding attempt at economic integration with a multiple currency system and fixed exchange rates today is the European Economic Community. The EEC, also known as the Common Market or the Community or simply as The Six, was created by the Treaty of Rome on March 25, 1957.[12] It is designed to become, eventually, a common market for goods and services, labor, and capital. In addition, there are provisions for the coordination of monetary and fiscal policies, as well as other economic and social policies, including agricultural. It is also envisioned that obstacles to competitive conditions will be removed. Original members are France, the Federal Republic of Germany, Italy, and the Benelux countries. We shall focus our discussion on these six original members.

The EEC's monetary arrangements are of special concern here. The Treaty of Rome, Article 6, Paragraph 1, states that member countries should "coordinate monetary policy in cooperation with Community organs, insofar as such coordination is necessary for the attainment of the goal of this treaty." In addition, in Article 3 the EEC is obliged to "make possible the coordination of economic policy of the member states and the alleviation of disturbances in the equilibrium of their balance of payments."

One of the permanent organs of the EEC is the Monetary Committee. Its purpose is to harmonize monetary policy among the several member countries. Its powers, however, are advisory. Two members who are experts in monetary and financial matters are elected to the committee by each EEC country. Typically, a country's representation on the committee consists of a high government official and a representative of its central bank, supported by two alternates. The more recently created Committee of Central Bank Governors works with the Monetary Committee in advising the Commission on ways and means of promoting the coordination of member countries' monetary policies.

It would seem that the influence of the Monetary Committee is growing, particularly in international monetary issues. There has been progressive coordination of external monetary policies of the several EEC members. By the late 1960s the committee in effect prepared decisions taken by the six finance ministers of the EEC countries regarding special drawing rights and reforms of the IMF.[13]

The treaty does provide for more specific forms of monetary cooperation. Article 107 states that each member shall treat its policy with regard to exchange rates as a matter of common interest. Article 108 provides that the Commission shall recommend the granting of mutual assistance. This may take the form of either support action in concert with another international organization or limited credits from other members. This latter may take the form of intercentral bank short-term support for balance-of-payments difficulties, which were brought into being in February 1970. It is in effect a swap network with each central bank assigned a quota. Another arrangement is a medium support program to be utilized by a member government that may find itself in serious balance-of-payments difficulties.

The establishment of a European fund for monetary cooperation to be integrated in a future common organization of central banks is another measure designed to push forth monetary cooperation with coordination among member countries. With the creation of the European Monetary System (EMS) in March 1979 Europe moved another step toward monetary integration.

As presently constituted, the EMS is, in some respects, an extension of the "joint float" or the "snake" monetary arrangements in which several EEC members have been participating for several years. A number of new features have been added making the EMS a more comprehensive system. Such additional arrangements as the European currency unit (ECU) serve as the linchpin of the EMS. The ECU is a composite unit, consisting of fixed amounts of currencies of EEC participants. It does not exist in a physical sense, as currencies of individual countries do. It is to serve as a monetary asset that can be held as resources by the participating central banks, borrowed and lent, and used in settlement of debts among them. While its use will be limited initially to participating in the EMS, it is expected that the ECU could eventually serve as an international reserve asset similar to special drawing rights and be held and used by central banks worldwide.

SOVEREIGNTY, MONEY CREATION, AND A
EUROPEAN FEDERAL RESERVE SYSTEM

The basic monetary problem, which is the creation and regulation of the supply of money and credit, has not been resolved. This is the issue of national monetary sovereignty. After all, the Monetary Committee's power is only advisory. The recommendations of the committee are not binding on EEC members; a member country can repudiate the recommendations of the Monetary Committee if they conflict with its national policy. The fact is that the Treaty of Rome did not create a supranational monetary authority. On the other hand, the sacrifice of sovereignty may have already taken place when members agreed to stable and apparently "fixed" exchange rates and free trade and investment within the area. How little sovereignty had been sacrificed was underscored by mid-1976 with the retirement of the French franc from "the snake," a joint float of strong EEC currencies that moves within prescribed limits (2.25 percent up or down) against the dollar. This demonstrated once again the shortcomings of the EEC's monetary arrangements. Apparently bolder political steps are going to be required if true progress toward monetary and economic union is to be accomplished. EMS may be viewed as one step—albeit an important step—toward integration. Full monetary union, with all its implications for national sovereignty, is simply left in the present catalog of goals. Indeed, national political leadership has resisted encroachment on its traditional decision-making authority.

One can speculate, of course, that the Monetary Committee and indeed EMS may evolve into a supranational monetary authority for the EEC, even though the creation of a common currency may be a long way off. This is possible, as in the case of the United States, beginning with the First National Bank of the United States in 1791, passing through a multiple currency system in the pre-Civil War period to a unified currency in the National Bank era, and culminating in the current Board of Governors of the Federal Reserve System. It could ultimately take the form and functions of the Board of Governors. This would be tantamount to the creation of a unified currency and a supranational central bank for the EEC.[14] The several central banks of member countries would then, presumably, become regional banks with roles and functions similar to those of the several Federal Reserve District Banks in the United States.

It is also possible that the Monetary Committee could develop traditional monetary policy tools such as open market operations and reserve requirements with which to implement and carry

out a centralized monetary policy. One barrier is that these
traditional instruments of monetary policy do not play the same
role in the several member countries. Their experiences with
these instruments differ significantly.[15] Some member countries
have little experience with the traditional instruments of monetary
policy. One would expect that substantial institutional changes
within these countries would be required before a supranational
monetary authority would be able to exercise a significant influence. The necessity for these changes could be reduced under
a system of flexible exchange rates since member states need
not sacrifice sovereignty over their internal affairs.

As its principal instrument of monetary policy, the National
Bank of Belgium employs changes in the discount rate and moral
suasion. Open market operations in Belgium are carried out
by the Securities Stabilization Fund. Resources for these operations are obtained in part by advances from the National Bank.
In 1957 the scope and activities of the fund were greatly enlarged
when it was permitted to issue its own certificates and to deal
in short- and long-term government securities. Reserve requirements for the country's banks are established by the Banking
Commission. Since 1962 this commission has been empowered to
impose compulsory cash reserve requirements for banks upon
proposal of the national bank.

Principal monetary instruments in France are: the terms
applied to rediscounts of short-term commercial paper, and the
minimum liquidity coefficient of the banks. Ceilings on rediscounts of short-term commercial paper other than for paper
originating in export trade are imposed by the Bank of France.
A penalty rate higher than the basic discount rate is applied
to rediscounts in excess of the ceilings. Frequent changes
occur in both the rates and ceilings. The liquidity coefficient,
first introduced in 1961, is the relationship between deposit
liabilities and such selected assets as cash, Treasury bills,
medium-term paper, and export paper. Since 1948, moreover,
banks are required to maintain a minimum ratio of deposit holdings to holdings of Treasury bills alone.

Open market operations of the Bank of France are of very
limited importance and completely different in character from
those in the United States. Thus, for example, the Bank of
France stands ready to buy from banks, up to given limits,
Treasury bills, bankers acceptance, as well as other types of
paper in the money market.

By way of contrast in neighboring Germany, the Bundesbank conducts open market operations in such securities as
Treasury bills and government bonds, as well as in other bonds

admitted to the official stock exchange. It may establish minimum
reserve requirements on credit institutions at any level up to
a maximum of 30 percent for demand deposits, 20 percent for
time deposits, and 10 percent for savings deposits. The Bundesbank may also change the discount rate and the rate it charges
for advances on eligible paper.

In addition to these conventional instruments of monetary
policy, the Bundesbank has developed a technique for influencing
the supply of funds on the domestic money market. The technique involves influencing the attractiveness of incentives to
German commercial banks in making covered investments on the
foreign exchange markets. By making it more expensive to banks
to make such covered investments, the supply of funds available
to the domestic market is increased, and conversely.

In Italy open market operations are not used to govern
bank liquidity, owing to the lack of a developed money market.
Compulsory reserve requirements were established in 1947, and
their level remained unchanged until 1962. Changes in the Bank
of Italy's rates of advances and discounts have been very infre-
quent.

The Bank of Italy's principal monetary instruments appear
to be moral suasion and the determination every four months on
the size of banks' lines of credit. Internal credit expansion is
also influenced by the Bank in actions affecting the foreign
borrowing and lending power of the country's banks. This is
accomplished by regulations concerning the amount of net foreign
borrowing in which banks are allowed to engage, and short-term
swaps of Italian lire for dollars between the Bank of Italy and
commercial banks.

In the Netherlands, on the other hand, the Governing
Board of the Netherlands Bank has authority to set discount
rates and conduct open market operations. In fact, since 1952,
when open market operations were first begun, the Netherlands
Bank has made extensive use of this instrument of monetary
policy. The maturities of the securities trade in open market
operations have been from one to five years and have consisted
of government securities and bonds quoted on the Amsterdam
Stock Exchange.

Reserve requirements are also an important instrument for
implementing the country's monetary policy. Under the terms
of the "gentlemen's agreement" of March 1954, the Bank is empowered to raise the cash reserve requirements of commercial
banks to 15 percent of total deposits. In the 1950s this ratio
was as high as 10 percent total deposits. In the 1960s this
ratio has been as high as 10 percent and as low as 4 percent.

The problem is compounded, moreover, by the fact that reserve ratios of commercial banks differ among the several countries. The net result is that the leverage effect of reserve changes produced by the execution of monetary policy would tend to differ among the several member countries. It would also very likely have a differential impact on money supplies, prices, and incomes in these countries.

In Belgium the existing commercial bank structure dates from 1935. Traditionally banks have granted all forms of credit and purchased shares of industrial and commercial enterprises. The "mixed" character of these banks was somewhat more clearly defined in 1935 when they were limited to collecting deposits and granting short-term credit. In 1967 banks were authorized to purchase enterprise bonds and most were also authorized by the government to grant loans under the Economic Laws of 1959 and 1966 whereby investment in selected sectors was encouraged through interest rate subsidies and loan guarantees.

A Post Office Giro System operates so as to facilitate the transfer of funds. Unlike commercial banks, however, the Post Office neither accepts time deposits nor does it pay interest on demand (sight) deposits. Belgian banks may pay interest on demand deposits. In large banks the rate of interest is 0.50 per annum on these deposits.

The Institute of Rediscount and Guarantee (IRG) established in 1935 assists banks and firms in dealing with temporary liquidity problems. In addition, and perhaps even more important, IRG operations in the so-called out-of-bank market, whereby it purchases commercial bills for its own account or as broker, serve as a mechanism linking banks or banks and other financial institutions purchasing bills, mortgage and savings companies, and semipublic credit institutions.

A "call-money" market exists and since 1959 has been merged with a similar market operating among certain public institutions that entrust temporary surpluses to the National Bank for allocation to organizations in need of liquidity. In order to prevent banks from depending permanently for funds on the call-money market, a 1959 regulation requires that each bank must lend the call-money market a larger amount than it has borrowed as computed at the end of each quarter.

Other important monetary and financial institutions are banks, insurance companies, the National Company for Credit to Industry (specializing in granting medium- and long-term credit to private enterprises), Caisse Generale d'Epargne et de Retraite (a public institution specializing in home construction loans, long-term loans, and government securities), and Credit

Communal de Belgique (a bank of the provinces and communes holding short-, medium-, and long-term loans).

Banks in France are highly structured and specialized. The system consists of so-called registered and nonregistered banks. Registered banks are under the direct control of the Bank of France and its two subsidiaries, the National Credit Council and the Banking Control Commission. The nonregistered banks are the Credit Populaire, the National Agricultural Credit Bank, and the French Foreign Trade Bank.

As of December 1970 the three categories of registered banks numbered 186 deposit banks; there were 16 merchant (commercial) banks and 33 banks extending long-term and medium-term credit. Although deposit banks may grant long-term loans, they generally confine their loans to the short term. Merchant or commercial banks are presumably limited to long-term loans; no difference in practice exists between deposit and commercial banks. Medium- and long-term credit banks accept deposits for two years or more and extend loans maturing in two years or more.

The nonbank financial intermediaries include financing companies, leasing companies, insurance companies, and, in general, all institutional savings groups. Among these intermediaries the National Credit Bank (NCB) holds a special position in the allocation of medium- and long-term credit to industrial and commercial enterprises. More important, perhaps, the NCB works very closely with the government in executing the French National Plan.

Another institution holding a special position is the Deposit and Consignment Office (DCO), which is a public agency founded by Napoleon. It is independent of the Bank of France. It serves as an investment clearinghouse. Its resources come mainly from savings banks, especially the National Savings Bank, which operates in all post offices, and from social insurance and social security institutions. These resources are directed toward investment in public or semipublic organizations or under DCO control. A portion of these resources (about 20 percent) is invested in liquid short- and convertible medium-term assets in order to be able to meet withdrawal requests. A portion is invested in public or semipublic institutions, thereby often serving to finance the national plan. The remainder is invested in the capital market. The DCO is also a major operator in the stock market. In effect, DCO converts sight or short-term deposits into long-term investments. It is in direct competition for deposits and loans with the country's banks and savings banks.

The French Treasury plays a role that is quite different from that in the United States or Great Britain. In France the Treasury is responsible for the execution of the budget and for public debt management. It does this through various sub-agencies with operations taking on monetary and banking characteristics. All of this is in addition to its traditional function of fiscal agent to the government. In the United States the Federal Reserve System, along with commercial banks, has an important role in Treasury operations. In Great Britain the Bank of England, through its services as fiscal agent and public debt manager, plays an important role in Treasury operations.

The country's money and capital markets have not played as important a role as elsewhere. This is particularly true since World War II. The French market has moved from "outside the Bank" to "inside the Bank," thanks to the fact that the Bank's discount rate is lower than the market rate. In effect the money market is no longer autonomous. It is narrow and its rates exceed central bank rates.

The fact that an inadequate capital market exists in the country contributes also to the narrowness of the money market. The lack of development of the capital market is in part the result of the dominant role the Treasury plays in the collection of savings and in budget investment policy. In part it is also the result of the lack of appeal that long-term securities have for French investors.

Thanks to the structural reforms in place since the late 1960s and early 1970s, many of the more obvious problems are being dealt with in a constructive way. For example, the Marjolin-Sadkin-Wormser report completed in June 1969 addresses itself to improving the conditions in the money and capital markets. Various other laws and ordinances passed since 1967 dealing with one aspect or another of the country's monetary and financial structure have, according to various observers, the objective of improving this structure.

The banking structure in the Federal Republic of Germany is relatively homogenous in that almost every bank will take on any banking transaction, though the significance of such a transaction may vary according to the type of bank. According to official banking data covering 3,600 banks at the end of 1970 and accounting for about 98 percent of the business volume of all credit institutions other than building and loan associations, not more than 260 institutions representing little more than 25 percent of the total resources belong to institutions carrying on specialized business. These are institutions extending long-term mortgages, institutions dealing with special transactions such as long-term industrial loans, or installment sales-financing institutions and the postal giro and savings facilities. Although the remaining banks may tend to specialize in one form of lending or borrowing, for the most part they all offer their customers the entire range of banking services, including long- and short-term lending. These banks are referred to as "universal banks" and cover commercial banks, savings banks, central giro institutions, and the cooperative banks with their central institutions.

In German "universal banks" as well as in specialized banks, long-term loans account for about one-half of all loans and investments. Other nonbank financial intermediaries specializing in long-term credit account for about 40 percent of loans granted for four years or more. This is in contrast to the situation in other countries where institutions specializing in the long-term market play a dominant role. The situation in Germany is accounted for by the activities of "universal banks" in the long-term market.

Banks and other financial institutions play a very significant role in the securities and capital markets in Germany. The markets are not confined to mutual claims and liabilities of nonbanks. An interbank market functions so as to convert funds placed with banks at short and medium terms with ultimately long-term loans. This is accomplished so as not to impose an undue liquidity risk on the lending bank. The risk is converted into a price risk. At the end of 1970, 158 billion deutsche marks (DM) of fixed interest securities issued by domestic borrowers were outstanding; of these, no less than DM 118 billion, or almost three-quarters, were bank bonds. Industrial bonds constituted little more than 5 percent of the total.[16] At the end of 1970 roughly half of the outstanding volume of bonds were in the portfolios of the banks, including the Deutsche Bundesbank. The remainder were in the portfolios of private households, industrial and commercial firms, other financial institutions, and social security funds.

The nominal value of total shares outstanding at the end of 1970 amounted to DM 56 billion. This figure is not strictly compatible with the fixed interest securities amount. The nominal value differs from the market value much more than in the case of bonds. Moreover, the interlinking of corporations must also be taken into account. In any case the figure is only a very rough measure of the amount finance corporations have been able to raise through the issue of securities.

In Italy the banking system operates under the Banking Law of 1936. At the end of 1970 there were 1,179 banks with 10,800 offices in Italy. A clear distinction is made between short-term, medium-term, and long-term banking operations. Banks can operate only in the short-term market. They may accept sight deposits and time deposits up to 18 months. They may make loans up to 12 months for working capital of enterprises—sometimes, however, fixed investments are also financed by "rolling over" loans through special credit institutions fully or partially owned by banks.

There has been a tendency in Italy, as elsewhere, for banks to take on a more universal character and provide their customers with a wide variety of services. Italy has also shared in the trend toward concentration in banking. Thus, at the end of 1970 the country's five largest banks accounted for 30 percent of resident deposits, 80 percent of foreign deposits, and 35 percent of total loans. Italian banking also has a developing network of cooperation and participation in such other financial institutions as mutual funds, credit institutes, leasing, and computer services, thereby providing an entire array of financial services.

A number of banks have what amounts to a group central bank. For example, the Credit Institute for Savings Banks holds the compulsory reserves of savings banks; the Central Institute holds reserves for Popular Banks; the Credit Institute holds for Rural and Handicraft Banks.

In the last decades large-scale growth has occurred in so-called special credit institutes. They are, in fact, medium-term banks for development of financing, typically capitalized by the government or commercial banks. These institutes account for more than one-third of total bank lending in the country. They obtain their funds by accepting long-term deposits of 18 months and more, issuing fixed income securities (which banks often buy and thus transfer liquid savings into long-term investments), and by borrowing abroad.

There is really no money market in Italy in the sense of a meeting point for the demand and supply short-term funds of banks, financial institutions, and other dealers. In fact, the money market in the country is little more than an interbank market where interest rates seldom change. Some attempt has been made to create a more effective money market by issuing Treasury bills in tranches, at variable prices, and according to Treasury requirements.

Moreover, banks must obtain prior authorization from the Bank of Italy before lending to any one customer more than one-fifth of the bank's capital. Thus the central bank reviews in advance all large loans and so maintains control of the economic and financial situation and of the investment programs of individual enterprises. Additional controls on the capital market are exercised by the monetary authorities on the basis of prior authorization for the establishment of new enterprises, increases in capital and bond issues by business, banks, and special credit institutes whenever the warrants exceed 500 million lire. This is also true for new equity issues by firms listed on the stock exchange when the shares of stock exceed 1,000 million lire, and for their underwriting by banks.

Rapid changes have occurred in recent years in the monetary and financial organization of many countries. They consist of new forms of financing, greater mobility of short- and long-term funds, and blurring of distinctions between the various forms of financial institutions.

The Netherlands shares in these changes. At the end of 1970 commercial banks in the Netherlands accounted for the buildup of financial resources in the country outside the central bank. In the second place are giro services followed by agricultural credit institutions. The number of commercial banks decreased from 117 at the end of 1960 to 70 at the end of 1971. The three largest banks conduct over 70 percent of the banking business.

Formerly the money market activities were detached from those in the field of credit to the private sector. Banks simply offered nothing in terms of funds to the private sector through the money markets. Nonbank financial institutions supplied only a very limited amount of short-term loanable funds. It is thus no surprise that the business sector obtained very few funds from the money market. All of this has changed in the past few years—albeit there is still nothing like a stampede for accommodations at the market. Discernible trends do exist that suggest that money will play a more important role in the future.

A close relationship exists between the supply of credit by the banking system to the private sector and the capital market. Interest rate differentials and expectations often influence the private sector in its choice between the two sources of finance. Indeed in periods when credit conditions are tight the relationship is underscored. The capital market that is left outside the direct influence of monetary policy is, in effect, the principal source of alternative financing, especially since borrowing abroad is subject to central bank control.

NOTES

1. Background material for these countries is drawn from several sources, including, George Macesich, "Supply and Demand

for Money in Canada, " in Varieties of Monetary Experience,
ed. David Meiselman (Chicago: University of Chicago Press,
1970); D. Dimitrijević and George Macesich, Money and Finance
in Contemporary Yugoslavia (New York: Praeger, 1973); George
Macesich, Money in a European Common Market Setting (Baden-
Baden: Nomos Verlagsgesellschaft, 1972); Karel Holbik, ed.,
Monetary Policy in Twelve Industrial Countries (Boston: Federal
Reserve Bank of Boston, 1973); George Macesich, ed., Proceedings and Reports (Tallahassee: Florida State University Center
for Yugoslav-American Studies, Research, and Exchanges),
Florida State University Slavic Papers 1963-74.

2. R. Craig McIvor, Canadian Monetary, Banking, and
Fiscal Development (Toronto: The Macmillan Company of Canada,
1958), pp. 236-37.

3. The so-called national banks are the commercial banks
chartered by the federal government. The banks chartered by
the federal government were permitted to issue their own notes
just as banks today can issue deposits. For a discussion of
the U.S. monetary and financial system, see Milton Friedman
and Anna J. Schwartz, A Monetary History of the United States
1867-1960 (Princeton, N.J.: Princeton University Press, 1963).

4. Commission on Money and Credit, "The Organization
of the Federal Reserve System," in Monetary Economics, ed.
Jonas Prager (New York: Random House, 1971), p. 103.

5. See George Macesich, Yugoslavia: Theory and Practice
of Development Planning (Charlottesville: The University Press
of Virginia, 1964), Chapter 9, "Major Trends in the Post-War
Economy of Yugoslavia," in Contemporary Yugoslavia: Twenty
Years of Socialism, ed. Wayne S. Vucinich (Berkeley: University
of California Press, 1969); and Macesich and Dimitrijević.

6. These funds were administered by banks, which were
obliged to follow the economic plans of the relevant government
bodies. In addition to specified projects that had to be financed,
the economic plans stipulated for one part of the resources only
the purpose for which it should be used, for example, a sugar
factory, so that the bank administering the fund had relatively
more room for decision making, mainly in deciding which project
among many in competitive bidding was the best.

7. Abolishment of investment loan funds does not mean
abolishment of a government role in investment financing.
Sources of these funds remained under government control,
and it continued to play a significant role in investment financing,
for example, using repayments and interest on credits as a
source of financing.

8. The new banking legislation could not be implemented
at once, and a one-year period was granted to banks to adjust

to the new legal provisions. These adjustments were not performed until the first quarter of 1966, so that for all practical
purposes the banking structure remained unchanged until the
reform in July 1965.

9. The bank was established in 1883 as the Privileged
National Bank of the Kingdom of Serbia (Privilegovana Narodna
Banka) by virtue of the Law of the National Bank. Thereafter
the name was changed several times. It was the National Bank
of the Kingdom of Serbs, Croats, and Slovenes in 1920, the
National Bank of the Kingdom of Yugoslavia in 1919, and the
National Bank of the Federal People's Republic of Yugoslavia in
1946. The present name was introduced in the Constitution of
the Socialist Federal Republic of Yugoslavia, 1963, Art. 29.

10. The operations of the National Bank of Yugoslavia
were significantly adjusted to the new needs in 1961, when
crediting of customers was transferred to other banks and the
National Bank of Yugoslavia became a regular central bank.
Consequently it was not necessary to introduce significant
changes in 1965.

11. Monetary float is on the liability side in the "giro"
payment system (European practice). In the checking payment
system monetary float is on the asset side (net), as is the case
with the Combined Balance Sheet of the Federal Reserve System
of the United States.

12. Treaty Establishing the European Economic Community
and Connected Documents (Brussels: Publishing Services of the
European Communities, 1958).

13. George Plescoft, "International Liquidity: The Cases
of the Common Market," American Economic Review, May 1968,
pp. 608-19.

14. See, for example, "Eminger Sees Need for a European
'Fed,'" European Community, June 1958, p. 18. See also Euro-
pean Economic Community, Commission Memorandum of the Com-
mission on the Action Programme for the Second Stage (Brussels,
October 24, 1962); and B. J. Cohen, "The Euro-Dollar, the
Common Market, and Currency Unification," Journal of Finance,
December 1963, pp. 605-21. A useful discussion of EMS is pre-
sented in P. H. Trezise, ed., The European Monetary System:
Its Promise and Prospects (Washington, D.C.: Brookings Insti-
tution, 1979).

15. "Comparative Features of Central Banks in Selected
Foreign Countries," Joint Economic Committee, 88th Cong. 1st
sess. (Washington, D.C.: U.S. Government Printing Office,
1963). See also George Macesich, Money in a European Common
Market Setting, and Economic Stability: A Comparative Analysis
(Belgrade: BGZ, 1973).

16. Monthly Report of the Deutsche Bundesbank, May 1954.

7

MONEY DEMAND AND SUPPLY:
EMPIRICAL RESULTS

STATISTICAL TESTS

In this chapter estimates are made of the parameters of
various demand and supply functions for money—functions that
have been suggested by theoretical and empirical considerations.
The general theoretical framework of the analysis was presented
in Chapter 3.

The essence of economic theory is the interdependence of
economic phenomena and the determination of the values of economic variables by the simultaneous interaction of relationships.
It is generally recognized that there are pitfalls in attempting
to estimate the parameters of a single structural equation taken
from a large economic model. This is because the minimum
assumption for the consistency of ordinary least squares—that
the explanatory variables are uncorrelated with the disturbance
term—cannot be maintained if the equation to be estimated is
one of a system of simultaneous structural equations. In this
case, ordinary least squares loses consistency when used as an
estimator of a structural equation. However, the difficulty dis-
appears when used to estimate the equations of the related form
as all explanatory variables in reduced-form equations are either
exogenous or lagged. Therefore, to take account of the simultaneous nature of the equations in the model to be estimated
and to get consistent estimates, we apply a two-stage least-
squares regression method (TSLS) to the model.

In order to test the various demand and supply functions
for different economies, it is desirable that the samples chosen
should have certain attributes and should be homogenous. In
particular, the size of the sample should be sufficiently large
to permit statistical inferences. The time series in this study
contain 20 observations. Since we also perform statistical tests

on two subsample periods—1951-65 and 1966-80—the size of
observations for these two subperiods is reduced to only 15.
Accordingly, statistical tests have been devised to permit the
evaluation of empirical results estimated on the basis of relatively
small samples.

The problem of undersized samples is characterized by the
serious implication that the TSLS estimators do not exist. The
Klein-Goldberger model provides an example, since it contains
more than 30 predetermined variables and is estimated for only
20 observations.[1] Note that this is no problem at all from the
standpoint of asymptotic theory.

Kloek and Mennes have suggested replacing the matrix of
endogenous variables on the right-hand side of the equation by
a small number of principal components in order to avoid these
difficulties.[2] This method does have certain merits, but a dis-
advantage is its arbitrariness caused by the fact that the com-
putation of principal components requires a certain normalization
rule on the variables (such as a unit mean square). The alternative based on causal orderings is suggested by F. M. Fisher.[3]
This procedure, however, is difficult to apply without extensive
prior information on the equation system. A third approach,
to be used in the following sections, is proposed by Henri Theil.[4]
This approach can be summarized as follows:

First stage: estimate each structural equation by least
squares and compute the reduced-form residual matrix $\bar{U}$, which
is implied by these structural coefficient estimates.

Second stage: take the submatrix $\bar{U}_j$ of $\bar{U}$, which corresponds
with endogenously explanatory variables Y_j, and reestimate the
j^{th} structural equation by running a least-squares regression
of y_j on $(Y_j - \bar{U}_j X_j)$, where y_j and x_j are the dependent and
the predetermined explanatory variables in the structural equation. The use of the reduced-form residual matrix $\bar{U}$ has the
advantage that this is a residual matrix that has been derived
subject to all overidentifying restrictions on the structural
equations.[5]

In the empirical analysis that follows, gross national product
and wholesale price index are used for the income and price
variables in the demand function. Interest rates in nominal
terms are used to incorporate inflationary expectation. The
notations and definitions of other variables entering the demand
and supply functions are as given in previous chapters. Both
M_1 and M_2 definitions are considered. The usual regression
criteria are used to evaluate the results of the statistical tests.

These are: goodness of fit, indicated by the multiple correlation coefficients, R; the t test for significance of regression coefficients; the Durbin-Watson d statistics for measuring the degree to which serial correlation exists in the residuals; the extent to which the signs of the regression coefficients agree with expectation; and lack of multicollinearity among the explanatory variables.

ESTIMATES OF MONEY DEMAND FUNCTIONS

Estimates of the money demand functions are given in Table 7.1. The results obtained from TSLS regressions are satisfactory for indicating the significance of the income variable. All the signs of the coefficients of Y/P are in conformity with economic theory—the Y/P coefficients are positive. Both M_1^D/P and M_2^D/P are significantly related to Y/P. All income elasticities at sample mean levels are highly significant at the 1 percent level and in most cases they are elastic when M_2/P is used, except the United Kingdom and Sweden, as shown in Table 7.2. In the case of the United Kingdom and Sweden, the income elasticities are less than unity, ranging from 0.7354 to 0.9675. However, when M_1 is used, most of the income elasticities are less than unity, with an exception of Germany, Canada, Italy, and Yugoslavia, which have income elasticities of 1.0537, 1.1362, 1.3431, and 1.2863, respectively. This suggests economies of scale in the transactions demand for real balances. Even so, the empirical evidence strongly suggests that money is something of a luxury in the sense that 1 percent increases in real income will entail more than 1 percent increases in the demand for real cash balances. In an economy that has experienced inflation, time and savings deposits are more like luxury goods than ordinary money since the former performs the function of a store of value only as compared to a means of payment that is required in all transactions. We may expect, therefore, that the inclusion of time and savings deposits in money will make it more like a luxury good.

The regression coefficients for the interest variable r^s are not all with expected negative signs. Equations 4, 6, 7, 8, 13, and 18 have the unexpected positive coefficients. However, most of them, with an exception of equation 8 for Italy and equation 18 for Canada, are all insignificant at the 5 percent level according to t-test. Although the signs of the r^s coefficients in the rest of the equations are in agreement with our expectations, only those coefficients in equations 1-2 (for

TABLE 7.1

TSLS Estimates of Money Demand Function, 1951–80

$$M_q^D/P = a_0 + a_1 r^S + a_2(Y/P) + a_3 Z$$

Country	Equation	M_q^D/P	R^{-2} / F	SEEB / SPCB	Constant t-ratios	r^S	Y/P	Z
Belgium	1	M_1^D/P	0.9544 / 203.2961	0.3022 / 6.2370	1.8712 / 13.9121	-0.1787 / -3.5077	0.2379 / 14.7365	0.9238 / 0.7522
	2	M_2^D/P	0.9980 / 4922.8659	0.1517 / 2.1170	0.0038 / 0.0563	-0.1142 / -4.4656	0.4967 / 61.2869	1.0422 / 1.6906
France	3	M_1^D/P	0.9495 / 182.5841	0.2811 / 9.6350	0.6572 / 4.9597	-0.0553 / -1.2241	0.2716 / 12.4289	-0.5552 / -0.7375
	4	M_2^D/P	0.9919 / 1185.5311	0.2500 / 5.7190	-1.1181 / -9.4871	0.0382 / 0.9500	0.5438 / 27.9875	0.0230 / 0.0344
Germany	5	M_1^D/P	0.9928 / 1342.3002	0.0482 / 4.2770	0.0788 / 2.8669	-0.0328 / -4.4726	0.1698 / 57.0397	0.5188 / 1.7052
	6	M_2^D/P	0.9872 / 748.1091	0.2525 / 7.4350	-1.0663 / -7.4098	0.0010 / 0.0268	0.6347 / 40.7075	0.6193 / 0.3887
Italy	7	M_1^D/P	0.9783 / 436.2711	0.0401 / 9.8780	-0.1491 / -6.2519	0.0006 / 0.1658	0.6335 / 24.7491	0.0766 / 0.6610
	8	M_2^D/P	0.9936 / 1507.6371	0.0356 / 5.2810	-0.3003 / -14.1902	0.0153 / 4.4969	1.0069 / 44.3172	-0.1207 / -1.1736

Country	No.	Variable						
Netherlands	9	M_1^D/P	0.9927	0.0117	0.0789	-0.0074	0.2087	-0.0251
			1311.7521	3.9170	8.5057	-2.1739	21.2481	-0.4811
	10	M_2^D/P	0.9845	0.0549	-0.0258	-0.0332	0.6965	0.1127
			616.2287	8.3360	-0.5898	-2.0821	15.0558	0.4584
United Kingdom	11	M_1^D/P	0.5323	0.0077	0.1347	-0.0040	0.0795	-0.0157
			12.0000	4.4220	19.9897	-3.9622	5.8513	-0.5452
	12	M_2^D/P	0.7997	0.0309	0.0942	-0.0047	0.2856	0.2737
			39.5984	9.8120	3.4695	-1.1742	5.2114	2.3512
Sweden	13	M_1^D/P	0.9710	0.0143	0.0974	0.0049	0.0976	0.0049
			324.5856	4.3060	12.1996	1.4474	9.4958	0.1036
	14	M_2^D/P	0.9851	0.0541	0.0337	-0.0012	0.5906	0.2745
			639.7180	4.2360	1.1162	-0.0932	15.2285	1.5476
Yugoslavia (1956–80)	15	M_1^D/P	0.9472	0.1751	-0.0570	-0.0169	0.3766	-1.0993
			144.6219	17.6220	-0.2553	-0.6117	16.7320	-1.9450
	16	M_2^D/P	0.9723	0.3291	-0.6261	-0.0116	0.9478	-1.3505
			281.5295	13.8060	-1.4907	-0.2247	22.4067	-1.2713
Canada	17	M_1^D/P	0.8394	0.0306	0.0244	-0.0096	0.1863	-0.0271
			51.5163	16.9890	1.7762	-2.4279	8.4005	-0.4620
	18	M_2^D/P	0.9743	0.0411	-0.0877	0.0158	0.4212	-0.0230
			368.1947	9.1020	-4.7580	2.9647	14.1330	-0.2911
United States	19	M_1^D/P	0.6580	0.2264	1.8609	-0.0971	0.1311	-1.2728
			19.6005	7.5090	11.9066	-2.4985	6.5810	-1.0082
	20	M_2^D/P	0.9877	0.2024	-0.1354	-0.1572	0.5116	3.7400
			778.8670	3.5390	-0.9688	-4.5226	28.7240	3.3134

Source: International Monetary Fund, International Financial Statistics, various issues for the years 1950–81 (Washington, D.C.: IMF).

TABLE 7.2

Income Elasticities at Sample Mean Levels, 1951-80

Country	M_1^D/P	M_2^D/P
Belgium	0.7476	1.0555
France	0.8998	1.2028
Germany	1.0537	1.3073
Italy	1.3431	1.2858
Netherlands	0.8867	1.3378
United Kingdom	0.3721	0.7354
Sweden	0.6132	0.9675
Yugoslavia	1.2863	1.3495
Canada	1.1362	1.0239
United States	0.5441	1.1190

Source: Compiled by the authors.

Belgium), 5 (for Germany), 9-11 (for the Netherlands, and the United Kingdom when M_1 is used), 17 (for Canada when M_1 is used) and 19-20 (for the United States) are significant at the 5 percent level. The insignificance of the interest rate in most of the M_2 functions may be due partly to the fact that the positive relationship between the demand for time deposits and the short-term market interest rate has neutralized the inverse relationship between money demand and the short-term market interest rate in the M_2^D function.

Another result that agrees with theoretical considerations and the findings of other econometric studies is that the interest elasticity of M_1^D/P, which excludes time and savings deposits, is in general greater than the interest elasticity of M_2^D/P, which includes these deposits. When money is defined inclusive of time and savings deposits, part of the substitution effect caused by interest rate changes takes place among monetary assets; that is, part of the substitution effect is hidden by changes within the composition of money itself. This suggests that the definition of money and the method of estimation are therefore important factors in the test of the Keynesian liquidity preference function. Interest elasticities of M_1^D/P and M_2^D/P at sample mean levels are tabulated in Table 7.3. They are extremely low

TABLE 7.3

Interest Elasticities at Sample Mean Levels, 1951-80

Country	M_1^D/P	M_2^D/P
Belgium	-0.1393*	-0.0602*
France	-0.1144	0.0527
Germany	-0.1368*	0.0014
Italy	0.0118	0.1709*
Netherlands	-0.1491*	-0.3040*
United Kingdom	-0.1432*	-0.0942
Sweden	0.0932	-0.0059
Yugoslavia	-0.1354	-0.0389
Canada	-0.2643*	0.1729*
United States	-0.1437*	-0.1226*

*Significant at the 5 percent level.
Source: Compiled by the authors.

and insignificant in half of the class under study. Only in the case of Canada and the Netherlands are comparatively high elasticities observed. This suggests that during the period 1951-80 cash balance holders in Canada and the Netherlands were sensitive to variations in the interest rates in their adjustment of desired real cash balances. The prompt and rational portfolio adjustments during this period were further confirmed by a comparison of the interest elasticities in the demand-for-money equations with the traditional (narrower) definition and those with the broader definition. In the latter sets of equations these interest elasticities are in general smaller in the absolute value. This illustrates the fact that a decline in the interest rate encouraged the holding of money proper but discouraged depositing money in time and savings accounts. This is partly due to the high correlations existing between real national income and the rate of price change.

As for the United Kingdom and the United States, there exists a significantly positive relationship between demand of M_2 and the rate of change of prices. This is owing to the high correlations existing between real national income and the rate of price change as shown in Table 7.1. Further studies have indicated that the Z coefficients are highly significant at both the 1 percent and 5 percent levels in equations, which regress the real cash balances on Y/P and Z separately. Their coefficients, however, do not have the expected negative signs. Not only do the $\bar{R}^2$s of each single regression equation not suggest that the rate of change in the price level are responsible for a major part of the variations of the demand for M_2, but also that this variable does not dominate the other two variables in the multiple regressions where there are multicollinearity problems, and hence variables of secondary importance have insignificant coefficients or coefficients of the wrong signs.

The elasticities of M_1^D/P and M_1^D/P with respect to Z at sample mean levels are extremely low in most of the cases under study. They are tabulated in Table 7.4.

In summary, estimates of the money demand functions for the period 1951-80 given in Table 7.1 indicate that real income is the most important factor influencing the demand for real cash balances in the economies under review. The interest rate apparently plays a supplementary role in augmenting the demand for real money. The rate of price changes is the least important. In the United Kingdom, the United States, and Yugoslavia the rate of change in the price level appears to play an important role in influencing the demand for real cash balances. To judge from the high value of $\bar{R}^2$ in most of our estimates, the demand for money functions includes most of the important factors that are responsible for the variations in the stock of real cash balances.

A comparison of the equations using M_1 as the regressand with those using M_2 indicates that the latter provide slightly better fits to the data. Thus, the equations employing the more inclusive definition of money possess somewhat better statistical properties than the equations in which the narrower money concept is used. The result also casts doubt on the hypothesis that the pressure from near money substitutes may be expected to be related to the maturity of an economy and that the more inclusive money total should, therefore, be used in the more mature economics.

The relative economic tranquility of the 1950s and early 1960s provided an opportunity to develop and test a number of hypotheses relating to the performance of the macroeconomy. One such hypothesis that received empirical support during this period held that monetary actions, as measured by movements in the monetary aggregates, have lasting effects on only nominal variables.

TABLE 7.4

Z Elasticities at Sample Mean Levels, 1951-80

Country	M_1^D/P	M_2^D/P
Belgium	0.0054	0.0041
France	-0.0108	0.0003
Germany	0.0133*	0.0053
Italy	0.0120	-0.0114
Netherlands	-0.0029	0.0058
United Kingdom	-0.0062	0.0594
Sweden	0.0008	0.0120
Yugoslavia	-0.0935*	-0.0479
Canada	-0.0072	-0.0024
United States	-0.0176*	0.0272*

*Significant at the 5 percent level.
Source: Compiled by the authors.

In contrast, the decade of the 1970s was marked by extensive experimentation with wage and price controls, energy
crises, and worldwide inflation. These events and developments
prompted many economists to question whether or not the performance of the industrial economies during this period was
consistent with prior hypotheses relating to the lasting impact
of monetary actions. In particular, the inability to accurately
simulate the movement of real money balances over the period
of third-quarter 1974 to fourth-quarter 1979 led to the general
conclusion that the money demand relationship shifted. In
reviewing the evidence, Ralph C. Kimball observes: "As these
overpredictions continued and increased in size through 1975
and 1976, many economists concluded that the money demand
function had shifted during 1974 by a substantial amount and
that this shift placed in doubt the usefulness of (old) M1 as
either an indicator of GNP or as a policy instrument."[6]
Several recent studies have demonstrated that the magnitude of downward shift in money demand relationships in the
1970s has been "exaggerated and the pattern of the precise
shifts has been obscured by reliance on the dynamic forecasting
procedure to evaluate the temporal stability of the money demand
relationship."[7]

By rejecting the notion of a constantly shifting money demand relationship, this study reaffirms the usefulness of money as a policy instrument. By dividing the 1951-80 full sample period into two subsample periods, 1951-65 and 1966-80, this study has further confirmed the findings above. Real income is the most important factor influencing the demand for real cash balances. The interest rate plays a supplementary role and the rate of price changes is the least important.

The regression coefficients for the income variable are all with expected positive signs and are all highly significant at the 1 percent level, with an exception of the United States when M_1 is used. For the subsample period 1951-65, income elasticities at sample mean levels are in most cases elastic and approximately equal to unity, except those of the United States (0.4211) when M_1 is used and the United Kingdom (0.2240 and 0.3810) when both M_1 and M_2 are used. The magnitude of income elasticity during this subperiod ranges from 0.2240 to 1.6071 when M_1 is used, and from 1.3810 to 1.4243 when M_2 is used. All income elasticities at sample mean levels with respect to M_2, except that of Yugoslavia, are greater than those with respect to M_1. This also is true for the subsample period 1966-80, except those of Italy and Yugoslavia, where income elasticities at the same mean levels with respect to M_1 are 1.7228 and 1.5661 compared to 1.2667 and 1.4674 for those of M_2, respectively.

During the subsample period 1966-80, most of the income elasticities at sample mean levels with respect to M_1 are less than unity, except those of Germany (1.1866), Italy (1.7228), and Yugoslavia (1.5661). They range from 0.1351 to 1.7228. On the other hand, all of the income elasticities at sample mean levels with respect to M_2 are greater than unity, ranging from 1.0264 to 1.4674.[8]

The interest rate plays a rather important role in demand-for-money functions for the Netherlands, Canada, the United Kingdom, and the United States in both subsample periods. However, the interest rate coefficients for Canada have unexpected positive signs during the subsample period 1966-80 when M_2 is used. The regression coefficients for other countries have the expected negative signs for both subsample periods but they are highly insignificant.

As for the Z variable, in the subsample period 1951-65, only the coefficients for Yugoslavia when M_1 is used are significant with the expected negative sign. However, in the subsample period 1966-80, Belgium and the United States have positive and significant Z coefficients. This may be partly a result of the high correlations existing between real national income and the rate of price changes during this period, and partly a result of inflationary expectation in consumer behavior since the energy crisis in 1973. The empirical results presented here deny the claim that monetary policy is important as a result of a shifting money-demand relationship. Those who argue the impotency of the monetary policy recently have suggested that attempts to control inflation through restrictive monetary policy will be unsuccessful, since the money demand relationship is unstable. Our findings of relatively stable money-demand relationships in the United States, Canada, and six EEC countries seriously question this assertion. The relationship between money demand, real income, and interest rates has not changed significantly over recent periods.

Other studies have also confirmed the surprisingly accurate predictions of money demand over the post-1973 period using the first-difference approach and have buttressed the conclusion that the money demand relationship has not suffered from any drastic shifts that would invalidate monetary policy. [9]

ESTIMATES OF MONEY SUPPLY FUNCTIONS

Estimates of the money supply functions for the period 1951-80 are given in Table 7.5. The analysis that follows is based on TSLS.

Estimates of M^S for every country are satisfactory from the point of view of the significance of coefficients, R^2. The R^2s for these countries range from the lowest 0.9046 (equation 4 for France) to the highest 0.9979 (equation 20 for the United States). However, in most of the cases studied, the Durbin-Watson tests fail. The highest Durbin-Watson statistic is 2.1447, which is within the range for confidently rejecting the hypothesis that there is serial correlation in the residuals. The lowest is 0.2575, which is not in the conclusive range for the Durbin-Watson test. Since the TSLS method has been used in estimating these money supply functions, the Durbin-Watson test should not be considered reliable for measuring the degree to which serial correlation exists in the residuals. The empirical results are analyzed below. Further investigation of the money supply functions are presented in Chapter 8 using the Dewald-Johnson model.

Coefficients of U measure the potential money multipliers of high-powered money (currency and reserves). Equations 1-20 in Table 7.5 show that both M_1^S and M_2^S are significantly related to high-powered money. Most of the regression coeffi-

TABLE 7.5

TSLS Estimates of Money Supply Function, 1951–80

$$M_q^S = s_0 + s_1 U + s_2 r^d + s_3 r^S + s_4 v_{-1}$$

Country	Equation	M_q^S	R^{-2} / F	SEEB	Constant t-ratios	U	r^d	r^S	v_{-1}
Belgium	1	M_1^S	0.9971	11.3977	-95.3815	2.4857	0.0703	-4.6503	56.6217
			2464.1701	2.9570	-3.6878	41.3246	0.0125	-0.8641	0.5535
	2	M_2^S	0.9872	50.5804	-429.8310	4.9476	4.8144	-0.9869	228.4890
			558.5246	8.4680	-3.7449	18.5348	0.1931	-0.0413	0.5033
France	3	M_1^S	0.9433	44.1263	-111.3150	4.9180	16.2899	13.0198	-306.0290
			121.5629	19.1460	-5.0150	9.5361	1.5409	1.1597	-1.4848
	4	M_2^S	0.9046	118.9553	-323.1890	9.5582	37.0897	28.0925	-790.4340
			69.7281	31.6720	-5.4012	6.8750	1.3015	0.9282	-1.4226
Germany	5	M_1^S	0.9526	15.0463	16.4041	2.0519	8.5800	-3.2073	-113.2610
			146.7464	15.7330	0.6605	18.6728	1.1874	-0.5986	-2.2253
	6	M_2^S	0.9642	46.9284	13.5334	7.1869	17.9575	5.5038	-447.9360
			196.2525	15.9050	0.1747	20.9695	0.7968	0.3293	-2.8217
Italy	7	M_1^S	0.9843	5.7697	19.8850	3.3065	0.5995	-3.1948	-25.9622
			456.9388	15.6420	2.3598	12.1995	0.6808	-2.0592	-1.4704
	8	M_2^S	0.9912	7.3007	10.3741	4.9832	0.1529	-1.4831	-9.1868
			817.3560	11.8220	0.9729	14.5298	0.1372	-0.7554	-0.4112

Netherlands	9	M_1^S	0.9492	4.2091	-6.2573	5.3550	1.0119	-3.1225	-29.6069
	10	M_2^S	136.5143	16.7250	-1.3306	9.4562	1.2230	-2.2756	-0.9829
			0.9210	15.8486	-36.6565	16.5626	7.5313	-13.5837	-72.1441
			85.5251	26.9420	-2.0703	7.7676	2.4176	-2.6291	-0.6361
United Kingdom	11	M_1^S	0.9924	0.6644	4.2282	2.7376	-0.7012	0.4358	-22.9517
			947.7034	5.8420	7.9892	29.8484	-6.2112	2.9874	-6.8454
	12	M_2^S	0.9874	2.0914	1.9672	5.7393	1.4537	1.7778	-48.3310
			567.9889	9.3220	1.1808	19.8801	-4.0910	3.8717	-4.5794
Sweden	13	M_1^S	0.9893	1.8391	-10.2506	1.3985	1.0490	1.2019	28.8985
			672.0207	7.3890	-5.7587	10.8312	2.1913	1.8812	4.4737
	14	M_2^S	0.9898	7.7550	-56.0431	5.6058	2.3468	8.7802	105.4590
			705.9309	7.8880	-7.4793	10.2958	1.1625	3.2591	3.8716
Yugoslavia	15	M_1^S	0.9853	15.3815	-0.9277	2.6876	1.1977	-0.0875	23.6658
			404.4521	16.9830	-0.0383	36.7274	0.8488	-0.0242	1.1011
	16	M_2^S	0.9866	37.5419	26.2338	6.8655	0.6885	-13.5953	184.1350
			444.2884	16.7810	0.4439	38.4400	0.1999	-1.5430	3.5101
Canada	17	M_1^S	0.9828	1.2732	11.1198	2.1844	-0.1068	-0.0807	-41.0256
			416.4461	9.0350	8.0142	15.8723	-0.2844	-0.1795	-7.5319
	18	M_2^S	0.9955	2.5850	-22.8242	7.5278	1.3959	-0.0970	40.7536
			1615.7526	6.6350	-8.1024	26.9420	1.8308	-0.1062	3.6853
United States	19	M_1^S	0.9969	4.7583	88.8792	2.3988	-11.5279	11.5502	-323.3790
			2332.9247	2.2330	7.5419	38.4750	-5.1027	5.1728	-5.6043
	20	M_2^S	0.9979	13.4066	-40.3045	7.9959	-25.2076	26.3446	-784.4890
			3367.4381	3.0670	-1.2139	45.5177	-3.9602	4.1875	-4.8253

Source: International Monetary Fund, International Financial Statistics, various issues for the years 1950–81 (Washington, D.C.: IMF).

127

TABLE 7.6

Elasticities of M_1^S and M_2^S with Respect to U at Sample Mean Levels, 1951-80

Country	M_1^S	M_2^S
Belgium	1.2751	1.6378
France	0.8209	0.9790
Germany	1.1420	1.2965
Italy	1.1374	1.0238
Netherlands	1.8691	2.4733
United Kingdom	1.1835	1.2577
Sweden	0.7372	0.7481
Yugoslavia	0.7862	0.8130
Canada	0.9280	1.1566
United States	0.8812	1.4316

Source: Compiled by the authors.

cients of U, except that of U coefficients for Sweden when M_1 is used, are very high. Elasticities of M_1^S and M_2^S with respect to U at sample mean levels are computed in Table 7.6.

In Belgium, Germany, Italy, the Netherlands, and the United Kingdom, the U elasticities of both M_1 and M_2 are slightly over unity, with the exception of the Netherlands, which ranges from 1.8691 to 2.4733. This also is true for Canada and the United States when the broader definition of money is used. This means that autonomous increases in the supply of currency can increase supplies of both "money proper" and money inclusive of time and savings deposits more than proportionately. In the case of France, elasticity of both M_1^S and M_2^S with respect to U at sample mean levels are 0.8209 and 0.9790, respectively. In the case of Sweden, elasticity of M_1^S with respect to U at sample mean levels is 0.7372 while U elasticity of M_2^S is 0.7481. Since banks keep lower reserve ratios for time and savings deposits, they can create more time and savings deposits with a given amount of reserves. The relatively high elasticity of M_2^S with respect to U in the Netherlands is therefore in accordance with banking theory.

As for the Yugoslav money supply function, elasticities of both M_1^S and M_2^S with respect to U at sample mean levels are only 0.7862 and 0.8130, respectively. This may be partly owing to the fact that there is a general lack of consensus as to what should be included in Yugoslav money stock. Furthermore, the evidence shows that in the Netherlands, Sweden, the United Kingdom, and the United States both M_1^S and M_2^S are highly sensitive to the interest rates. This suggests that the stocks of money in these economies are not wholly determined by the amount of the monetary base. This, however, is not the case in Belgium, France, Germany, and Yugoslavia. In the Netherlands, Germany, Sweden, Canada, the United States, and the United Kingdom both M_1^S and M_2^S are significantly related to the reserve ratios. This is in contrast to the results obtained for Italy, Belgium, France, and Yugoslavia.

Elasticities of M_1^S and M_2^S with respect to r^d and r^s at sample mean levels are listed in Table 7.7 for comparison. Most interest elasticities of M_1^S and M_2^S at sample mean levels, except those for the Netherlands, are very low. The relatively higher interest elasticities of M_2^S in comparison to those of M_1^S in most of the countries under study probably reflect higher interest elasticity of the supply of time and savings deposits in comparison to demand deposits. This suggests that in these countries changes in interest rates may affect banks' supply of time deposits more significantly than demand deposits.

Elasticities of M_1^S and M_2^S with respect to v_{-1} at sample mean levels are given in Table 7.8.

Further investigation was done by dividing the 1951-80 full sample period into two subsample periods, 1951-65 and 1966-80. The empirical results are consistent with results for the entire 1951-80 period.

Unborrowed monetary reserves are important factors affecting money supply in all countries under study except Yugoslavia for both subsample periods. During the first subsample period, unborrowed monetary reserves play no role at all in Yugoslavia. The results of v_{-1} for both subperiods are in most cases different from those obtained for the full sample period, which indicates that v_{-1} is one of the factors affecting the money supply in Belgium, France, Germany, Sweden, the United Kingdom, and Yugoslavia. During the second subsample period, v_{-1} coefficients are significant at the 5 percent level for those money supply functions in Italy (M_1 and M_2), the United Kingdom (M_1 and M_2), Sweden (M_1 and M_2), and Yugoslavia (M_1).

Neither government-controlled rate of interest nor the short-term market rate affects money supply significantly during

TABLE 7.7

Elasticities of M_1^S and M_2^S with Respect to r^d and r^s at Sample Mean Levels, 1951–80

Country	r^d		r^s	
	M_1^S	M_2^S	M_1^S	M_2^S
Belgium	0.0100	0.0441	-0.0455	-0.0062
France	0.4205	0.5876	0.3408	0.4512
Germany	0.3813	0.2587	-0.1576	0.0876
Italy	0.0961	0.0146	-0.6546*	-0.1815
Netherlands	0.1913	0.6092*	-0.7489*	-1.3938*
United Kingdom	-0.4563*	-0.4795*	0.2397*	0.4956*
Sweden	0.2279*	0.1291	0.3027*	0.5598*
Yugoslavia	0.0603	0.0140	-0.0077	-0.4845
Canada	-0.0444	0.2099*	-0.0283	-0.0123
United States	-0.2615*	-0.2787*	0.2419*	0.2689*

*Significant at the 5 percent level.
Source: Compiled by the authors.

TABLE 7.8

Elasticities of M_1^S and M_2^S with Respect to v_{-1} at Sample Mean Levels, 1951-80

Country	M_1^S	M_2^S
Belgium	0.0169	0.0440
France	-0.0992	-0.1572
Germany	-0.5372*	-0.6886*
Italy	-0.1181	-0.0250
Netherlands	-0.0629	-0.0656
United Kingdom	-0.3386*	-0.3615*
Sweden	0.1441*	0.1331*
Yugoslavia	0.1715	0.5401*
Canada	-0.6443*	0.2315*
United States	-0.2787*	-0.3295*

*Significant at the 5 percent level.
Source: Compiled by the authors.

the first subsample period, 1951-65. However, this was not half of the case for the second subsample period, 1966-80. These results may imply the change of economic structure.

U elasticities at sample mean levels are in most cases greater than unity, except those of France and Yugoslavia in both sub-sample periods.

In summary, satisfactory results are obtained for France, Italy, Sweden, the Netherlands, the United Kingdom, and the United States in the first subsample period; similar results are also obtained in the second subsample period. We may seemingly conclude that the model works well for these six countries.

THE INCOME VELOCITY OF MONEY

A concept closely related to demand for money is the income velocity of money. The pre-Keynesian literature of economics emphasized the quantity of money as a determinant of spending and tended to regard the velocity of income as a constant in the short run. In the post-Keynesian era, however, economists realized that the velocity of money is influenced not only by institutional factors, which can be assumed to be constant, but it is quite variable even in the short run. Many economists have stated that changes in the rate of inflation are one of the important factors affecting the velocity of money, causing it to rise if the rate of inflation accelerates and fall if the rate of inflation slows up.[10] Recent empirical work based on the data of the United States further suggests that the interest rate, current income, permanent income, and private wealth are important factors in affecting the income velocity of money.[11] The role of velocity, nevertheless, has not been clarified, although the behavior of that variable has always been crucial in evaluating the fruitfulness of any quantity theory, new or old, relative to alternative analytical methods. Friedman has frequently testified to the empirical stability he finds in velocity of money, noting that the velocity of M_2 has been stable.[12]

NOTES

1. L. R. Klein and A. S. Goldberger, An Econometric Model of the United States, 1929–1952 (Amsterdam: North-Holland, 1955).

2. T. Kloek and L. B. M. Mennes, "Simultaneous Equation Estimations Based on Principal Components of Predetermined Variables," Econometrica 28 (1960): 45–61.

3. F. M. Fisher, "The Relative Sensitivity to Specification Error of Different k-Class Estimators," Journal of the American Statistical Association 61 (1966): 345–56.

4. Henri Theil, Principles of Econometrics (New York: John Wiley, 1971).

5. Ibid., pp. 532–36.

6. Ralph C. Kimball, "Wire Transfer and the Demand for Money," New England Economic Review, Federal Reserve Bank of Boston, March/April 1980, p. 14.

7. Scott E. Hein, "Dynamic Forecasting and the Demand for Money," Review, Federal Reserve Bank of St. Louis, June/July 1980, p. 30.

8. Gregory C. Chow, "Tests of Equality between Sets of Coefficients in Two Linear Regressions," Econometrica 28 (1960): 591–604.

9. R. W. Hafer and Scott E. Hein, "The Dynamics of Estimation of Short-Run Money Demand," Review, Federal Reserve Bank of St. Louis, March 1980, pp. 26–35.

10. See Reuben A. Kessel and Armen A. Alchian, "Effects of Inflation," Journal of Political Economy 70 (1962):521-37; M. Friedman, "The Quantity Theory of Money—A Restatement," in Studies in the Quantity Theory of Money, ed. Milton Friedman (Chicago: University of Chicago Press, 1956); and D. H. Robertson, Money, 6th ed. (New York: Pitman, 1948), pp. 17-19.

11. See the works of Latane, Friedman, Meltzer, and Teigen cited in Chapter 4.

12. Milton Friedman, The Optimum Quantity of Money and Other Essays (Chicago: Aldine, 1969), pp. 114-15, 212-15, and 265.

8

GOALS OF MONETARY POLICY

STATED GOALS

If we are willing to allow for a certain amount of vagueness, defining the goals of monetary policy is slippery but not impossible. It is generally agreed that by goals of monetary policy we mean the ultimate aims or objectives. These agreed-upon goals are price stability, economic growth, "full" or maximum employment, and balance-of-payments equilibrium. Moreover, these objectives are shared by the countries under review in this study.

When viewed individually, each of these goals appears straightforward. It is, however, another matter to achieve all of them at the same time. Conflicts among goals may and indeed do arise. Reaching one goal may make it impossible to reach another. Thus the closer an economy is to full (or maximum) employment the faster will prices rise—the so-called Phillips curve analysis; under a system of fixed exchange rates and in the absence of exchange controls, balance-of-payments equilibrium requires that the domestic economy be systematically inflated and deflated. Moreover, the goal of economic growth may conflict with any or all of these other goals.

As an aid to understanding potential conflict among goals it is useful to distinguish between a necessary conflict and a policy conflict. A necessary conflict means that an achievement of one goal necessarily means the unachievement of another. An example of such a conflict is suggested in the Phillips curve analysis whereby a trade-off occurs between full employment and price stability. A policy conflict example is furnished in the case where monetary policy cannot pursue both price stability and economic growth at the same time. The evidence suggests that any rate of economic growth is consistent with any rate of price increase. Other examples of potential conflict come readily to mind from the experiences of other countries.

The goals of monetary policy in Canada during the post-World War II period varied from combatting inflation to reducing unemployment to defending the foreign exchange of the Canadian dollar under fixed and flexible exchange rates. Moreover, the official view of monetary policy in Canada switched from a "quantity theory" to a "credit conditions" approach with corresponding reversals in the choice of the appropriate targets and indicators of policy.

The repudiation of cheap money policies in the United States after the war with the Federal Reserve-Treasury accord of 1951 and the formal abandonment of pegging government bond prices in 1953 led to a revival of belief in the potency of monetary policy. The goals of monetary policy are the promotion of full employment, economic growth, while maintaining internal and external balance. The basic document in the area of macroeconomic objectives in the United States is the Employment Act of 1946, which marks the government's official acceptance of responsibility for the state of the U.S. economy.

The goals of the act are to "promote maximum employment, production, and purchasing power." Ambiguous and imprecise though they are, anything more specific would probably not be politically acceptable. This is different from the goals assigned to monetary policy during the prosperity of the 1920s. At that time, the chief roles assigned to monetary policy were to promote price stability and to preserve the gold standard.

Monetary policy in Sweden remained largely passive in the early postwar years. The objective of monetary policy up to 1960 was to stabilize the interest rate level considered essential to rapid economic progress and full employment. During the 1960s such goals of monetary policy as price stability, internal or external balance, stability, or growth occurred in Sweden, and the country opted for growth and full employment relative to balance in international payments.

Postwar objectives of monetary policy in the United Kingdom are more difficult to grasp. It would appear that by 1969 and 1970 some improvement in the country's balance-of-payments and external balance emphasis shifted to maintaining internal equilibrium, avoiding both inflation and excessive unemployment. A major wage explosion shortly thereafter complicated the internal situation.

Nevertheless, there has been a change in stance regarding the objectives of monetary policy in the United Kingdom. This, in effect, involves the withdrawal by the Bank of England of automatic support for financial markets. Support of prices in financial markets made it impossible to use the price mechanism to limit the rate of growth of such monetary aggregates as bank advances, domestic credit, and the money stock. Any attempt by the monetary authorities to combine a deflationary monetary policy with continuing support for prices in financial markets would in fact require controls of one kind or another designed to ration available financial resources.

The shift in policy of providing automatic support for the gilt-edge securities market became apparent in late 1968. Official sanction was provided in 1971 whereby the vast and compli-cated structure of direct controls that had encumbered the U.K. banking system were finally removed. One would expect that in the future the banking system would have an opportunity to play a positive role in assisting the economy toward a freely competitive internal and external equilibrium.

The goals of monetary policy in Yugoslavia focus on eco-nomic development, employment, price stability, and achievement of balance-of-payments equilibrium. Institutional and other changes after the 1965 reform have required significant adjust-ments in the pattern of monetary policy goals and produced fundamental changes in the interrelationship of individual goals, their conflicting effects and complementarities. The basic change in the pattern of monetary policy goals has been the increased importance of stabilization and balance-of-payment goals, so that they have become as significant as the previously dominating economic growth and employment goals. Thus the list of basic goals of monetary policy was extended fundamentally after the reform. It is obvious that this change has made the problem of trade-offs far more complex and similar in difficulty to those in market economies.

In Belgium, conflict between internal and external balance tilts in favor of the latter, owing to the very strong influence of foreign trade and powerful economic neighbors. The country's foreign trade represents about 50 percent of its total economic activity. Over the long term, the country's balance of payments has had a surplus. One effect of such a surplus has been to increase the supply of money—much as though a specie-flow mechanism were in operation.

France shares in the goals of monetary policy outlined above, though at times in the postwar period it was not always clear that this was in fact the case. Since 1963 considerable emphasis has been placed on the goal of price stability. Rapid price rises, most notably in 1958-59, 1963-64, as well as 1969-70, have underscored the urgency for pursuing internal stability. Balance-of-payments problems were particularly acute in the period 1956-58 when pronounced deficit was registered. The

situation improved in 1959-63 to the extent that France was able
to repay borrowings from the International Monetary Fund, the
European Payments Union, and the United States. Indeed by
1963 French reserves were built up to almost 22 billion francs.

Price stability, economic growth, maximum employment,
and balance-of-payments equilibrium are also goals of monetary
policy in the Federal Republic of Germany. The Bundesbank
was able to concentrate monetary policy on domestic goals through
the revaluation of the deutsche mark in 1961 and 1969 as well
as during much of 1971 when flexible exchange rates were in
force. The strict orientation of German monetary policy to
domestic requirements, however, is incompatible with the requirements of the Common Market. This also holds, of course, for
other EEC members. If the Common Market is to work it is
necessary that its members pursue a common monetary policy
in relation to the other countries of the world.

The stated goals of monetary policy in Italy are almost
identical to those already discussed. Monetary authorities
have succeeded in the two past decades of achieving a rather
rapid economic growth. Except for a period in the early 1960s
when inflationary pressures threatened internal stability and
monetary policy was focused on cooling the economy, the monetary
authorities throughout much of the postwar period have provided
the economy with liquidity to push the process of economic
development. Indeed, the currency and bank deposits in public
hands grew at a much faster rate than the value of GNP.

The Social Economic Council of the Netherlands sets the
goals of economic policy, including monetary policy, to be satisfactory economic growth, full employment, the greatest possible
price stability, equilibrium in the balance of payments, and a
reasonable income distribution. Monetary policy aims at establishing monetary conditions that will further economic equilibrium.
This may result at times in monetary policy encroaching on the
objectives of other policy instruments. Moreover, the internal
value of the currency and equilibrium in the balance of payments
are the specific responsibilities of the Netherlands Bank as laid
down by the Bank Act of 1948.

LIMITS TO MONETARY POLICY

It is argued that monetary policy influences primarily the
value and composition of assets. As a consequence, it is more
circuitous than, for example, fiscal policy, which directly influences income and therefore economic activity. A contrary position

is the argument that decisions regarding the demand to hold money really involve a decision as to whether it is best to hold wealth in this form or in securities or physical assets. Against such a background asset holdings may be as significant as income in directly influencing economic activity. Monetary policy through its effect upon assets may theoretically have as direct an impact on economic activity as fiscal policy operating through income. The empirical evidence cited elsewhere also tends to support this view.

Prior to the 1930s theoretical and empirical research in monetary theory focused on the institutional determinants of velocity. Since that time considerable attention has been given to the relation between velocity—or its alternative formulation, the demand for money—and interest rates. The possible existence of the Keynesian liquidity-trap and the consequent ineffectiveness of monetary policy probably motivated much of this research. In themselves many of these studies left much to be desired. To judge from results reported in this study, the demand for cash balances does in fact depend partly on interest rates. A promising explanation seems also to be contained in the permanent income hypothesis discussed by Milton Friedman.

Another aspect deals with the effect of the discount rate on market rates of interest and thus on investment. The sensitivity of investment to interest rates has triggered much theoretical debate, with some empirical results.[1] These results do not strongly support what has come to be considered as the Keynesian view of monetary effects on investment expenditures. Canadian results reported on elsewhere, for example, contradict studies that claim to find no relation between interest rates and investment. One consequence of these results is that they cast doubt on the usefulness of a narrow and restrictive interpretation of changes in the money stock.

The length of time over which interest rate effects appear to be distributed in Canada should be cause for sober reflection on the part of those people who expect to observe a rapid response of investment to interest rate changes. It simply takes time to plan and execute investment projects. Obviously, this lag may differ among industries and sectors of the economy. This is one important reason for the failure on the part of some empirical studies to find any relation between interest rates and investment. Existence of such lags, however, indicates that the effect of monetary changes may not be as quick-acting as some would argue.

Though opinions differ, evidence does suggest that, in general, monetary authority can control nominal quantities and the quantity of its own liabilities.[2] By manipulating the quantity of its own liabilities it can fix the exchange rate, the price level, the nominal level of national income, and the nominal quantity of money. It can also influence directly the rate of inflation or deflation, the rate of growth of the nominal stock of money, and the rate of growth or decline in nominal national income. Again, though opinion differs, the bulk tends to tilt on the side that the monetary authority cannot, through control of the nominal quantities, fix the real quantities such as the real interest rate, the rate of unemployment, the level of real national income, the real quantity of money, the rate of growth of real national income, or the rate of growth of the real quantity of money.

Economists are quick to point out, however, that this does not mean that monetary policy does not have important effects on these real magnitudes. Indeed, when money gets out of order, important repercussions are felt throughout the economy. Monetary history provides ample evidence on this point. Indeed the debate between Milton Friedman and the Keynesians is over the effectiveness of governmental monetary policy and whether it has little or no impact on income and employment, particularly during severe economic depressions. Moreover, government taxation and spending, in effect fiscal policy, are most effective when dealing with problems of inflation and unemployment.

Monetarists and Milton Friedman, as we have noted elsewhere, stress the importance of money. They argue that a rule that requires the monetary authority to cause the nominal stock of money to increase by a fixed percentage annually would effectively reduce fluctuations in prices, real output, and employment.

Much of the discussion, the evidence presented, and policy prescription, which were discussed elsewhere in this study, resemble very much the debates of British economists that have raged off and on for more than 200 years. For example, the differences between Keynesians and Friedman on employment of fiscal and monetary policy to achieve economic stability may be attributed in part to differences in the economic conditions at the time each wrote their theories and in part to differences in political philosophies.

DO POLICY GOALS CONFLICT? A QUANTITATIVE
ANALYSIS

Monetary authorities are fond of talking about the mutual consistency of policy goals. In fact, however, they appear to act as though these goals do indeed conflict. Economists, on their part, have attempted to shed light on the issue of priorities used by monetary authorities in resolving conflicts among the goals of monetary policy. One such study for the United States, which covers the period 1952-61, was conducted by W. G. Dewald and Harry Johnson. [3]

The principal assumption in this study is that monetary authorities formulate monetary policy in response to the economic goals we have discussed. Consider that the Dewald and Johnson study, although more recent, applies the same method for the United States as G. L. Reuben does for Canada. [4] They formulate the conduct of monetary policy in terms of "reaction function" originally discussed and applied to Canadian data by Reuben. This function relates a statistical indicator of monetary policy to statistical indicators of the degree to which the various objectives of policy have been achieved. The form of the reaction function expresses the weights attached by the monetary authority to the various objectives and the lag in the reaction of monetary policy to changes in the performance of the economy.

Dewald and Johnson seek to determine the weights attached to the various policy objectives and the lag response of monetary policy simultaneously, by a multiple regression analysis relating the monetary policy indicator as a dependent variable to its own past values and the statistical indicators of achievement of objectives as independent variables. It is possible to calculate the trade-offs between the various objectives, as revealed by the behavior of the monetary authority, from the weights attached to the objectives of policy. They correctly point out that the trade-off so derived must be interpreted with some caution for at least three reasons. One is that the statistical indicator of monetary policy selected may not correspond with the true monetary control variable, and its correlation with the independent variables may reflect endogenous relationships other than policy reactions. It may also be that the monetary indicator most highly correlated with the independent variables is not necessarily that which the monetary authorities are attempting to control. The results, therefore, should be read as conditional on the validity of the monetary policy indicator selected. Second, the coefficients relating the monetary policy indicator selected to the independent variables may in fact reflect the monetary authorities' preference among the policy objectives as well as the assessment of the trade-offs between objectives actually existing in the structure of the economy. Third, the technique they employ assumes that both the structure of the economy and the way in which monetary policy is integrated with other policy instruments in stabilization policy have not altered substantially over the period.

Dewald and Johnson experimented with three types of monetary policy indicators in recognition of the disagreement in the literature over what it is that the monetary authorities control or seek to control in the implementation of policy. The three indicators they selected are money supply, money market interest rates, and member bank reserve positions. Their best results were obtained with the money supply series and these are the results we will discuss here. With respect to the performance characteristics of the economy, Dewald and Johnson use the consumer price index, the unemployment percentage, and the balance-of-payments deficit as the variables relevant, respectively, to the objectives of price stability, high employment, and a satisfactory balance of payments. They employed real GNP as an indicator of economic growth. A stepwise regression program was applied to the U.S. quarterly data for the period 1952 to 1961.

The regression result, for the variables expressed in linear form, was

$$M_t = 26.87991 + \underset{(.07182)}{.75385M_{t-1}} + \underset{(.13691)}{.45733U_t} + \underset{(.01509)}{.03767Y_t}$$

$$- \underset{(.05536)}{.08825P_t} + \underset{(.00020)}{.00036B_t} \tag{1}$$

$$\bar{R}^2 = .99056$$

where M represents currency, plus demand deposits, in billions of dollars; U is the percentage unemployment rate; Y is real GNP in billions of 1954 dollars; P is the consumer price index in percentage points; and B is the balance-of-payments deficit in millions of dollars. The standard error of estimate is .61884; the standard errors of the regression coefficient are shown in parentheses below the associated coefficients. Only the first three regression coefficients are statistically significant at the 5 percent level.

The regression equation can be "decoded" into a reaction function for the monetary authorities and the distributed lag reaction structure. The reaction function obtained by solving for the equilibrium value of $M_t = M_{t-1}$ is

$$M = 109.20125 + 1.85793U + .15304Y - .35852P$$

$$+ .00146B \tag{2}$$

What this reaction function tells us is that during the period 1952-61 a percentage increase in the price level is associated with a $0.36 billion reduction in the money stock on the average, while a percentage point increase in the unemployment rate was associated with an average increase of $0.2 billion in the money stock, while $1.0 billion increase in the balance-of-payments deficit was on the average associated with a $1.5 billion increase in the money stock. Dewald and Johnson point out, correctly, that the last result makes no sense in terms of appropriate monetary policy. The fact is, however, the coefficient of the balance-of-payments variable is not significant. This suggests that the monetary authorities either ignored the balance of payments or assigned little importance to it.

From the point of trade-offs between policy goals—which is to say compensating changes in two performance indicators that would result in a zero change in the monetary policy indicator—the evidence does shed light on the questions we posed at the outset of this section. Suppose, for example, we treat M as constant, what will happen to Y and U if P rises by 1 percent? From the reaction function our answer is that U will rise by 0.19 percent (Y constant) and that Y will rise by $2.34 billion ($U$ constant). In effect, if the price level rises by 1 percent and the unemployment rate also rises by 0.19 percent, GNP remaining the same, then the monetary authorities will do nothing. They will be willing to "trade" a 1 percent rate of inflation for a 0.19 percent increase in the unemployment rate. They will similarly trade a 1 percent increase in the price level for a $2.34 billion increase in GNP with U constant.

The evidence presented by Dewald and Johnson is only suggestive. Some of the coefficients are not significant; the study is out of date and subsequent studies have indicated that the authorities change priorities. Nevertheless, the results do suggest that no matter what monetary authorities say about the consistency of policy goals, they act as though these goals conflict. We shall apply the Dewald-Johnson Model to the ten countries under review in this study.

The Dewald-Johnson Model

The regression results for the period 1956-80 for the variables expressed in linear form are listed in Tables 8.1 and 8.2, where M_q^S represents M_1^S or M_2^S, in billions of dollars (local currency), U is the percentage unemployment rate (in the case of France, the unemployment number is used), Y/P is real GNP in billions of 1975 dollars, P is the consumer price index in percentage points, and B is the balance-of-payments deficit in millions of U.S. dollars.

The standard error of estimates is less than 6.0 percent for every case under study; in the cases of Yugoslavia and Canada, when M_1^S is used the t-ratios of the regression coefficients are shown below the associated coefficients. The regression coefficients for M_{-1}^S are all statistically significant at the 5 percent level, with an exception of Canada and Germany and the Netherlands when M_1^S is used. The magnitude of M_{-1}^S coefficients ranges from 0.1892 to 1.0655 for M_1^S and from 0.4847 to 1.0328 for M_2^S. In general, the results seem to indicate that the Dewald-Johnson Model works better for most of the countries under study.

The regression equations can be "decoded" into a reaction function for the monetary authorities and distributed lag reaction structure. The reaction functions, obtained by solving for the equilibrium value of $M_t = M_{t-1}$, are listed in Table 8.2. The information contained in the reaction function is also expressed in terms of trade-offs between policy objectives; that is, compensating changes in two performance indicators that would result in a zero change in the monetary policy indicator.

European Experience, 1956-80

The purpose of this section is to present the results of an objective investigation, employing the methods of statistical inference using the Dewald-Johnson Model, of the objectives that have governed monetary policy in selected European countries in the period 1956-80 and the lag in the translation of those objectives into concrete monetary policy.

The application of the Dewald-Johnson Model described requires specification of statistical indicators for both monetary policy and the performance characteristics of the economy relevant to the objectives listed. For simplicity, we select the money supply as the control variable actually used by the monetary authorities, the consumer price index, the unemployment rate, and the balance-of-payments deficit as the variables relevant, respectively, to the objectives of price stability, high employment, and a satisfactory balance of payments, with real GNP as an objective of economic growth. Annual data for the period 1956-80 are used in the ordinary least-squares regression.

Consider the reaction function in Belgium as shown in equation 1, Table 8.2. According to this reaction function, a percentage point increase in the unemployment rate was associated with a $10.6 billion reduction in the money stock on the average during the period 1956-80, while a percentage point increase in the price level was associated with an increase of

TABLE 8.1

Estimates of Money Supply Function (Dewald-Johnson Model), 1956–80

$$M_q^S = s_0 + s_1 M_{-1} + s_2 Um + s_3 (Y/P) + s_4 P + s_5 B \quad q = 1,2$$

Country	Equation	M_q^S	$\bar{R}^2$ / F	DW / R	SEEB / SPCB	Constant t-ratios	M_{-1}	Um	Y/P	P	B
Belgium	1	M_1^S	0.9945	1.9382	15.2094	-78.6467	0.5494	-4.8094	1.8111	3.8029	0.0105
			840.0591	0.9979	3.4880	-2.4178	2.6185	-1.3765	0.5137	3.1702	1.8690
	2	M_2^S	0.9988	2.1161	15.3587	-195.5920	0.7831	-0.2052	4.1458	4.3680	0.0217
			3918.1555	0.9995	2.2091	-1.9518	4.0023	-0.0553	0.9283	2.0167	3.3542
France	3	M_1^S	0.9981	2.0869	7.9471	-254.2450	0.5650	2.0033	1.6978	2.3774	0.0028
			2378.5638	0.9992	2.8850	-1.7696	3.1697	1.2789	0.5066	3.3433	3.1612
	4	M_2^S	0.9988	1.9153	13.8070	-108.6020	1.1411	1.0761	1.8091	-0.2285	0.0036
			3684.2631	0.9995	3.0250	-0.4400	6.0770	0.3624	0.3193	-0.1357	2.3297
Germany	5	M_1^S	0.9931	2.2801	5.5153	-50.2466	0.5899	0.4874	1.1201	1.0688	0.1163
			660.2654	0.9973	4.8670	-1.5942	2.6967	0.2320	0.4432	1.2018	0.8884
	6	M_2^S	0.9949	1.9580	17.0257	-89.0504	0.7725	5.2621	17.4080	0.2973	0.2688
			899.6452	0.9980	4.7570	-0.8925	3.9322	1.0211	2.2149	0.1537	0.6657
Italy	7	M_1^S	0.9976	1.8539	2.3499	-10.1237	1.0655	0.7580	8.9654	0.0412	0.5361
			1935.7134	0.9991	5.2090	-1.6960	6.8063	1.7014	2.1148	0.3535	2.0666
	8	M_2^S	0.9979	1.3917	3.7427	-26.3207	0.8761	1.2372	19.4504	0.2859	0.2953
			2168.5203	0.9992	4.9420	-1.9983	3.8628	1.7955	2.8391	0.9643	0.7744
Netherlands	9	M_1^S	0.9966	1.7484	1.0866	-13.4761	0.1892	0.7969	4.6986	0.3876	-514.8690
			1354.4666	0.9987	3.7030	-4.4002	1.0001	1.2508	2.3291	2.8909	-0.9489
	10	M_2^S	0.9990	2.1643	1.8324	-12.4783	0.8979	1.4227	5.5809	0.1938	0.0001
			4509.9431	0.9996	2.5980	-1.4365	6.0716	1.1118	1.0546	0.5145	0.0736

Sweden	11	M_1^S	0.9968	2.1739	1.0179	1.8705	1.0360	-0.5772	-2.3260	0.0707	0.0013
			1417.2614	0.9987	3.5370	0.6323	4.9380	-0.8935	-2.4216	0.7935	2.7444
	12	M_2^S	0.9969	2.1304	4.2929	-13.3737	0.8965	2.5959	-2.6105	0.4607	0.0039
			1466.5900	0.9988	3.7140	-0.8886	4.7923	0.9414	-0.5532	1.4079	2.0242
United Kingdom	13	M_1^S	0.9951	2.2170	0.5572	-1.1170	0.8663	0.9019	0.2391	0.0077	-0.0737
			935.9309	0.9981	4.3720	-1.1256	4.6811	4.1900	0.1558	0.2548	-1.6407
	14	M_2^S	0.9943	1.2297	1.4614	-5.7706	1.0910	-0.5570	7.2009	-0.0260	0.1063
			804.9432	0.9978	5.6500	-1.4734	2.1201	-1.0846	1.5850	-0.1541	0.3152
Yugoslavia	15	M_1^S	0.9951	1.4945	8.8614	5.5622	0.8699	-0.6647	-7.6963	1.3157	0.0151
			983.1218	0.9981	9.7840	0.5312	8.7972	-0.2680	-1.6669	5.8590	3.7551
	16	M_2^S	0.9983	2.1245	13.3483	50.0320	1.0328	-6.5433	-19.7836	2.6371	0.0262
			2839.2887	0.9993	5.9670	3.1003	11.6788	-1.7590	-2.7096	5.6474	4.3151
Canada	17	M_1^S	0.9802	2.3379	1.3392	-6.4214	0.3138	-0.0433	10.5478	0.0688	0.0893
			228.4509	0.9922	8.1480	-2.2985	1.2400	-0.1598	2.6938	1.8309	0.3219
	18	M_2^S	0.9984	2.2261	1.6230	-34.7707	0.4847	0.1188	0.3797	0.7698	0.4557
			2803.4540	0.9994	3.5090	-2.3994	1.5503	0.3113	0.0930	1.8420	0.6351
United States	19	M_1^S	0.9989	2.2503	2.8293	-26.3825	0.7735	1.9336	4.9619	0.1312	0.4113
			4086.0487	0.9996	1.2140	-3.6834	6.0667	3.1227	4.0555	0.5410	-4.3949
	20	M_2^S	0.9982	1.8629	12.1020	-242.8260	0.5444	5.0098	16.7205	3.1025	-0.5971
			2611.0027	0.9993	2.4090	-2.8203	2.6606	1.7643	2.9390	2.3374	-1.4885

Source: International Monetary Fund, International Financial Statistics, various issues for the years 1956–80 (Washington, D.C.: IMF).

TABLE 8.2

Reaction Function of Money Supply (Dewald-Johnson Model), 1956–80

$$M_q^S = a + bUm + c(Y/P) + dP + eB \qquad q = 1,2$$

Country	Equation	M_q^S	Constant	Um	Y/P	P	B
Belgium	1	M_1^S	-174.5377	-10.6733	4.0193	8.4396	0.0233
	2	M_2^S	-901.7612	-0.9461	19.1139	20.1383	0.1000
France	3	M_1^S	-584.4713	4.6053	3.9030	5.4653	0.0064
	4	M_2^S	769.6811	-7.6265	-12.8214	1.6194	-0.0255
Germany	5	M_1^S	-122.5228	1.1885	2.7313	2.6062	0.2836
	6	M_2^S	-391.4303	23.1301	76.5187	1.3068	1.1815
Italy	7	M_1^S	154.5603	-11.5725	-136.8763	-0.6290	-8.1847
	8	M_2^S	-212.4350	9.9855	157.7111	2.3075	2.3834
Netherlands	9	M_1^S	-16.6207	0.9829	5.7950	0.4780	-635.0136
	10	M_2^S	-122.2165	13.9344	54.6611	1.8981	0.0010

Sweden	11	M_1^S	-51.9583	16.0333	64.6111	-1.9639	-0.0361
	12	M_2^S	-129.2145	25.0812	-25.2222	4.4512	0.0377
United Kingdom	13	M_1^S	-8.3545	6.7457	1.7883	0.0576	-0.5512
	14	M_2^S	63.4132	6.1209	-79.1308	0.2857	-1.1681
Yugoslavia	15	M_1^S	42.7533	-5.1091	-59.1568	10.1130	0.1161
	16	M_2^S	-1525.3659	199.4909	603.1585	-80.3994	-0.7988
Canada	17	M_1^S	-9.3579	-0.0631	15.3713	0.1003	0.1301
	18	M_2^S	-67.4766	-0.2296	0.7369	1.4939	0.8843
United States	19	M_1^S	-116.4790	8.5369	21.9068	0.5792	-1.8159
	20	M_2^S	-532.9807	10.9960	36.7000	6.8097	-1.3106

Source: International Monetary Fund, International Financial Statistics, various issues for the years 1956-80 (Washington, D.C.: IMF).

$8.4 billion; a $1.0 billion increase in real gross national product was associated with a $4.0 billion (Belgian francs) increase in the money stock; a $1.0 million (U.S. $) increase in the balance-of-payment deficit was associated with a $2.3 billion (Belgian francs) reduction in money stock.

The results of the unemployment rate and real GNP do not make sense from the point of view of appropriate monetary policy, but since the regression coefficients of the unemployment rate and GNP are not significant, it seems reasonable to conclude that on the average for the period as a whole the monetary authorities either ignored the unemployment rate and real GNP or attached so little weight to them that other performance economic variables, possibly including some not considered here, dominated in the management of the money stock.

Further evidence shows that an increase of 1 percentage point in the consumer price index would have been associated with an increase in the money supply equal in magnitude to the reduction in the money supply associated with an increase of $36.2 million in the balance-of-payments deficit. In other words, the behavior of the money supply indicated an average trade-off of $36.2 million additional balance-of-payments deficit for a 1 percentage point increase in prices. Similar analysis can be applied to the reaction functions for other countries under study.

To summarize the results of this section, we have been able to find reasonably good statistical explanations of changes in the money supply in terms of lagged reaction of the money supply to changes in statistical indicators of the performance of the economy relevant to the main objectives of economic policy for most of the countries under study. If we assume that the money supply is the control variable the monetary authorities actually employ, our empirical reaction functions suggest that during the period 1956-80 the main concerns of monetary policy in each country are:

Country	Price Stability	Economic Growth	Full Employment	Balance of Payments
Belgium	X			X
France	X			X
Germany	X	X	X	X
Italy	X	X		X
Netherlands	X	X	X	X
Sweden	X	X		X
United Kingdom			X	
Yugoslavia	X	X	X	X
Canada	X	X		
United States	X	X	X	X

NOTES

1. See Phillip Cagan, "A Commentary on Some Current Issues in the Theory of Monetary Policy," in Patterns of Market Behavior, ed. Michael J. Brennan (Providence: Brown University Press, 1965).

2. See, for example, Milton Friedman, "The Role of Monetary Policy," American Economic Review, March 1968, pp. 1-17.

3. W. G. Dewald and Harry G. Johnson, "An Objective Analysis of the Objectives of American Monetary Policy," in Banking and Monetary Studies, ed. Deane Carson (Homewood, Ill.: Richard D. Irwin, 1963), pp. 171-89.

4. G. L. Reuben, "The Objectives of Canadian Monetary Policy, 1949-1961," Journal of Political Economy, April 1964, pp. 109-32.

9

THE PROBLEM OF TIMING

THE U.S. AND CANADIAN EXPERIENCE

A satisfactory solution to the problem of timing changes in monetary policy must be found if monetary policy is to promote economic stability. If monetary policy is badly timed it may promote instability rather than stability in the several economies. A variable period of time may elapse between action taken by a central bank and the effect of such action on economic activity. The problem is likely to be made even more complicated by the existence of several central banks, as in the Common Market, particularly since each country is apt to have different lags.

We have evidence for the United States and Canada on the importance of lags in monetary policy. It is useful to go into this evidence at some length. In a study published in 1958 for the U.S. economy, Thomas Mayer takes the position that the lag between the taking of action and its effects on the economy can be divided into two distinctly separate lags: the credit market lag and the output lag.[1] The credit market lag refers to the time lapse from the application of a change in policy to changes in the availability of credit to changes in GNP.

To determine the estimated effects on GNP, Mayer worked with a simple multiplier model in which he assumed a multiplier coefficient of 2.5 and a time period of four months. With this model he estimated that it would take 11 months for an increase in credit availability to offset the persistent effects of the previous restrictive policy and to begin to influence current GNP. If policy and credit market lags are included it would take even longer. Thus if monetary policy is changed two months after the cyclical peak, and the monetary authority gradually intensifies the new policy over an 8-month period, the new policy would not begin to influence GNP until 17 months after the cyclical peak. The lag was the same for expansionary policies enacted after the trough. Comparing this with the NBER (National Bureau of Economic Research) average contraction and expansion periods of 23 months, anticyclical measures would begin to work only six months before the peak or trough of the cycle. Applying this to six NBER cycles starting with the years 1919 through 1945, Mayer determined that only 5 to 10 percent of the cycle amplitude could have been expected to be canceled by anticyclical monetary policy. On the basis of this, Mayer concluded that while monetary policy itself may be changed quickly, its effects may not. Therefore, monetary policy, in Mayer's estimation, is a most inflexible tool.

In a subsequent article, W. H. White indicated a number of shortcomings in Mayer's study.[2] When these are corrected the effect would be presumably to shorten the estimate of the lag sufficiently to imply that anticyclical measures should be used aggressively. He indicates that a lag of roughly 12 months was probably more accurate.

Another study that reports on the lag in the effect of monetary policy was conducted by John Karaken and Robert Solow for the Commission on Money and Credit.[3] It constitutes a part of a larger study on lags in fiscal and monetary policy undertaken by the commission.

Insofar as Karaken and Solow reach a conclusion in their study, they note that full results of policy changes on the flow of expenditures may be a long time coming.[4] The effects are spread out over a wide interval of time, however, so some effect comes fairly quickly. They build up over time, so that some substantial stabilizing power results after a lapse of approximately six to nine months.

The principal criticism of the work turns on the statistical tool used throughout by the authors. They estimate an infinite distributed lag function by using multiple regression in which prior values of the independent variable enter as dependent variables, along with the current value of the variable suspected of having a lagged effect (the operational variable). Milton Friedman has noted that this procedure will yield a valid estimate of the lag, if such a lag exists.[5] However, by itself, it does not provide any evidence on the existence of a lag, since it cannot discriminate between serial correlation in the dependent variable that arises from other sources and that which arises from the distributed lag effect of the operational variable. As a result, doubt is cast on the validity of the results presented in the study.

Another statistical estimate of the lag has been made by
Friedman. This was an outgrowth of extensive empirical studies
conducted on the relation between the stock of money and economic activity.[6] One principal empirical finding is the conclusion
that monetary actions affect economic conditions only after a
lag that is both long and variable. The technique employed in
arriving at this conclusion is a comparison of the timing of peaks
and troughs in the rate of change of the stock of money relative
to peaks and troughs in general business. This comparison,
covering 20 business cycles from 1867 to 1960, disclosed that
at upper turning points the lag ranged from 13 to 24 months
for specific cycles and averaged 16 months. At lower turning
points, the lag ranged from 5 to 21 months and averaged 12
months.

Friedman's measurement of the lag assumes that the primary
direction of influence is from money to business rather than
from business to money. Instead of interpreting the rate of
change of the money stock as conforming to the business cycle
with a lead, it could be interpreted as conforming inversely with
a lag. To test the assumption that the primary causal direction
is from money to business, timing observations were computed
both ways. The stability of timing observations was much
greater when the monetary series led the output series. The
amplitude of the cyclical movement in money was also found to
be highly correlated with the amplitude of the cyclical movement
in general business.

Friedman and Schwartz observe, moreover, that the relation
between money and business has remained largely unchanged
over a period that has seen substantial changes in the arrangements determining the quantity of money. Over the period 1867-
1960, which they studied, the United States was on, successively,
a gold standard, an inconvertible paper standard with floating
exchange rates, and a managed paper standard with fixed exchange rates. In addition, government arrangements for monetary
control altered. If the predominant direction of influence has
been from business to money, these changes might have been
expected to alter the relation between business changes and
monetary changes, but the relation has remained fairly constant
in both timing and amplitude. They admit to the existence of
a significant feed-back effect from business to money, but this
is viewed as an important reason for the lags being both long
and variable.[7]

Canadian experience is very similar to that of the United
States reported on by Friedman and Schwartz. Tables 9.1 and
9.2 present data from 1867 to 1965 and from 1868 to 1908, respec-

tively, the specific cycles in the monthly rate of change in the
Canadian stock of money and its relation to Canadian cycles.[8]
The specific cycles are dated according to National Bureau
criteria. These criteria include dating on the cycle by at least
three judges. Five people (including Milton Friedman and
Anna J. Schwartz for the period 1924-58) assisted in dating the
cycles. It is obvious from an examination of the evidence when
plotted that the Canadian indicator falls short of satisfying
criteria set out by the NBER for an "ideal" statistical indicator.
It leads the cyclical revival center by variable amounts; it does
not sweep smoothly up or down; its cyclical movements are not
always pronounced.

By way of contrast, the indicator does seem to approximate
closely the last "ideal" criterion that it be "so related to general
business activity as to establish . . . confidence . . . that its
future behavior in regard to business cycles will be like its
past behavior."[9] Moreover, the indicator does satisfy the NBER's
"two-thirds rule" for acceptable indicators. Table 9.1 indicates
that between 1867 and 1900 the peak in the rate of change of
the money stock preceded the peaks in general business activity
by an average of almost 7 months at peaks and almost 8 months
at troughs. For the postwar period and six complete reference
cycles between 1924 and 1964, peaks in money precede peaks
in general business by an average lead of 15.5 months at peaks
and about 7 months at troughs. These results are consistent
in direction and of roughly the same order of magnitude with
the 15-month leads at peaks and 12-month leads at troughs for
reference cycles since 1907, found for the United States.

Evidence presented in Table 9.2 indicates that peaks and
troughs occurring in the Macesich monthly money series are
clearly approximated by Chambers' quarterly money series.
Indeed, in almost every instance, the turning points in both
monthly and quarterly money series precede their counterpart
cyclical reference dates. One exception is August 1874 when,
according to Chambers, special circumstances were presented—
namely, the transfer of Canadian bank deposits following the
New York financial panic.

In the post-World War I period there are several extra
cycles in the Canadian money series. One is in 1925-26. There
is some uncertainty connected with the dating in Canada of a
reference cycle in 1926-27.[10] The occurrence of an extra cycle
in the money series in 1925-26 corroborates the observed slowing-
down of economic activity in 1926-27.[11]

Another extra cycle occurs in 1930-31. This is consistent
with U.S. experience where a similar but less obvious movement

TABLE 9.1

Specific Cycles in Canadian "Leading Monetary Indicator"
and Its Relation to Canadian Cycles, 1867 to 1965

	Specific Cycle Date	Material Reference Date	Lead (−) or Lag (+) of Canadian Reference Date	
			Peak	Trough
P	12/68			
T	5/69			
P	6/70			
T	9/71			
P	5/74	10/73	+7	
T	5/75			
P	4/76			
T	5/79	5/79	0	
P	12/81	7/82	−7	
T	9/84	3/85		−6
P	11/86	2/87	−3	
T	9/87	2/88		−5
P	6/88	7/90	−25	
T	9/89	3/91		−18
P	12/92	2/93	−2	
T	9/93	3/94		−6
P	4/94	8/95	−16	
T	4/96	8/96		−4
P	1/99			
T	4/00			
P	1/06			
T	9/07			
P	1/13			
T	—			
P	7/20	6/20	+1	
T	10/22	9/21		+11
P	9/25			
T	11/26			
P	12/27	4/29	−16	
T	5/30	—		

(continued)

154

Table 9.1 (continued)

	Specific Cycle Date	Material Reference Date	Lead (−) or Lag (+) of Canadian Reference Date	
			Peak	Trough
P	5/31	—		
T	11/31	3/33		
P	9/35	7/37	−22	
T	10/37	10/38		−12
P	5/42	—		
T	2/47	—		
P	10/48	10/48	0	
T	1/51	9/49		+16
P	12/51	5/53	−17	
T	10/53	6/54		−8
P	12/54	4/54[a]	−28	
T	3/57	4/58[a]		−13
P	8/58	3/60	−19	
T	3/60[b]	4/61		−13
P	6/63[b]	3/64	−9	

[a]D. J. Daly suggests these tentative reference dates.
[b]These reference dates are very tentative.
Sources: Material Reference Dates are from Edward J. Chambers, "Late Nineteenth Century Business Cycles in Canada," Canadian Journal of Economics and Political Science, August 1964, pp. 391-412, and "Canadian Business Cycles Since 1919: A Progress Report," Canadian Journal of Economics and Political Science, May 1958, p. 181. See also Canadian Statistical Review, January 1963 and January 1965, and Bank of Canada, Annual Report of the Governor to the Minister of Finance, 1959-65.

TABLE 9.2

Monthly and Quarterly Turning Points in Rate of Change
in the Canadian Money Stock, 1868 to 1908

	Monthly: Macesich	Quarterly: Chambers
P*	12/68	11/68
T*	5/69	5/69
P	6/70	5/70
T	9/71	8/71
P	5/74	8/74
T	5/75	5/75
P	4/76	5/76
T	5/79	5/79
P	12/81	11/81
T	9/84	8/84
P	11/86	11/86
T	9/87	11/87
P	6/88	8/88
T	9/89	8/89
P	12/92	11/92
T	9/93	8/93
P	4/94	5/94
T	4/96	2/96
P	1/99	2/99
T	4/00	2/00
P	1/06	2/06
T	9/07	11/07

*P = peak; T = trough.
Source: Chambers' quarterly dates from personal correspondence with the author dated November 5, 1962.

occurs. It may be that but for the departure of Canada and
Great Britain from the gold standard in the fall of 1931, the
1930 trough would have corresponded to a reference trough in
the summer of 1931. This was cut short because of the departure
from the gold standard.

The other extra cycle occurs during the war period. Although these data are difficult to read when plotted because of

the extraordinary gyrations, some of these of approximately seven to nine months, like corresponding movements in U.S. figures, are associated with the bond drives; others, perhaps, with inadequate seasonal adjustment. Thus in the case of government bond drives, the estimates exclude government cash balances. During a war bond campaign, deposits were transferred from public to government accounts. When the public paid them out again they came back into the hands of the public, and this accounts for the sharp gyrations in the figures.[12]

Although the "leading monetary indicator" roughly satisfies the NBER's criteria for an adequate indicator, its usefulness for accurately predicting turning points is very limited. For the several reference cycles the lead in months at peaks ranges from 0 to 28. At the trough the lead of the indicator ranges from 4 to 18 months. The evidence, however, is consistent with U.S. results, where similar difficulties occur in attempting to use this indicator alone to predict turning points in economic activity.

It is partly on the basis of such evidence for the United States that Milton Friedman and others argue against the use of discretionary monetary policies and for the pursuit of policies that would require that the money supply increase at a constant rate. The basic problem is that the effects of actions taken currently by the monetary authority may be felt at some variable future date;[13] thus the difficulty of knowing what measures the monetary authority ought to take at any given time. A possible consequence of this imperfect knowledge is that the policies of the monetary authority may contribute to the instability of the economy.

The behavior of the rate of change of the money supply in Canada during the period 1867-1958 tends to support Friedman's position. During periods when gyrations in the money series are very sharp, great economic instability also occurs. When the data are relatively free of gyrations there is relative stability in economic activity.

Of course, it is not possible on the basis of evidence presented in this chapter to argue unequivocally that money factors are the principal causal elements generating stability or instability in Canada. The evidence, however, is suggestive. Other factors undoubtedly also contributed to Canadian difficulties during the period 1867-1964.

If we restrict ourselves to the post-World War II period when quarterly data on variables other than money are available, lagged relations and relations between first differences may be tried. The evidence is that money is more highly correlated with consumption from one to four quarters later than with consumption in an earlier or later quarter. Autonomous expenditures are more highly correlated with consumption one quarter later than in the same or any later quarter. When first differences are considered, money is more highly correlated with consumption one or two quarters later than in the same quarter. One implication of these results is that the argument that changes in induced expenditures brought about changes in money loses force. This does not mean, of course, that money causes induced expenditures just because they precede them. It may be that both are responding to a third variable that lags neither. In any case such a third variable argument can be made against any theory of causality. The point is that the evidence in its support should be presented.[14] Some evidence relating to what caused changes in the money supply to come about is presented in the references provided in this chapter.

Another important implication of the results summarized is that they tend to provide an independent check on the observation that the timing and duration of Canadian and U.S. reference cycles have been very similar, especially since the 1920s.[15] The behavior of the rate of change of the Canadian money stock and its relation to reference cycles has been similar to U.S. experience, thereby reinforcing the observation of similarity of timing and duration of reference cycles in the two countries. They also tend to support the view that a variable lag exists between the implementation of monetary stock and the effects of such policies on economic activity. On this score the Canadian results are consistent with those found by others for the United States.

On the other hand the existence of a lag need not necessarily hamper the effectiveness of monetary policy. In fact, the lag in the effects of a change in policy could make a positive contribution on stabilization.[16] At the beginning of a recession, output does not fall to its lowest level, but falls steadily over some time period. The reverse is true for recovery periods. Given this tendency to continuing movements, first in one direction and then in the other, a given policy change will work to counteract these movements. For example, if a downturn is recognized sufficiently quickly, a given policy reaction will work to counteract these movements. For another example, if a downturn is recognized sufficiently quickly, a given policy reaction will work to increase output only a little at first, when output has fallen only a little, and will work to increase it by more later, when it otherwise would have fallen by more. This is true only if the relevant lags are sufficiently short.

THE EUROPEAN EXPERIENCE

Scattered evidence for France, Italy, and Germany also suggests the existence of a variable lag between the implementation of monetary policy and the effects of such policies on economic activity.[17] Its precise length, however, is more difficult to determine from available evidence for these countries. We would judge it to be on the average two to three quarters in the period 1956 to 1967. The variable nature of the lag is indicated in the case of France. In mid-1962 France gradually tightened monetary conditions. The impact of these changed monetary conditions was felt by decelerated economic activity in late 1963. In late 1964 and early 1965 monetary conditions were made easier, and economic activity picked up in mid-1965. In mid-1966, French monetary authorities operated so as to decelerate the money. These actions apparently resulted in a deceleration in economic activity by 1967.

In the same period (1956-67) Italy experienced two business cycles. The variability of the lag is once again underscored. For example, the money supply, which was growing at a 20 percent annual rate, reached a peak in the first quarter of 1963 and declined to a 4 percent annual growth rate in the fourth quarter. Economic activity as represented by domestic production fell from an 11 percent increase in the second quarter of 1963 to a 9 percent rate of decrease in the second quarter of 1964. By the second half of 1964 the monetary authorities allowed the money supply to grow, but at a significantly lower rate than in early 1963. In spite of this more conservative monetary policy, domestic production responded promptly and registered a 10-12 percent growth rate in 1965-66.

Germany did not experience any serious cyclical movements from 1951 until 1965. A sharp deceleration in the money supply occurred in early 1965 and continued more or less through mid-1966. A substantial decline in the rate of growth of industrial output occurred by the middle of 1965, or in about two quarters from the time that a deceleration in the money supply occurred.

The evidence suggests that in France, Italy, and Germany, three principal members of the EEC, a case can be made against the use of discretionary monetary policies and for the pursuit of policies outlined by Milton Friedman, which require that the money supply increase at a constant rate. If the money stock is to be increased at a constant rate, monetary policy cannot be used to counter balance-of-payments disequilibrium. A system of flexible exchange rates could keep the balance of payments in equilibrium, as Friedman suggests.

The implementation of such an arrangement with the EEC, however, would require a change in monetary policy objectives. For example, the monetary policies of France, Italy, and Germany are intimately linked with the target of balance-of-payments equilibrium.[18] In France monetary authorities have allowed the operation of a mechanism similar to the international gold standard, which largely determined the growth in the money supply. By allowing changes in its international reserves to dominate growth in the money stock, France has in effect followed a discretionary monetary policy in response to the balance of payments. Thus, for example, the gradual weakening in the French trade position from late 1961 was accompanied by a gradual tightening of monetary conditions beginning in mid-1962. Production and imports decelerated by late 1963, leading to an improvement in the trade balance beginning in mid-1964. Monetary policy was moderately easier after recovery in the trade balance in late 1964 and 1965.

Even Germany, with a large level of international reserves, imposed a restrictive monetary policy to correct a deterioration in the trade balance. Only in late 1966 and early 1967, after the trade balance was again in substantial surplus, did the authorities allow the money supply to increase. Italy has also allowed the balance of payments to dictate its monetary policy. Thus in 1956 a weakening trade balance led to a moderately tight monetary policy that, in turn, led to a deceleration of domestic output. The trade balance improved by the middle of 1957 and monetary policy was eased toward the end of the year.

In Yugoslavia the evidence suggests that monetary policy measures have always been taken too late and therefore necessarily have been too strong.[19] This is, however, mainly because of rapidly changing institutional conditions. As a result monetary policy has had to bear an additional burden, thereby complicating the problem of timing.

NOTES

1. Thomas Mayer, "The Inflexibility of Monetary Policy," Review of Economics and Statistics 40 (1958). See also Gene C. Uselton, Lags in the Effects of Monetary Policy: A New Parametric Analysis (New York: Marcel Dekker, 1974) for a useful summary discussion of the problem of lags in monetary policy.

2. W. H. White, "The Flexibility of Anticyclical Monetary Policy," Review of Economics and Statistics 43 (1961).

3. Commission on Money and Credit, Stabilization Policies (Englewood Cliffs, N.J.: Prentice-Hall, 1963).

4. Ibid., p. 30.

5. Milton Friedman, "Note on Lag in Effect of Monetary Policy," American Economic Review, September 1964, p. 760.

6. See Milton Friedman, "The Supply of Money and Changes in Prices and Output," in U.S. Congress, Joint Economic Committee, The Relation of Prices to Economic Stability and Growth: Compendium (Doc. No. 23734) (Washington, D.C.: U.S. Government Printing Office, March 31, 1958), pp. 241-56; Milton Friedman and Anna J. Schwartz, "Money and Business Cycles," Review of Economics and Statistics 45, no. 1, pt. 2 (February 1963):32-75, "The Lag Effect of Monetary Policy," Journal of Political Economy 69 (1961):452, and The Optimum Quantity of Money and Other Essays (Chicago: Aldine, 1969).

7. Several criticisms have been presented against measurement of the lag by Friedman and Schwartz. In the main the criticisms have revolved around the accusation that the lag as measured by Friedman and Schwartz is "a statistical artifact," arising because they compare the rate of change of the money supply with the level of economic activity. Friedman deals with these criticisms in studies cited elsewhere.

For all practical purposes, much of this criticism may be semantic squabbling. After all, statistical considerations require separation of cyclical behavior from secular behavior. The two most common methods are either to express the data in terms of deviations from trend or to use first differences. Friedman chose the latter method for its simplicity. The comments of at least one critic imply that the former method would have met with wider acceptance largely, it seems, because that method yields an average lag of five months at peaks. John M. Culbertson, "Reply," Journal of Political Economy 69 (1961). Friedman had already noted, however, that the two methods are simply two ways of presenting similar information. Neither method provides a full description of the behavior of the money stock. Rather, they are both summary measures.

8. George Macesich, "Supply and Demand for Money in Canada," in Varieties of Monetary Experience, ed. David Meiselman (Chicago: University of Chicago Press, 1970).

9. Ibid.

10. Edward J. Chambers, "Canadian Business Cycles Since 1919: A Progress Report," Canadian Journal of Economics and Political Science, May 1958, p. 172.

11. Ibid., p. 180.

12. For a discussion of Canadian war finance, see R. Craig McIvor, Canadian Monetary Banking and Fiscal Development (Toronto: The Macmillan Company of Canada, 1958).

13. See Macesich.

14. K. A. J. Hay, "Money and Cycles in Post Confederation Canada," Journal of Political Economy, June 1967, pp. 263-73, for example, argues that in Canada money is passive in the upswing of the cycle but an active agent in promulgating recessions in the country and at this time in keeping with Douglass North's suggestion in Economic Growth of the United States, 1790-1860 (Englewood Cliffs, N.J.: Prentice-Hall, 1961) that money has had a role in curtailing long upswings in U.S. growth. This may be a surface manifestation of even more fundamental forces that appear to a considerable extent to be monetary in nature. Macesich argues that defunct ideas, including the Real Bills' Doctrine and the specie standard with its fixed exchange rates, operating through the monetary mechanism, have made significant contributions to the economic stagnation. See George Macesich, Commercial Banking and Regional Development in the United States, 1950-60 (Tallahassee: Florida State University, 1965), and "A Monetary Hypothesis and Southern Development," Revista Internazionale di Scienze Economiche e Commerciali, February 1966, pp. 128-47. Macesich also argues that the problems of the turbulent 1830s and early 1840s in the U.S. economy in no small part derive from capital flows and the operation of the specie-flow mechanism under fixed exchange rates. See his "Sources of Monetary Disturbance in the United States, 1834-45," Journal of Economic History, September 1960, pp. 407-34. See also Clark Warburton, "Variations in Economic Growth and Banking Development in the U.S. from 1835 to 1885," Journal of Economic History, September 1958, pp. 283-97; Milton Friedman and Anna J. Schwartz, A Monetary History of the United States 1867-1960 (Princeton, N.J.: Princeton University Press, 1963); Phillip Cagan, Determinants and Effects of Changes in the Stock of Money, 1875-1960 (New York: National Bureau of Economic Research, 1965), and "The First Fifty Years of the National Banking System: An Historical Appraisal," in Banking and Monetary Studies, ed. Deane Carson (Homewood, Ill.: Richard D. Irwin, 1963).

15. Chambers, p. 186.

16. Martin J. Bailey, National Income and the Price Level (New York: McGraw-Hill, 1962), pp. 174-75.

17. See, for example, Michael W. Keran, "Monetary Policy, Balance of Payments and Business Cycles," Review, Federal Reserve Bank of St. Louis, November 1967, pp. 7-20.

18. Ibid.

19. See D. Dimitrijević and George Macesich, <u>Money and Finance in Contemporary Yugoslavia</u> (New York: Praeger, 1973), pp. 188ff.

10

RULES VERSUS DISCRETIONARY AUTHORITY IN MONETARY POLICY

THE MERITS

Discussions regarding the merits of rules versus discretionary authority date to the early 1930s. Henry Simons in his classic "Rules versus Authorities in Monetary Policy," set the stage for subsequent discussions.[1] Milton Friedman, as we have noted, took up the charge and pressed it for a constant rate of increase in the money supply no matter how defined, although theoretically a discretionary monetary policy is superior to a fixed rule. As we have seen, the argument is that the economy would function better in that it would prevent the Federal Reserve (or central bank) from making things worse. The real sector of the economy is in the main stable. In the absence of monetary disturbances, economic cycles would leave only very shallow peaks and troughs.

Another benefit from a fixed rule, according to Friedman, is that it would eliminate destabilizing expectations. Not only must those in charge of firms handle the uncertainties they face on the micro level, but they must also cope with the uncertainties of general and erratic movements in the price level. As a consequence a considerable amount of time and energy is expended in trying to forecast the future. A constant growth in the money supply reduces the scope of the problem facing firms on the macro level.

Still another benefit, according to proponents of the fixed rule, is that government intervention in the economy is reduced. The monetary authorities would not need to make judgments about the ultimate goals of society. Instead they would concern themselves with the technical aspects of expanding the stock of money.

All these positive aspects of a fixed rule, according to its proponents, flow from the fact that monetary authorities deal with conflicting goals, among which they may shift as a matter of course. Moreover, monetary policy takes effect only after a lag of variable and uncertain length, and consequently may make the economy more rather than less stable. Finally, the record, according to Friedman, supports the view that the Federal Reserve has made and continues to make significant errors of judgment.

The fixed-rule idea has not been received enthusiastically by all economists. One reason perhaps is that in the Keynesian tradition many view the real economy as inherently unstable. This would leave the economy without means for coping with business cycles. Booms and depressions would be treated identically under a fixed rule. Proponents of a fixed rule deny that such major swings in the economy would in fact occur if a fixed rule were adopted.

To these objections, critics of the fixed rule also add that the case for a causal link between changes in the money supply and income has yet to be adequately demonstrated. Moreover, it is impractical for at least two reasons: one political and the other technical. Politically, it is unlikely that a monetary authority would in the near future accept a rule that effectively reduces its options. Technically, the monetary authority cannot assure a smooth and steady growth because the money supply is determined through the interactions of the banking system, the public, and the central bank.

DISCRETIONARY AUTHORITY AND THE POLITICAL-ADMINISTRATIVE SYSTEM

Proponents of discretionary authority base their argument in part on the Keynesian view that the real economy is inherently unstable. In doing so they overlook the imperfections in the political-administrative system. Some students of stabilization policies consider it more reasonable to approach these policies from the vantage point that there are instabilities and imperfections in both the real economy and the political-administrative system and that these interact in a complex way.[2] Fluctuations in the economy are so intimately connected with government policies that realistic explanations and economic forecasts require that government behavior be analyzed as an essential element. Imperfections in the political-administrative system together with a penchant on the part of some governments in stabilizing

votes in the short run is very likely destabilizing. Policy measures meant to be short-run and temporary are often in fact
permanent. As a result distortions in the allocation of resources
by way of deformations of the price system are the result.
Accordingly, the basic problem is not that economists do not
understand analytically what is happening, but rather that the
institutional changes and the discretionary policies that are
necessary for macroeconomic stability seem to be politically difficult to implement.[3]

It may be necessary to improve the functioning of the
political-administrative system, if confidence in discretionary
authority is to be promoted. Such concrete suggestions may
include limiting the "misuse" of short-term stabilization policy
as an element in party-political competition; a more critical view
by the citizens of attempts by governments to buy votes by way
of unsustainable expansion; a more conscious view of the inter-
nationalization of the economic system in the post-World War II
period and the limits of national governments relative to international coordination in the field of stabilization policy. These
international aspects are perhaps the most important. Ready
examples such as the need to control and coordinate the international monetary system and the 1974-75 worldwide recession
when most countries based their hope for an export expansion
generated by expansionary policies in other countries, underscore these international requirements.

QUANTITATIVE TESTS FOR RIVAL MONETARY RULES

Consider now how well the monetary authority in the several
member European countries has managed the money supply and
compare its performance with what might have happened had
the money supply been managed according to some well-defined
"automatic rules."[4] Such a comparison provides some gauge as
to the difficulty of the task of properly managing the money
supply by a supranational monetary authority, for example, the
International Monetary Fund and the European Monetary System,
and the problem of international monetary coordination. It also
sheds light on the continuing controversy over "rules versus
discretion" in monetary management.

The empirical tests that follow are those designed by Martin
Bronfenbrenner to test the performance of the monetary authority
in the United States for various concepts of the money supply
under given assumption as to the nature and timing of the effects
of monetary changes, the actual price-level history of the United

States with its hypothetical history under alternative monetary rules.[5] For the purposes of his tests, Bronfenbrenner defines as "ideal" monetary behavior the constancy of the price level and thus leaves to other branches of economic policy such other objectives of policy as stabilizing interest rates, protecting the gold stock, promoting full employment, balance-of-payments equilibrium, and so on. The alternative rules tested by comparison with Bronfenbrenner's "ideal" rule are:

The "judgment rule," which holds that monetary authorities deal with each situation as it arises according to their best judgment of circumstances present and future. This particular rule is assumed to have been the one actually in practice during the period under review.

The "inflexible rule," under which the money stock grows at a steady annual rate of 3 percent, and which he calls the "3 percent variant of the inflexible rule."

The "4 percent variant of the inflexible rule."

A "lag rule," which provides for money stock expansion according to a percentage equal to the sum of the prior year's percentage increase in the labor force, the prior year's percentage increase in man-hour labor productivity, and the prior year's percentage decrease in the velocity of circulation of money. In effect, if M is the money supply, N the labor force, O an index of output per employed worker, and V the income velocity of circulation of money, the rule may be written as:

$$(dM/M)_t = (dN/N + dO/O - dV/V)_{t-1} \qquad (1)$$

The equation for Bronfenbrenner's "ideal" rate of monetary growth is derived from Irving Fisher's equation of exchange in its income form, $MV = PY$, where P is a price index, Y a measure of real national income, M the money supply, and V the income velocity of circulation of money, and differentiating so that

$$dM/M + dV/V = dP/P + dY/Y \qquad (2)$$

The "ideal" pattern preserves price level stability or in effect

$$(dM/M)_0 = dY/Y - dV/V \qquad (3)$$

When the price level, however, has not remained constant, the actual rate of growth of the money supply is determined by

$$dM/M = dY/Y - dV/V + dP/P \qquad (4)$$

so that

$$(dM/M)_0 = dM/M - dP/P \qquad (5)$$

Thus the "ideal" pattern can be defined as the growth rate of real income minus the growth rate in velocity or the observed growth in the money supply minus the growth rate in the price level. We have $(dM/M)_0$ as the "ideal" pattern of growth rate and (dM/M) as any annual growth other than the ideal. The actual growth rate observed is indicated by $(dM/M)_1$; the 3 percent rule is presented by $(dM/M)_2$; the 4 percent rule is $(dM/M)_3$; the lag rule is $(dM/M)_4$. If we let d_i stand for the annual growth rate of the price level, then

$$d_i = (dM/M)_i - (dM/M)_0 = (dM/M)_i - (dY/Y - dV/V) \qquad (6)$$

where $i = 2$, 3, 4. The changes in real income and velocity are observed changes in (6). The d_i indicates the deviation of the growth of the money supply from the ideal under the various rules. The lower on the average is d_i, the better is the performance of the rule being tested.

Two principal assumptions underline Bronfenbrenner's tests, both of which may be debilitating. One is that the effect of the money supply changes in the price level is usually worked out within one year or one quarter, depending upon whether annual quarterly data are used in the analysis. The evidence cited elsewhere in this study clearly indicates that the lags in the effect of money supply changes on economic activity including prices are variable. Another assumption is that changes in the velocity are independent of monetary policy and changes in the money supply. The tests and their results do provide, as a first approximation, useful insights into problems of monetary management, especially in such multicountry and multinational arrangements as the EEC—and, indeed, for worldwide monetary coordination by such aspirants as the International Monetary Fund.

For the purposes of this study two definitions of the money supply are employed. One is the narrow (conventional) definition and includes demand deposits and currency outside the commercial banking system. The second broader (expanded) definition includes time deposits held in commercial banks. The consumer price index and the wholesale price index are used as a measure of the price level.

We may compare the performance of the several rules by means of a pairwise test that may be represented symbolically as

$$d_{ij} = d_j - d_i \qquad\qquad (7)$$

The statistic d_{ij} measures the extent to which rule i comes closer than does rule j to the ideal behavior in any given year. If d_{ij} should be negative, then the performance of rule j is judged superior to rule i.

QUANTITATIVE TESTS FOR RIVAL MONETARY RULES: EUROPEAN AND NORTH AMERICAN EXPERIENCE, 1956-80

The four monetary rules—judgment rule, 3 percent rule, 4 percent rule, and lag rule—are applied to Belgium, France, Germany, Italy, the Netherlands, the United Kingdom, Sweden, Yugoslavia, Canada, and the United States for the years 1956-80 (1958-80 for Yugoslavia) using annual data.[6] The results of comparing the average deviations of each rule from ideal behavior for price stability are summarized below.

In the tables, the figures outside the parentheses are the deviations from the ideal. The figure is computed by summing all the deviations, neglecting the sign of the deviation, and dividing by the number of observations. The figures within the parentheses are the average algebraic deviations and account is taken of the signs. A positive figure indicates an inflationary bias, the average change in the money supply is greater than ideal, and a negative figure indicates a deflationary bias, which means that the average change in the money supply has been less than ideal.

Belgium

To judge from the test results, the judgment rule that holds that the monetary authority deals with each situation as it arises according to its best judgment of circumstances present and future performs significantly better than any of its rivals in Belgium, when both definitions (narrow and broader) of money and wholesale prices are used in the test (see Table 10.1). However, the judgment rule is inferior when consumer prices are used in the analysis. The 4 percent rule does better than the lag rule in all cases considered. It performs better than the 3 percent rule when a broader definition of money is used. On the other hand, the 3 percent rule does better than the 4 percent rule only when a narrow definition of money together with consumer price is used.

TABLE 10.1

Overall Tests: Average Deviation of dM/M from Ideal Values under Alternative Money Rules, Belgium, 1956–80

Judgment Rule	3 Percent Variant	4 Percent Variant	Lag Rule
	I. Narrow (Conventional) Money: Wholesale Prices		
0.0480 (0.0389)	0.0669 (−0.0030)	0.0644 (0.0097)	0.0915 (0.0018)
	II. Narrow (Conventional) Money: Consumer Prices		
0.0595 (0.0595)	0.0436 (0.0184)	0.0485 (0.0312)	0.0587 (0.0019)
	III. Broader (Expanded) Money: Wholesale Prices		
0.0480 (0.0389)	0.0602 (−0.0345)	0.0556 (−0.0217)	0.0730 (−0.0003)
	IV. Broader (Expanded) Money: Consumer Prices		
0.0595 (0.0595)	0.0337 (−0.0130)	0.0311 (−0.0002)	0.0404 (0.0005)

Source: All tables in this chapter have been compiled by the authors, using data from various issues of the IMF's International Financial Statistics.

The small negative or deflationary bias is indicated in both the 3 and 4 percent rules. The inflationary pattern, however, is evident in the judgment rule and the lag rule. The judgment rule aside, the absolute deviations tended to be smaller when consumer prices were used. Again, the judgment rule aside, the use of wholesale prices and consumer prices yields clear-cut results as to which might give the lower absolute figure. Consumer prices do apparently yield a lower absolute value of deviation in the 3 percent, 4 percent, and lag rules. The evidence indicates a different pattern in the judgment rule, which yields a smaller absolute value when wholesale prices are used in the test.

France

The 3 percent, 4 percent, and lag rules all perform significantly better than the judgment rule when consumer prices are used in the analysis (see Table 10.2). Nonetheless, the judgment rule does better than the 3 percent rule and the lag rule when wholesale prices are used. It also performs better than the 4 percent rule when a broader definition of money together with wholesale price is used; and it is inferior compared to the 4 percent rule when a narrow definition of money and wholesale prices are used in the test. On the other hand, the 4 percent rule does better than the 3 percent rule when wholesale prices are used.

The lag rule is better than the 3 percent rule when a broader definition of money with consumer prices is used, but the 3 percent rule is better using a narrow definition of money. A similar pattern is also observed between the lag rule and the 4 percent rule.

A deflationary bias is revealed in the 3 percent and 4 percent rules, whereas an inflationary pattern is strongly suggested in the judgment rule. The small negative bias indicated in the lag rule, however, may be the result of statistical artifact since the data indicate that the fluctuations from year to year are large and tend to alternate from positive to negative every two or three years. The range of the values of bias is only 0.0037-0.0089.

The use of consumer prices yields clear-cut results that it might give the lower absolute figure. The evidence also indicates that the algebraic deviations from year to year for the 3 percent and 4 percent rules are almost identical for the money supply, irrespective of which price index is used in the analysis.

TABLE 10.2

Overall Tests: Average Deviation of dM/M from Ideal Values under Alternative Money Rules, France, 1956–80

Judgment Rule	3 Percent Variant	4 Percent Variant	Lag Rule
		I. Narrow (Conventional) Money: Wholesale Prices	
0.0809 (0.0717)	0.0818 (−0.0214)	0.0775 (−0.0086)	0.0996 (0.0037)
		II. Narrow (Conventional) Money: Consumer Prices	
0.0901 (0.0901)	0.0562 (0.0002)	0.0563 (0.0130)	0.0605 (0.0089)
		III. Broader (Expanded) Money: Wholesale Prices	
0.0809 (0.0717)	0.0923 (−0.0575)	0.0862 (−0.0448)	0.0938 (0.0038)
		IV. Broader (Expanded) Money: Consumer Prices	
0.0901 (0.0901)	0.0631 (−0.0359)	0.0581 (−0.0231)	0.0538 (0.0089)

Germany

The results indicate that the judgment rule performs better than the 3 percent, 4 percent, or lag rules (see Table 10.3). The average absolute value of the deviations for the judgment rule is consistently lower than the 3 percent, 4 percent, or lag rules regardless of the definition of the money supply or price index used, except in the case of the lag rule, in which a broader definition of money together with consumer prices is used in the analysis. The magnitude of these deviations for the judgment rule ranges from 0.0392 to 0.0452. In most of the cases the absolute value for the judgment rule is less than half its rivals.

The 4 percent rule performs better than the 3 percent rule in all cases considered. This is an overwhelming result. The lag rule is significantly better than the 4 percent variant in all cases considered, when a broader definition of money is used. Similar results are also observed between the lag rule and the 3 percent rule, which is inferior. In order of performance it is the judgment rule that scores better in Germany. It is followed by the lag rule, the 4 percent, and 3 percent rules.

In the second test, which deals with the algebraic deviations, an inflationary bias is revealed in the judgment rule and the lag rule. On the other hand, a deflationary pattern is suggested in the 3 percent and 4 percent rules. The lag rule appears to reduce the inflationary bias as compared to the judgment rule, and the 4 percent rule has less of a deflationary bias than the 3 percent rule.

The judgment and the lag rules aside, the absolute deviations tended to be smaller when a narrow definition of money was used in the study. Again, the judgment rule aside, the use of consumer prices apparently yields a lower absolute figure.

Italy

To judge from the test results, the judgment rule performs better by comparison to the lag rule in all respects (see Table 10.4). However, it is better than the 3 percent rule only when a narrow definition of money together with wholesale prices is used in the analysis. The 4 percent rule is insignificantly better than the 3 percent rule in all cases considered. In fact, they are almost identical in performance. There appears to be little to choose from between the 3 percent and 4 percent rules. Both perform about equally poorly. On the other hand, the lag rule

TABLE 10.3

Overall Tests: Average Deviation of dM/M from Ideal Values under Alternative Money Rules, Germany, 1956–80

Judgment Rule	3 Percent Variant	4 Percent Variant	Lag Rule
I. Narrow (Conventional) Money: Wholesale Prices			
0.0392 (0.0361)	0.0682 (−0.0359)	0.0621 (−0.0231)	0.0659 (0.0097)
II. Narrow (Conventional) Money: Consumer Prices			
0.0452 (0.0452)	0.0559 (−0.0258)	0.0498 (−0.0130)	0.0581 (0.0084)
III. Broader (Expanded) Money: Wholesale Prices			
0.0392 (0.0361)	0.0941 (−0.0622)	0.0849 (−0.0494)	0.0579 (0.0116)
IV. Broader (Expanded) Money: Consumer Prices			
0.0452 (0.0452)	0.0747 (−0.0521)	0.0662 (−0.0393)	0.0447 (0.0104)

TABLE 10.4

Overall Tests: Average Deviation of dM/M from Ideal Values under Alternative Money Rules, Italy, 1956–80

Judgment Rule	3 Percent Variant	4 Percent Variant	Lag Rule
	I. Narrow (Conventional) Money: Wholesale Prices		
0.1057 (0.1003)	0.1182 (−0.0677)	0.1087 (−0.0549)	0.1040 (0.0047)
	II. Narrow (Conventional) Money: Consumer Prices		
0.1026 (0.1020)	0.0942 (−0.0619)	0.0873 (−0.0491)	0.0666 (0.0051)
	III. Broader (Expanded) Money: Wholesale Prices		
0.1057 (0.1003)	0.1095 (−0.0672)	0.1007 (−0.0544)	0.0958 (0.0080)
	IV. Broader (Expanded) Money: Consumer Prices		
0.1026 (0.1020)	0.0809 (−0.0614)	0.0726 (−0.0486)	0.0506 (0.0084)

is superior to both the 3 percent and 4 percent rules. The overall test results suggest that the lag rule performs best in Italy during the period 1951-80, even though a slight inflationary bias is evident in the lag rule. The judgment rule reveals a significant inflationary bias and both the 3 percent and 4 percent rules tend toward a deflationary direction. In Italy, the 4 percent rule appears to perform slightly better than the 3 percent rule. In all cases, the 3 percent rule is the poorest performer.

The absolute deviations tended to be smaller when consumer prices were used in the analysis. The use of different definitions of money does not yield clear-cut results as to which might give the lower absolute value of deviations from the ideal value.

The Netherlands

In the first test, the judgment rule performs better than the 3 percent and 4 percent rules when wholesale prices together with both definitions of money are used in the test (see Table 10.5). However, the 3 percent, 4 percent and lag rule variants are better performers when consumer prices are used. The lag rule is better than the other three rules when a broader definition of money is used, regardless of price index used. The order of better performance is: the judgment rule, the lag rule, the 4 percent rule, and the 3 percent rule.

In the second test, which deals with the algebraic deviations, an inflationary bias is revealed in the judgment rule. On the other hand, a deflationary bias is suggested in all three other rival rules. However, the smaller negative or deflationary pattern indicated in the lag rule may be a statistical artifact since the data fluctuate from year to year and tend to alternate from positive to negative. The judgment rule aside, the absolute deviations tended to be smaller when consumer prices are used in the analysis. The use of wholesale prices does apparently yield a lower absolute deviation in the case of the judgment rule. Again the judgment rule aside, the use of a different definition of money does not yield clear-cut results as to which might give the lower absolute value of deviation.

The United Kingdom

To judge from the overall test results, the 3 percent rule performs best and the judgment rule the poorest in the United Kingdom during the period 1951-80 (see Table 10.6). The 4 per-

TABLE 10.5

Overall Tests: Average Deviation of dM/M from Ideal Values under Alternative Money Rules, the Netherlands, 1956–80

Judgment Rule	3 Percent Variant	4 Percent Variant	Lag Rule
I. Narrow (Conventional) Money: Wholesale Prices			
0.0484 (0.0439)	0.0571 (−0.0308)	0.0532 (−0.0180)	0.0682 (0.0011)
II. Narrow (Conventional) Money: Consumer Prices			
0.0670 (0.0662)	0.0426 (−0.0077)	0.0413 (0.0050)	0.0648 (−0.0019)
III. Broader (Expanded) Money: Wholesale Prices			
0.0484 (0.0439)	0.0743 (−0.0681)	0.0637 (−0.0553)	0.0466 (0.0041)
IV. Broader (Expanded) Money: Consumer Prices			
0.0670 (0.0622)	0.0514 (−0.0450)	0.0420 (−0.0323)	0.0404 (0.0011)

TABLE 10.6

Overall Tests: Average Deviation of dm/M from Ideal Values under Alternative Money Rules, the United Kingdom, 1956–80

Judgment Rule	3 Percent Variant	4 Percent Variant	Lag Rule
	I. Narrow (Conventional) Money: Wholesale Prices		
0.0983 (0.0983)	0.0690 (0.0394)	0.0751 (0.0522)	0.0838 (0.0051)
	II. Narrow (Conventional) Money: Consumer Prices		
0.1012 (0.1012)	0.0716 (0.0430)	0.0766 (0.0558)	0.0787 (0.0058)
	III. Broader (Expanded) Money: Wholesale Prices		
0.0983 (0.0983)	0.0646 (0.0153)	0.0690 (0.0281)	0.0760 (0.0003)
	IV. Broader (Expanded) Money: Consumer Prices		
0.1012 (0.1012)	0.0626 (0.1089)	0.0683 (0.0317)	0.0767 (0.0011)

cent rule and the lag rule perform equally well. The judgment
rule aside, there are no clear-cut results as to which might give
the lower absolute deviations. An inflationary bias is revealed
in all cases considered, irrespective of which price index or
which definition of money is used.

Sweden

To judge from the overall test results, the 4 percent rule
performs best in Sweden during the period 1951-80 (see Table
10.7). The 3 percent rule suggests a slight deflationary bias
when a broader definition of money together with either wholesale or consumer price is used in the analysis. On the other
hand, the judgment rule, the 4 percent rule, and the lag rule
during the same period tend toward an inflationary direction.
In all cases, the judgment rule is the poorest performer. The
3 percent rule is poorer than the 4 percent rule only when a
broader definition of money together with wholesale prices is
used. On the other hand, the lag rule is significantly poorer
than the 3 percent and the 4 percent variants regardless of
which price index or which definition of money is used. Thus,
the order of better performance is the 3 percent rule, the 4
percent rule, the lag rule, and the judgment rule.

Yugoslavia

In Yugoslavia the judgment rule does better than the 3 percent, the 4 percent, and the lag rules when wholesale prices are
used, irrespective of which definition of the money supply is used
in the test (see Table 10.8). The 3 percent, 4 percent, and lag
rules, in turn, are the better performers when consumer prices
are used. The 4 percent rule performs slightly better than the
3 percent rule in all cases considered. However, there are no
clear-cut results as to which might give the lower absolute deviations. On the other hand, the lag rule performs better than
both the 3 percent and the 4 percent rules in the case that uses
a broader definition of money together with wholesale prices.

A deflationary bias is revealed in the 4 percent and 3 percent rules, while an inflationary bias is suggested in the judgment and lag rules. However, the inflationary bias in the lag
rule is relatively small compared to that of the judgment rule.
The small negative algebraic deviation in the lag rule may be a
statistical artifact as a result of fluctuation of annual data.

TABLE 10.7

Overall Tests: Average Deviation of dM/M from Ideal Values under Alternative Money Rules, Sweden, 1956–80

Judgment Rule	3 Percent Variant	4 Percent Variant	Lag Rule
I. Narrow (Conventional) Money: Wholesale Prices			
0.0769 (0.0745)	0.0454 (0.0001)	0.0456 (0.0129)	0.0814 (0.0111)
II. Narrow (Conventional) Money: Consumer Prices			
0.0790 (0.0790)	0.0465 (0.0063)	0.0484 (0.0191)	0.0787 (0.0094)
III. Broader (Expanded) Money: Wholesale Prices			
0.0790 (0.0745)	0.0540 (-0.0095)	0.0528 (0.0032)	0.0742 (0.0155)
IV. Broader (Expanded) Money: Consumer Prices			
0.0790 (0.0790)	0.0418 (-0.0033)	0.0431 (0.0095)	0.0628 (0.0138)

TABLE 10.8

Overall Tests: Average Deviation of dM/M from Ideal Values under Alternative Money Rules, Yugoslavia, 1956–80

Judgment Rule	3 Percent Variant	4 Percent Variant	Lag Rule
	I. Narrow (Conventional) Money: Wholesale Prices		
0.1174 (0.1174)	0.1552 (−0.1021)	0.1502 (−0.0893)	0.1596 (0.0016)
	II. Narrow (Conventional) Money: Consumer Prices		
0.1826 (0.1826)	0.1351 (−0.1381)	0.1323 (−0.0253)	0.1623 (0.0037)
	III. Broader (Expanded) Money: Wholesale Prices		
0.1174 (0.1174)	0.1419 (−0.1311)	0.1303 (−0.1183)	0.1211 (0.0014)
	IV. Broader (Expanded) Money: Consumer Prices		
0.1826 (0.1826)	0.0892 (−0.0672)	0.0831 (−0.0544)	0.1173 (0.0035)

Canada

To judge from the overall test results, the judgment rule appears superior during the period 1951-80 when the narrow definition of money is used in the analysis (see Table 10.9).

The average absolute value of the deviations for the judgment rule is consistently lower than the other three rules when the narrow definition of money is used. The judgment rule, however, has the larger average value of the deviations than these three rules when a broader definition of money and consumer prices are used in the test.

In the second set of tests the results indicate a tendency toward an inflationary bias in the judgment rule, whereas a deflationary bias appears in the 3 percent, 4 percent, and lag rules. The judgment rule aside, the absolute deviations tended to be smaller when consumer prices were used in the analysis. Again the judgment rule aside, the use of broader definition of money yields the lower absolute deviations.

The United States

To judge from the overall test results, the judgment rule performs consistently more poorly by comparison to the other three rival rules regardless of the definition of the money supply or price index used (see Table 10.10). The average absolute value of deviations for the judgment rule ranges from 0.0618 to 0.0626. The use of consumer prices seems to yield lower absolute deviations in all cases considered.

In the second set of tests the results indicate a strong tendency toward an inflationary bias in the judgment rule, while a deflationary bias appears only in the 3 percent rule when the broader definition of money is used. However, these deflationary biases are too small to be significant. This might be a statistical artifact. In order of performance it is the lag rule that scores better in the United States. It is followed by the 4 percent, 3 percent, and judgment rules.

IMPLICATIONS

What implications can we draw from this evidence with respect to the long-standing debate on "rules versus discretion" and a supranational monetary authority for coordinating stabilization policies? From the point of view of the individual EEC

TABLE 10.9

Overall Tests: Average Deviation of dM/M from Ideal Values under Alternative Money Rules, Canada, 1956–80

Judgment Rule	3 Percent Variant	4 Percent Variant	Lag Rule
I. Narrow (Conventional) Money: Wholesale Prices			
0.0833 (0.0464)	0.1259 (−0.0282)	0.1263 (−0.0155)	0.2194 (−0.0161)
II. Narrow (Conventional) Money: Consumer Prices			
0.0628 (0.0628)	0.0843 (−0.0003)	0.0862 (0.0125)	0.1297 (−0.0004)
III. Broader (Expanded) Money: Wholesale Prices			
0.0833 (0.0464)	0.0871 (−0.0710)	0.0803 (−0.0583)	0.1396 (−0.0164)
IV. Broader (Expanded) Money: Consumer Prices			
0.0628 (0.0628)	0.0526 (−0.0431)	0.0450 (−0.0303)	0.0551 (−0.0008)

TABLE 10.10

Overall Tests: Average Deviation of dM/M from Ideal Values under Alternative Money Rules, the United States, 1956–80

Judgment Rule	3 Percent Variant	4 Percent Variant	Lag Rule
	I. Narrow (Conventional) Money: Wholesale Prices		
0.0626 (0.0618)	0.0496 (0.0370)	0.0562 (0.0497)	0.0492 (0.0029)
	II. Narrow (Conventional) Money: Consumer Prices		
0.0618 (0.0618)	0.0446 (0.0383)	0.0526 (0.0511)	0.0396 (0.0021)
	III. Broader (Expanded) Money: Wholesale Prices		
0.0626 (0.0618)	0.0542 (−0.0024)	0.0532 (0.0104)	0.0535 (0.0011)
	IV. Broader (Expanded) Money: Consumer Prices		
0.0618 (0.0618)	0.0425 (−0.0011)	0.0417 (0.0117)	0.0456 (0.0003)

countries, that combination of forecasting ability, political pressure, and administrative routine that passes as "judgment" or "discretionary" monetary policy has an edge. The individual records in these countries seem favorable to such policy, at least in comparison to the other three rules considered—provided, of course, that the monetary authority makes use of its discretion in the pursuit of price stability as the stated goal.

The evidence with respect to the other rules, though on balance not spectacular, is not irrelevant. On the contrary, in the experience of all six countries the 3 percent and 4 percent versions of the inflexible rule came close to the record registered by the judgment rule. This is particularly significant for a supranational monetary authority. The formulation and implementation of a judgment rule by such a supranational authority for the entire community so that the rule is compatible for and in all six member countries may very well out-tax the ingenuity of such an organization. It would probably lead to oligopolistic reaction on the part of each of the countries and to squabbles that would undermine the EEC as an effective organization. A useful alternative would be the obligation on the part of the EEC monetary authority to adhere to, say, a 4 percent increase in the money supply designed to serve the goal of price stability. This rule does perform reasonably well in most member countries. Its adoption would serve to defuse the explosive nature of the situation by making it unnecessary for a central monetary authority to thrash about in search of a judgment rule acceptable to all member countries, individually and collectively.

To be sure, rules can provide only a rough guide to monetary management. Rules designed to serve specific goals nevertheless do focus attention on areas of conflict and lay open to public debate both the goals and means for reaching them. This is particularly important in such a multinational and multistate organization as the EEC. A given rule at least avoids one of the principal objections to discretionary policy, which is that such a policy may be used to serve goals other than those agreed upon by all participants within the community.

Events since the financial crisis in May 1971 underscore the difficulties of putting together a European monetary union and coordinating monetary policy. Indeed, it is doubtful whether any of the rules discussed would have been appropriate under the circumstances. French enthusiasm for exchange controls and German opposition to such controls generated differences that even the Council of Finance Ministers failed to resolve. In the end, each country went its own separate road.

Some countries resorted to exchange controls, while others allowed their currencies to find their own levels on the international exchange markets. These difficulties have in fact been compounded by Great Britain's entry into the EEC and the Nixon administration's efforts on behalf of the dollar. By 1976, monetary turbulence divided Europe into weak and strong currency zones and compounded problems of making the EEC simply function as an area of free trade and equal competition. Indeed, a question being asked nearly 20 years after the EEC was created by a generation of Europeans that knew two world wars is whether the EEC can survive half submerged by currency turbulence, divisions between its rich and poor members, and mounting waves of protectionism.

NOTES

1. Henry Simons, "Rules versus Authorities in Monetary Policy," Journal of Political Economy, February 1936.
2. Assar Lindbeck, "Stabilization Policy in Open Economies with Endogenous Politicians," American Economic Review, May 1976, pp. 1-19.
3. Ibid., p. 18.
4. See, for example, George Macesich, "Monetary Policy in Common Market Countries: Rules versus Discretion," Weltwirtschaftliches Archiv 108, no. 1 (1972):29-52, and Geldopolitik in Einem Gemeinsamen Europaischen Markt (Baden-Baden: Nomos Verlagsgesellschaft, 1972).
5. M. Bronfenbrenner, "Statistical Tests of Rival Monetary Rules," Journal of Political Economy 69 (1961):7, and "Statistical Tests of Rival Monetary Rules: Quarterly Data Supplement," in ibid., p. 621. See also Franco Modigliani, "Some Empirical Tests of Monetary Management and of Rules versus Discretion," Journal of Political Economy 72 (1964):211; and Donald P. Tucker, "Bronfenbrenner on Monetary Rules: A Comment," Journal of Political Economy 71 (1963):173.
6. The tests are also conducted for EEC data as a whole by summing the data for income, employment, and monetary variables from six EEC countries. By so doing, we hope to justify the goal and purpose of EEC monetary unity. However, limitations are encountered in combining the price variables. It is meaningless to sum all price indexes across countries, for the definition of each price index may not be the same for each country. Using a proxy such as the price variable from France, Germany, and the United Kingdom, we do find evidence indicating

that the judgment rule performs consistently better in comparison to the other three rival rules regardless of the definition
of the money supply or price index used. The results also
indicate a strong tendency toward an inflationary bias in the
judgment rule, while a deflationary bias appears in the 3 percent,
4 percent, and lag rules.

11

MONETARISM AND THE INTERNATIONAL ECONOMY: SOME OUTSTANDING ISSUES

MONETARISM AND THE MONETARY APPROACH
TO THE BALANCE OF PAYMENTS

The reemergence of the long-dormant view, with roots going back more than 200 years, that money and monetary policy are indeed important is underscored by the work on the monetary approach to the balance of payments undertaken by James Mead, Harry Johnson, Robert Mundell, Jacob Frenkel, J. Richard Zecher, Bluford H. Putnam, D. Sykes Wilford, and others.[1] This approach can be summarized in the proposition that the balance of payments is essentially a monetary phenomenon.

> In general the approach emphasises the budget constraint imposed on a country's international spending and views the various accounts of the balance of payments as the "windows" to the outside world, through which excesses of domestic flow demands over domestic flow supplies over domestic flow demands are cleared.
>
> Accordingly surpluses in the trade account and the capital account respectively represent excess flow supplies of goods and of securities, and a surplus in the money account reflects an excess domestic flow demand for money. Consequently, in analysing the money account, or more familiarly the rate of increase in the country's international reserves, the monetary approach focuses on the determinants of the excess domestic flow demand for a supply of money.[2]

Though the approach is described as "monetary," it should not be confused with the term "Monetarist" used in policy debates, especially over the use of monetary policy as contrasted with fiscal policy in economic stabilization. As Frenkel and Johnson put it:

> The monetary approach to the balance of payments asserts neither that monetary mismanagement is the only cause, nor that monetary policy change is the only possible cure, to balance of payments problems; it does suggest, however, that monetary processes will bring about a cure of some kind—not necessarily very attractive—unless frustrated by deliberate monetary policy action, and that policies that neglect or aggravate the monetary implications of deficits and surpluses will not be successful in their declared objectives. . . .[3]

As in the quantity theory statement of Milton Friedman, the essential assumption in the monetary approach is that there does exist an aggregate demand function for money that is a stable function of a relatively small number of aggregate economic variables. In this sense it makes the same assumptions as in the moderate Keynesian view. Like the classical quantity theory of money, the monetary approach assumes the longer-run view for the most part of a fully employed economy as the norm rather than the exception.

A country's size is irrelevant to the monetary approach. A small country viewed as facing a parametric set of world prices and interest rates presents no theoretical difficulty in regarding demand and supply functions depended on prices rather than prices themselves as parameters. Frenkel and Johnson note that country size is important on the monetary side of analysis. For instance, a large country such as the United States, whose national currency is internationally acceptable, may, as a result of following an inflationary domestic credit policy, force an accumulation of its money in foreign hands and so lead to world inflation rather than a loss in its international reserves. The postwar era is a good illustration of such a case.

Of the several studies reported on by Harry Johnson up to about 1975, one is by N. Parkin, I. Richards, and G. Zis. An

> empirical study of the determination and control of the world money supply under fixed exchange rates 1961-1971 reaches the important general conclusions that the growth of the world money supply in the

study period was influenced in an important and predictable way by the growth of the world reserve
money, but that even if there had been firm control
of the growth of world high-powered money, this
would not have prevented national control banks from
pursuing domestic credit expansion policies uncon-
ducive to world price stability. [4]

Zecher properly puts the issues in perspective when he
writes that

the emergence of the monetary approach in the late
1960's and 1970's marks a major swing in economic
thought back to the concepts of Hume and Smith,
and away from the balance of payments theories that
emerged from the Keynesian revolution. . . . At the
same time domestic monetarism was a rising force,
emphasizing the importance of money and the general
equilibrium nature of domestic economies. Given the
world goods and capital markets were becoming more
and more integrated, international theorists were
forced to rework their models; simultaneously, the
importance of monetary demand and supply relationships on a world level was becoming integrated with
this new general equilibrium approach to balance of
payments questions. [5]

MONETARISM AND FLEXIBLE EXCHANGE RATES

Another major issue is the effectiveness of flexible exchange
rates in achieving balance-of-payments adjustments. Some
observers claim that exchange-rate changes can only raise
world prices and do nothing to foster payments equilibria.
Others view flexibility as a major deterrent to world inflation,
either because it "bottles up" inflation in individual countries
or because depreciations trigger tougher stabilization policies
than do losses of reserves. [6] The question is whether floating
exchange rates have provided more or less stability than fixed
exchange rates.

The strongest argument traditionally made in favor of
flexible exchange rates has been that they allow countries, not
committed by buying and selling currencies at fixed prices, to
pursue independent monetary policies according to their own
welfare criteria. [7] Milton Friedman argues that if internal prices

and wages were inflexible, it would be preferable to allow adjustment to occur through a depreciation of domestic currency.[8] Svend Laursen and Lloyd Metzler, Egon Sohmen, and Murray Kemp argue in favor of floating exchange rates by the familiar insulation properties of free rates;[9] while Robert Mundel, in his advocacy of fixed exchange rates, has been considered as more in the tradition of rules-over-authority than Friedman, in his advocacy of floating exchange rates.[10]

The fact that the fixed exchange-rate system creates substitutability among money assets and produces policy-offsetting flows of money and common rates of inflation among countries is undesirable from a closed economy monetarist perspective. Some monetarists argue that the money supply instead should be used to help achieve internal stability and a perfectly flexible exchange rate system for external stability.

Under a perfectly flexible exchange rate system, the central bank does not intervene in the foreign exchange market to guarantee the value of domestic money. There are two assumed benefits as a result of this lack of intervention. First, foreign money is no longer a perfect substitute for domestic money on the supply side, because the central bank no longer guarantees the value of the domestic money. Holding a given quantity of foreign currency no longer means holding a specific quantity of domestic currency. Consequently, no central bank is willing to convert domestic and foreign currency at some constant rate. Second, since the central banks no longer intervene in the foreign exchange market, the net movements of money among countries is assumed to be zero. There are no longer leakages in the money supply, and all the effects of domestic monetary policy are felt within the domestic country. "Flexible exchange rates then are assumed to provide countries with the monetary independence that permits the implementation of the monetary policies proposed by the closed economy monetarists.[11]

Several questions, however, are raised by the above arrangement: Can a floating exchange rate confer national monetary autonomy? Can it insulate an economy against exogenous disturbances from abroad? Can it enhance the effectiveness of domestic monetary and fiscal policies? Actual experience with limited exchange rate flexibility since 1973 suggests that a floating exchange rate cannot confer complete monetary autonomy. Recent developments in the literature further suggest that monetary independence may be illusory: From Dornbush it can be concluded that independent monetary policies ultimately affect only nominal variables, simply altering inflation and exchange rate paths.[12] In his study based on a generalization of a flexible exchange rate system of the "monetary" or "asset" view of balance-of-payments adjustment under fixed exchange rates, J. Frenkel suggests that "monetary independence in any real sense may be largely chimerical, even in the short run."[13]

Although a floating exchange-rate system would prevent the transmission of excess demand from one country to another, it does not imply that there would be less inflation in the world as a whole. If a country generates domestic excess demand, the spilling-over to other countries would be hindered by a depreciation in the exchange rate. Inflation in the depreciating country would be worse than under fixed exchange rates because the excess demand is "bottled" within the country.[14]

There are two bodies of current literature on the determination of exchange rates relevant to the issues under discussion here. One is an outgrowth of the efficient market analysis of securities markets, while the other is the monetary approach. The efficient market approach to foreign exchange rates is based on rational microeconomic behavior by individual economic agents. The monetary approach, prominent among competing theories of exchange rate determination in a regime of floating exchange rates, is a macro theory that attempts to equilibrate the international demand for stocks of assets rather than the international demand for flows of goods as under the more traditional view. This approach rests on the view that the exchange rate between two national currencies is endogenously determined by stock equilibrium conditions in markets for national monies. The major theoretical focus is the supply and demand functions for monetary stocks.[15]

Within the monetary view, there are two very different approaches: the "Chicago" theory and the "Keynesian" theory. The Chicago theory assumes that prices are perfectly flexible, in contrast to the Keynesian theory that prices are sticky, at least in the short run. As a consequence of the flexible price assumption in the Chicago theory, changes in the nominal interest rate reflect changes in the expected inflation rate. Thus there exists a positive relationship between the exchange rate and the nominal interest differential. In the Keynesian theory, however, changes in the nominal interest rate reflect changes in the tightness of monetary policy, and the exchange rate and the nominal interest differential are thus negatively related.[16]

Jeffrey Frankel develops a model that is a version of the asset view of the exchange rate in that it emphasizes the role of expectations and rapid adjustment in capital markets.[17] By so doing, the model combines the Keynesian assumption of sticky prices with the Chicago assumption that there are secular rates of inflation. It shares with the Frenkel-Bilson (Chicago) model an attention to long-run monetary equilibrium. The Frenkel-Bilson model suggests that a monetary expansion causes a long-run depreciation because it is an increase in the supply of the currency and an increase in expected inflation causes a long-run depreciation because it decreases the demand for the currency. The model also shares with the Dornbusch (Keynesian) model the assumption that sticky prices in goods markets create a difference between the short run and the long run. The result is that the exchange rate is negatively related to the nominal interest differential but positively related to the expected long-run inflation differential.

Other recent contributors to the balance-of-payments literature include Robert Barro, Rudiger Dornbusch, Jacob Frenkel, Hans Genberg and Hary K. Kierzkowski, Donald Kemp, Michael Mussa, and Michael Parkin.[18] They have focused on the determination of the exchange rate viewed as a relative price of two national monies. The exchange rate is seen as endogenously determined by the respective national money supplies and demands in the two countries and the resulting effects on their general price levels. The demand functions are typically specified to correspond to conventional macro-model money demand functions involving income, the interest rate, and expectations concerning future exchange rates. Some specifications permit the simultaneous determination of the exchange rate and the expected future exchange rate by imposing restrictions that characterize rational expectation formation. Other models include broader specifications and additional asset supply and demand equations. Despite their differences, a common theme runs through all these studies: "While it is recognized that the exchange rate is not purely a monetary phenomenon (being affected in part by the real determinants of the demand for money), the thrust of the new asset approach to exchange rates is that the exchange rate is primarily determined by current and past innovations in the relative supplies of national monies."[19]

Caves and Feige present a bivariate model of the determination of exchange rates that is

> sufficiently rich to incorporate the major features of
> the simple monetary approach to exchange-rate deter-
> mination, the efficient markets view of foreign ex-
> change markets, and the systematic intervention
> effects from monetary authorities. The model allows
> some refining of past concepts of market efficiency,
> and of the testable hypothesis of incremental effi-

ciency. It also highlights the conceptual difficulties involved in empirical observation of the monetary mechanism in markets that may be characterized by incremental efficiency. Finally, it permits testing of the hypothesis of monetary authority.[20]

They test six propositions relating to the money supply/exchange rate relationship. Their finding of causality from exchange rates to the money supply is consistent with the hypothesis of government intervention in the foreign exchange market. Their results provide yet another example of the "reverse causality" phenomenon that has appeared in other economic contexts.

On the other hand, Dornbusch and Fischer develop a model of exchange-rate determination that integrates the roles of relative prices, expectations, and the assets markets.[21] It emphasizes the relationship between the behavior of the exchange rate and the current account, in contrast to the early theories of the exchange rate that singled out purchasing power parity or the current account as the chief determinants of the exchange rate. Most of the recent models of exchange-rate determination and dynamics emphasize asset stock equilibrium as the relevant framework. The study of exchange-rate dynamics typically formulates in a macroeconomic setting that emphasizes the speeds of adjustment of goods and assets markets and in which expectations dominate the short-run behavior of the exchange rate. Dornbusch and Fischer focus instead on the association between the current account and the exchange rate. Although their approach retains many elements of the recent approaches including asset equilibrium, and the distinction between anticipated and unanticipated disturbances to the economy, they do extend recent approaches by giving an important role to the accumulation of assets over time through the current account. Asset accumulation, together with expectation, dominates the dynamic behavior of the exchange rate.

NOTES

1. For example, papers in Jacob A. Frenkel and Harry G. Johnson, eds., The Monetary Approach to the Balance of Payments (London: George Allen and Unwin, 1978), and Bluford H. Putnam and D. Sykes Wilford, eds., The Monetary Approach to International Adjustment (New York: Praeger, 1978) contain useful theoretical and empirical studies on the monetary approach to international adjustment as well as a statement by J. Richard

Zecher and a bibliography of relevant studies. See also George
Macesich, The International Monetary Economy and the Third
World (New York: Praeger, 1981), Chapters 2 and 3.

2. Frenkel and Johnson, p. 21.

3. Ibid., p. 24.

4. Harry G. Johnson, "Monetary Approach to the Balance
of Payments: A Nontechnical Guide," in The Contemporary Inter-
national Economy: A Reader, ed. John Adams (New York: St.
Martin's Press, 1979), p. 205. The empirical study is N. Parkin,
I. Richards, and G. Zis, "The Determination and Control of the
World Money Supply under Fixed Exchange Rates, 1961-71,
Manchester School 43 (September 1975):293-316.

5. J. Richard Zecher, "Preface" to The Monetary Approach
to International Adjustment, pp. ix-x.

6. Fred C. Bergsten and William R. Cline, "Increasing
International Economic Interdependence: The Implications for
Research," American Economic Review 66, no. 2 (May 1976):157.

7. David T. King, Bluford H. Putnam, and D. Sykes
Wilford, "A Currency Portfolio Approach to Exchange Rate
Determination: Exchange Rate Stability and the Independence
of Monetary Policy," in Putnam and Wilford, p. 199.

8. Milton Friedman, "The Case for Flexible Exchange
Rates," in Essays in Positive Economics, ed. M. Friedman
(Chicago: University of Chicago Press, 1953).

9. Egon Sohmen, Flexible Exchange Rates (Chicago:
University of Chicago Press, 1969); D. S. Kemp, "A Monetary
View of Balance of Payments," in Putnam and Wilford; S. Laursen
and L. Metzler, "Flexible Exchange Rates and the Theory of
Employment," Review of Economics and Statistics 32 (1950):
251-99.

10. R. A. Mundell, International Economics (New York:
Macmillan, 1968).

11. Marc A. Miles, "Currency Substitution: Perspective,
Implementations, and Empirical Evidence," in Putnam and Wilford,
pp. 173-74.

12. Rudiger Dornbusch, Open Economy Macroeconomics
(New York: Basic Books, 1980).

13. King, Putnam, and Wilford, p. 199.

14. Helmut Frisch, "Inflation Theory 1963-1975: A 'Second
Generation Survey,'" Journal of Economic Literature 15, no. 4
(December 1977):1909.

15. See John F. O. Bilson, "The Current Experience with
Floating Exchange Rates: An Appraisal of the Monetary Approach,"
American Economic Review: Papers and Proceedings 68, no. 2
(May 1978):392-97; Jacob A. Frenkel, "A Monetary Approach to

the Exchange Rate: Doctrinal Aspects and Empirical Evidence,"
Scandinavian Journal of Economics 78, no. 2 (May 1976):200-24.

16. Jeffrey A. Frankel, "On the Mark: A Theory of Floating Exchange Rates Based on Real Interest Differentials,"
American Economic Review 69, no. 4 (September 1979):610-22.

17. Jeffrey Frankel.

18. See, for example, papers in Frenkel and Johnson,
and Putnam and Wilford.

19. Douglas Caves and Edgar L. Feige, "Efficient Foreign
Exchange Markets and the Monetary Approach to Exchange-Rate
Determination," American Economic Review 70, no. 1 (March
1980):120-34.

20. Ibid., p. 131.

21. Rudiger Dornbusch and Stanley Fischer, "Exchange
Rates and the Current Account," American Economic Review 70,
no. 5 (December 1980):960-71.

12

MONEY AND THE ECONOMIC ORGANIZATION: A SUMMARY VIEW

MONETARY APPROACH

Monetary theory is relevant whatever a country's economic and political system. It is ideologically neutral. Economics cannot (or should not) make value judgments about society. What it can do is develop measures of the way a society is functioning, and of whether—given a particular set of objectives—it is functioning well. Whatever their ideologies, all governments' economic performances are judged by the relentless statistics for economic growth, unemployment, inflation, and the balance of payments.

A "monetary" approach to economic policy emphasizes two aspects of economic policy problems: the relation between monetary growth and the basic rate of inflation (or deflation); and the relation between unanticipated monetary growth and temporary changes in output and unemployment. The first relation determines the monetary view about antiinflationary policies. The second relation focuses on the need for a stable and predictable course of monetary policy. The monetary view is also sceptical about monetary manipulation aimed at influencing real economic growth.

It is erroneous to attribute to money and monetary policy an all-embracing power. In fact, Milton Friedman writes:

> I stress nonetheless the similarity between the views
> that prevailed in the late twenties and those that
> prevail today because I fear that, now as then, the
> pendulum may well have swung too far, that, now as
> then, we are in danger of assigning to monetary
> policy a larger role than it can perform, in danger
> of asking it to accomplish tasks that it cannot achieve

and, as a result, in danger of preventing it from
making the contribution that it is capable of making. [1]

Moreover, to use the monetary system to pursue changing
goals and objectives is incompatible with monetary order. [2] Such
manipulation will make the monetary system, writes Herbert
Frankel, "capricious and uncertain and prey to conflicting and
varying political objectives." [3] Intended to reduce uncertainty,
monetary manipulation actually increases it by casting in doubt
the monetary system itself. A monetary policy, writes Frankel,
"which is directed to shifting goals—as for example, full employment, economic growth, economic equality or the attempt to
satisfy conflicting demands of capital and labour—cannot but
vary with the goals adopted." [4]

These views are in marked contrast to views held by some
economists that we now possess the technical tools and scientific
knowledge to enable us to control monetary behavior. We should
keep in mind that Frankel's views on money and the monetary
system derive from Georg Simmel and are close to those of the
"Austrian school," which differs significantly from both Keynesian
and Monetarist (Friedman) views. [5] According to the Austrian
view, money and the monetary system is the unintended product
of social evolution in much the same fashion as the legal system.
"Money" is a social institution—a public good. It is not simply
another durable good held in the form of "real balances" by
utility-maximizing individuals or profit-maximizing firms as
Keynesian and Monetarist views hold. However useful the tools
of demand and supply analysis applied to money as a private
durable good, Keynesians and Monetarists miss the full consequences of monetary instability.

In essence, the monetary system is an integral part of the
social fabric whose threads include faith and trust, which make
possible the exercise of rational choice and the development of
human freedom. This is misunderstood by the very people who
benefit from it. It is this misunderstanding of the social role
of money as a critical element in the market mechanism and the
need for confidence in the stability of its purchasing power that
came to dominate much of the Keynesian and Monetarist monetary
thought in the postwar period. This misunderstanding is the
"ideological" key to the use of discretionary monetary policies
for monetary expansion as an unfailing means of increasing output and employment and reducing interest rates.

Both Keynes and Friedman (and their intellectual associates)
deplore the uncertainty generated by monetary disturbances,
that marked instability of money is accompanied by instability

of economic activity. They both desire a stable growth rate in the money supply as a way of minimizing fluctuations in prices, output, and employment. They differ, however, in how to achieve the benefits of monetary stability. Keynes thought that exclusive reliance on monetary policy was unrealistic on political grounds and opted for fiscal policy. Friedman has little confidence in the role political authorities may play in providing monetary stability and opts from both monetary and fiscal authorities to a fixed rule.

To judge from the evidence presented in our study for individual countries, that combination of forecasting ability, political pressure, and administrative routine that passes as "judgment" or "discretionary" monetary policy has an edge, albeit not a spectacular edge, over the "fixed rule." The individual records in these countries seem favorable to such a "discretionary policy," at least in comparison to the other three rules considered—provided, of course, that the monetary authority makes use of its "discretion" in the pursuit of price stability as the stated goal.

Price stability, however, does not appear to be the principal concern of monetary policy in all countries reviewed in our study. To judge from our test results it is in France that monetary policy appears to focus on the price level. In other countries, the price level shares along with economic growth, unemployment, and the balance of payments a major concern of monetary policy. Monetary authorities apparently do act as though these policy goals conflict while at the same time talking about their mutual consistency.

Our results are also suggestive to the on-going debate for a supranational monetary authority, such as the International Monetary Fund, to coordinate multinational monetary policies. This debate is accentuated by the burden of reconciling domestic and international goals that have fallen on U.S. monetary policy and the Federal Reserve System.[6] The monetary authorities have had to intervene all too frequently in the foreign exchange markets to prevent wild fluctuations in the dollar. The consequence has been that U.S. interest rates were higher than political authorities favored. This has prompted the U.S. administrations to push for a stronger IMF to manage the international monetary system, thereby restoring the Federal Reserve's independence to concentrate on domestic problems. This requires that the IMF must become more like a supranational central bank and be given additional surveillance power over the economic policies of its 140 members. It also means that the IMF's reserve asset (Special Drawing Rights) should be given a more important role in the international monetary system.

The formulation and implementation of a "judgment rule" by a supranational monetary authority—for instance, for the entire EEC—may very well out-tax the ingenuity of such an organization. Extending such an arrangement to 140 member countries of the IMF would surely compound the problem faced by the authority. In such multinational and multistate organizations as the EEC and the IMF, a given monetary rule at least avoids one of the principal objectives to discretionary policy, which is that such a policy may be used to serve goals other than those agreed upon by all participant countries.

Our evidence also suggests why central banks have not adopted a "fixed monetary rule." It may well be, as some economists argue, that discretionary policies serve the established bureaucracies. Such a policy permits them to take credit when economic conditions are good and allow for disclaimers of responsibility when economic conditions deteriorate.

Another reason for such reluctance may be in the degree of independence possessed by central banks in executing monetary policy.[7] Such independence depends on: the method of appointment of governors; the length of time they serve; whether they have legislated objectives clear enough to be a barrier to government intervention; and whether their constitutions provide the bank or the government with the final authority for monetary policy. In practice, central banks may have rather less, or rather more, freedom than their charters suggest. This is likely to depend on tradition as well as on the personalities involved.

In our study only the German Bundesbank has final authority for monetary policy. The governor, moreover, is not directly appointed by the government. The National Bank of Yugoslavia is an independent federal institution, established by federal law. The bank is managed by the governor, who is appointed by the Federal Assembly on the recommendation of the Federal Executive Council. He is responsible to both of these institutions for the implementation of bank operations and targets. The Federal Assembly and the Federal Executive Council decide monetary policy targets and the National Bank is responsible only for their implementation. In policy formation the National Bank, nonetheless, plays a significant, if not dominant role in monetary policy thanks to ready acceptance of its proposals by policy workers.

The central bank of the Netherlands has a clearly defined objective of price stability built into its constitution. On no other score could it be considered independent. In fact, the world's two oldest central banks, Riksbank of Sweden (1668) and the Bank of England (1694), are clearly subservient to their governments in the formation of monetary policy. In the United States and Germany, central bank control rests with a board composed of the heads of the several regional banks, thereby allowing for greater independence from the central government.

It is not surprising that central banks find themselves in the uncomfortable position where monetary and fiscal policies meet. They must meet the requirements of their governments. This means ensuring that the government is able to function smoothly in meeting its financial obligations. In many countries government borrowing in the 1970s resulted in regular deficits and debt rose as a proportion of gross national product.

Concern with inflation calls attention to the growth in the money supply. Governments have reacted by setting formal targets for monetary growth. Since central banks must now try to achieve monetary targets while at the same time financing much larger public-sector borrowing, their job is made all the more difficult.

The evidence summarized from the Economist and presented in Table 12.1 suggests that central banks only rarely succeed in hitting monetary targets. When they miss, it is nearly always in overshooting, creating "base drift." The base drift problem occurs if the supply of money ends up above its ceiling, raising the issue of what should be used as the starting point for the next target. By unsettling financial markets, base drift creates additional difficulties for the monetary authority in its efforts to achieve longer-term monetary goals.

The Economist correctly calls attention to the issue of means and ends raised in several countries regarding the methods of monetary control. How can a central bank control monetary growth? One approach is through interest rates. The other is by controlling the monetary base directly. Interest rates affect the demand for money as suggested by our results; but the interest rate effects may be overwhelmed by other effects. This suggests that the central bank is better advised to operate more directly on the supply of money through the monetary base—cash and bank reserves held in the central bank. These magnitudes can be controlled. As a result monetary growth can be affected in more predictable ways than through interest rates.

Methods and monetary targets differ in the several countries under review in our study. The German Bundesbank sets targets for "central bank money" fixed in such a way as to more or less reflect rather than influence overall monetary growth. Since 1979 the U.S. Federal Reserve System switched from controlling interest rates to setting intermediate targets for the monetary

TABLE 12.1

Target Practice: The United Kingdom, Canada, France, West Germany, Italy, and the United States

Country	Monetary Aggregate	Period	Monetary Targets and Overrun	
			Target	Outturn
United Kingdom	Sterling M3	Year to April 1977	9-13	7.2
		Year to April 1978	9-13	15.9
		Year to April 1979	8-12	10.9
		Year to Oct. 1979	8-12	13.2
		June 1979-Oct. 1980	7-11*	17.2
		Feb. 1980-April 1981	7-11*	23.4
Canada	M1	2nd qtr. 1975-Feb.-Apr. 1976	10-15	12.0
		Feb.-Apr. 1976-2nd qtr. 1977	8-12	9.2
		June 1977-June 1978	7-11	8.5
		June 1978-2nd qtr. 1979	6-10	8.1
		From 2nd qtr. 1979	5.9*	6.3
France	M2	Year to Dec. 1977	12.5	13.9
		Year to Dec. 1978	12.0	12.3
		Year to Dec. 1979	11.0	14.3
		Year to Dec. 1980	11.0	10.0

		Target	Actual
West Germany	Central bank money		
	Average 1975–Avg. 1976	8.0	9.2
	Average 1976–Avg. 1977	8.0	9.0
	Average 1977–Avg. 1978	8.0	11.4
	Year to 4th qtr. 1979	6–9	6.3
	Year to 4th qtr. 1980	5–8	4.8
Italy	Total domestic credit		
	Year to Dec. 1977	15.0	17.8
	Year to Dec. 1978	19.4	20.6
	Year to Dec. 1979	18.5	18.6
	Year to Dec. 1980	17.5	21.5
United States	M1		
	Year to 4th qtr. 1976	4.5–7.5	5.8
	Year to 4th qtr. 1977	4.5–6.5	7.7
	Year to 4th qtr. 1978	4.0–6.5	7.4
	Year to 4th qtr. 1979	1.5–4.5	5.5
	revised to	3.0–6.0	
	M1B Year to 4th qtr. 1980	4.0–6.5	7.5

*At annual rate: to latest month at annual rate.

Source: Adapted from Economist, November 29, 1980, p. 13.

base. The result has been greater fluctuations in interest rates;
for example, the prime lending rate went from 11.5 percent in
October 1979 to over 20 percent in January 1981. The United
Kingdom also appears to be drifting toward the idea of monetary-
base methods.

Again the target variable in use by the several countries
differs. Our evidence reported in this study suggests interest
rates exert important influence on the movement of the general
measures of the money supply, for example, movement between
interest-bearing time deposits and demand deposits that in the
United States should be less important in the future owing to
interest payment on demand deposit (NOW accounts). The United
States sets targets for several definitions of the money supply
from the narrow M1A to the broad M3. The United Kingdom,
on the other hand, sets one target M3 defined as notes and coin
plus sterling deposits of U.K. public and private sectors.
Germany focuses on the monetary base as the ultimate target,
which is the same as its intermediate target. In France the
broader definition of money M2 (cash plus demand and time
deposits) is used as the target.

It is important to distinguish what central bankers say they
do and what in fact happens. A case in point is that since 1976
annual messages from central bankers intone that monetary growth
is to be squeezed in the forthcoming year. In fact, what has
happened is that monetary growth targets are informally raised.

According to the Economist this happens "by letting monetary growth overshoot—and then not lowering next year's target
to offset it—central banks have been much less tight-fisted than
their statements suggest. Since the mid-1970s the cumulative
overrun has been as much as 19.6 percent in Britain and as
little as 1 percent in Japan. . . ."[8]

The evidence summarized in Table 12.2 suggests that this
is what happened. It is one reason for the skepticism about
monetary targets. Another is that the money supply definition
used may not give a full picture of the situation in financial
markets. There is, in fact, divergence between such narrow
definitions of money as M1 and central bank money and such
broader definitions as M2 and M3. In fact, M3 has been growing
much more rapidly than M1 thanks to rising interest rates en-
couraging depositors to shift deposits in response to such rates.
Not all divergence, however, can be so readily explained.

How seriously, then, should governments react to such
signals? If the monetary target is a single measure, there is
little choice with which to judge policy. In low-inflation countries
this would not seem to be a problem, for example, Japan, Switzer-

TABLE 12.2

Monetary Targets and Outturns

Country	Monetary Aggregate	Period	Target	Growth to Latest Month[a]	Excess over Targeted Growth, 1975–76 to Latest (percentage points)
United States	M1b	Year to 4th qtr. 1980	4.0–6.5[b]	7.5	9.3
Japan	M2 and CDs	Year to 4th qtr. 1980	10.0	9.5	1.0
		Year to 4th qtr. 1981	9.5		
West Germany	Central bank money	Year to 4th qtr. 1980	5–8	4.7	3.0
		Year to 4th qtr. 1981	4–7		
France	M2	Year to Dec. 1980	11.0	9.9	5.6
		Year to Dec. 1981	10.0		
United Kingdom	M3	Feb. 1980 to Apr. 1981	7–11	23.4	19.6
Switzerland	Monetary base	Year to Nov. 1980	4.0	0	—[c]
		Year to Nov. 1981	4.0		

[a] At annual rate.
[b] Switzerland had no target in 1979.
[c] Where ranges were set their midpoint is assumed to be the target.
Source: Economist, December 6, 1980, pp. 70–71.

land, West Germany. Their narrow and broad definitions of money have been moving closely in line with each other. When they decide to change target rates the choice is clear. The United States uses several target definitions so as to assure itself that a broad thrust of policy is correct. If all targets are missed then clearly something is wrong and presumably something else is required. [9]

There is a general consensus in Yugoslavia that changes in the money supply are used as targets of monetary policy. This consensus is based on the prevailing quantity theory of money approach and on empirical evidence suggesting that there is a close association between changes in the money supply and real developments (investment and such other developments as expenditures for goods and services, rate of increase in production changes in the price level, imports and exports). [10]

Alternative indicators might be the monetary base (high-powered money), bank credit, and interest rate. Not all of these indicators can be used under specific Yugoslav conditions. Interest rates cannot be used since they do not reflect correct market conditions. High-powered money can be used as a subsidiary monetary indicator substituting for the money supply. This is possible because of the close association between changes in the monetary base and changes in money supply, at least in the long run.

Similar arguments hold for the choice between the money supply and bank credit. Bank credit has at least two advantages over high-powered money. First, it is related more closely to the money supply, as well as to expenditures for goods and services, than high-powered money. Second, bank credit is conceptually and statistically simpler (at least under Yugoslav conditions). Thus, bank credit may be a better substitution for the money supply as a monetary indicator than high-powered money. There is, however, a significant field of monetary action where bank credit serves as an independent indicator. This is the field of selective credit policy goals. In this instance bank credit, classified according to selective credit policy goals, presents the targets of credit policy that have to be implemented in supporting specific economic policy goals.

Declarations of the Federal Assembly on economic policy goals, which define monetary policy goals and targets, include the rate of increase in the money supply and in bank short-term credit. Changes in the money supply are considered a primary monetary target, whereas changes in bank credit are treated as a secondary target.

As to the "efficiency" of monetary policy in Yugoslavia the evidence suggests that changes in money supply may deviate significantly from planned targets. Thanks to errors in the projection of monetary targets (a definite rate of change in money supply) as well as the uncertainties in the adjustment processes of demand to supply of money, monetary policy is less efficient in implementing the planned set of policy goals.

A strong "monetarist" tradition exists in Yugoslavia that is in keeping with the ideological neutrality of monetary theory. The prewar quantity theory tradition is unbroken by Keynesian views. Keynesian monetary theory did not reach Yugoslav economists before World War II, and after the war the central planning framework was unsuited to Keynesian views.[11] By the end of the 1950s when Yugoslavia was more receptive, the rigid Keynesian views already had been substantially revised, and at the same time a revised and sophisticated quantity theory was rapidly gaining acceptance.

Moreover, the prewar quantity theory was not inconsistent with the dominant Marxian theory after the war. Both the theoretical and practical approaches to monetary problems are very close to the quantity theory views under conditions of noncommodity, fiduciary money. Indeed, even in the central planning system the quantity of money (currency in circulation) was strongly regulated by cash planning.

Finally, one of the most decisive arguments for the prevailing monetarist approach has been the experience of strong inflationary impacts produced by sharp monetary expansion.

As a result, there always has been a general consensus that "money matters" and that there is a need for an efficient monetary policy. This does not mean, however, that there has been complete agreement about the goals and targets of monetary policy or about its efficiency. On this score it is possible to distinguish two groups of views. On the one hand there are the "neutral money policy" views and on the other there are the "easy money policy" views. The first group of views is related to the post 1965-reform developments, when stabilization goals became as significant as production and development goals. The "easy money" views dominated monetary policy before the 1965 reform. They continue to exist and exert some influence. The rationale for these views is that production and economic growth are the basic economic policy goals and that an easy money policy is presumably more helpful toward these goals. The risk of inflation apparently ranks lower than the risk of deceleration of production and economic growth. Although significantly different, Yugoslav experience is useful for the insights it provides into the economies of Eastern Europe.

MONEY, POLITICS, AND IDEOLOGY

The scope for money and monetary theory is limited in East European economies and the Soviet Union.[12] If coordination of economic activity is accomplished by the command principle, then planning is necessarily biased in the direction of physical magnitudes. Nonetheless, Gregory Grossman writes:

> Over the decades East European planners have devel-
> oped a technique of monetary planning, especially in
> regard to currency (as against bank money), which
> is the money of the household sector. The chief
> purpose of this planning has been anti-inflationary
> (and presumably, though operationally less signifi-
> cant, also anti-deflationary). The main planning
> technique has been the drawing up of so-called
> balances of money receipts and expenditure of the
> population. . . .[13]

In addition to Grossman's introductory statement, contributions by other authors dealing with monetary experiences in the economies of the East European countries are useful if somewhat dated. George Garvy provides a useful summary in his essay, "East European Credit and Finance in Transition." In Poland, writes Andrzej Brzeski, "most economists favor instead [of the Quantity Theory of Money] an Aftalion-like income theory of money. But this is because they wrongly associate the Quantity Theory with a constant velocity of circulation. . . ."[14] Indeed, Brzeski continues:

> Monetary explanations alone are insufficient for an
> understanding of the vicissitudes of production and
> distribution of the wealth of nations. But neither
> must they be neglected. This is true of Soviet-style
> socialism as it is of capitalism. There, as here,
> money is more than a mere veil. . . . Poland, like
> other East European countries is believed to have
> dispensed with "monetary policy." This is not so,
> unless very narrow definitions are accepted. . . .
> Poland's monetary policy appears clear: nearly
> perfect flexibility—unlimited supply of money in
> the service of industrialization. . . .[15]

The demand for money in Poland is for <u>real</u> balances. Even in a Soviet-type economy the public cannot be forced to hold much more <u>real</u> money than it desires, if there is a significant free market sector (food) and the possibility of withdrawing the supply of labor (for example, housewives quitting their jobs).[16]

"It may surprise most readers to learn," writes Milton Friedman,

> that in today's terminology Karl Marx could be labeled a "monetarist"—a term that is currently, if incorrectly, regarded as synonymous with "conservative" or "pro free market." Similarly, the same ideas guide monetary policy in Russia and Yugoslavia as those in Chile, Brazil and Argentina, or in Germany, Great Britain and Japan.[17]

The results presented in our study are consistent with these observations. Monetary theory cuts across a wide spectrum of economic systems and a variety of ideologies. There may well be a "fallacy of association," one perhaps more accidental than systematic that can be attributed to equating monetarism, conservatism, and a "free market."[18] Even so, Yugoslav experience suggests that as the decentralization process gathered force in that country, so too did movement toward a free market coupled with an increasing role for money and monetary policy.

It is perhaps the "fallacy of association" along with differences in interpretation of theoretical and empirical evidence generated for the most part from the U.S. experience that has led to a curious exchange between Friedman and his detractors. Attempts to sort out hidden ideological bias in the controversy between Monetarists and Keynesians suggest little if any evidence on this score.[19] Such differences as exist can be traced to the political ideologies and value judgments of politicians and commentators on the debate rather than to the participants themselves. In a sense, it is a nondebate as far as political ideologies and value judgments are concerned.

A case in point is the storm raised over Professor Friedman's series of lectures in Chile in 1975. He is taken to task by leading U.S. newspapers and commentators for having given advice to an authoritarian government. In fact, he writes that that visit

> launched a campaign of abuse that has continued sporadically ever since. The campaign peaked after the news broke that I was to receive the Nobel Prize in Economics in 1976. Four Nobel laureates in the

natural sciences wrote indignant letters to The New York Times asserting that my visit to Chile disqualified me from joining their select company. In Stockholm the authorities were sufficiently concerned about organized protests that they assigned my wife and me a 24-hour police guard. In this country I have been subjected to hostile demonstrations at lectures ranging from New York to San Diego. . . .[20]

What is curious about this tragic affair is that Friedman is not taken to task for similar lectures given elsewhere. In Yugoslavia, for instance, his lectures were well received. Indeed, many are published and in wide circulation among academics and professionals. His book of essays, Theory of Money and Monetary Policy, has not lost its appeal to the Yugoslav audience.[21] In the People's Republic of China in 1980 he lectured under the auspices of the Institute of World Economics of the Chinese Academy of Social Sciences, a government body, as part of a cultural-exchange program between the United States and China. The ideological differences between Yugoslavia, China, and Chile are clear. In all these countries, nonetheless, Friedman's lectures generated (and indeed continue to generate) interest and enthusiasm.

This does not mean that any given economic theory is without its ideological bias. If we are to take the pronouncements of the modern philosophy of science seriously, no theory is without ideology. Indeed, very different political ideologies do exist, in fact, among monetarists.[22] What they share is the view that money and monetary theory are important. That they share a common abstract idea of political economy is not to be inferred.

NOTES

1. Milton Friedman, "The Role of Monetary Policy," in The Optimum Quantity of Money and Other Essays, ed. Milton Friedman (Chicago: Aldine, 1969), p. 99.

2. See George Macesich, The International Monetary Economy and the Third World (New York: Praeger, 1981). The reemergence of the long dominant view, that money and monetary policy are indeed important, is underscored by work on the monetary approach to the balance of payments undertaken by James Mead, Harry G. Johnson, Robert Mundell, Jacob Frenkel, and others. See, for example, papers in Jacob A. Frenkel and

Harry G. Johnson, eds., The Monetary Approach to the Balance of Payments (London: George Allen and Unwin, 1978); International Monetary Fund, The Monetary Approach to the Balance of Payments (Washington, D.C., 1977).

3. S. Herbert Frankel, Two Philosophies of Money: The Conflict of Trust and Authority (New York: St. Martin's Press, 1977), p. 89.

4. Ibid., p. 92.

5. See, for example, David Laidler and Nicholas Rowe, "Georg Simmel's Philosophy of Money: A Review Article for Economists," Journal of Economic Literature, March 1980, pp. 97-105; Herbert Frankel, and a review of Frankel's study by David Laidler in Journal of Economic Literature, June 1979, pp. 570-72; and Macesich.

6. See Macesich.

7. See, for example, Economist, January 28, 1978, pp. 91-93.

8. Economist, December 6, 1980, p. 70.

9. See, for instance, Milton Friedman, "A Memorandum to the Fed," Wall Street Journal, January 30, 1981, p. 20. According to Friedman "the key defect in trying to control the [U.S.] money supply by pegging the federal funds rate is that mistakes are cumulative and self-reinforcing, and lead to the kind of wide swings in monetary aggregates that we have experienced in recent years."

10. D. Dimitrijević and George Macesich, Money and Finance in Contemporary Yugoslavia (New York: Praeger, 1973), Chapter 10.

11. See ibid.

12. On the history of views on the role of money in centrally planned economies, see P. J. D. Wiles, Economic Institutions Compared (New York: John Wiley, 1977), Chapters 12-14. See also L. Szeplaki and R. A. Taylor, "Banking Credit and Monetary Indicators in Reformed Socialist Planning," Journal of Money, Credit, and Banking, August 1972, pp. 572-81.

13. Gregory Grossman, ed., Money and Plan (Berkeley: University of California Press, 1968), pp. 10-11.

14. A. Brzeski, "Forced-Draft Industrialization with Unlimited Supply of Money," in ibid., p. 28.

15. Ibid., pp. 34-35.

16. Ibid., pp. 36.

17. Milton Friedman, "Marx and Money," Newsweek, October 27, 1980, p. 95.

18. Walter W. Heller, in "What's Right with Economics," American Economic Review, March 1975, p. 5, writes:

These associational claims are not linked together in any inexorable logic—in part they seem to be accident of birth as in the case of the Chicago twins of monetarism and laissez-faire rules. A belief in the supremacy of monetary over fiscal tools could quite logically go hand-in-hand with avid interventionism. But this escapes the jaundiced eye of the outside observer who takes the ideological lineup as further evidence that economics is riven to its core.

19. See, for example, Dieter Robert, Makroökonomische Konzeptionen in Meinungsstreit: zur Auseinandersetzung zwischen Monetaristen und Fiskalisten (Baden-Baden: Nomos Verlagsgesellschaft, 1978).
20. Milton Friedman, "A Biased Double Standard," Newsweek, January 12, 1981, p. 68.
21. Milton Friedman, Teorija Novca I Monetarna Politika (Belgrade: RAD, 1973).
22. Much has been written on monetarism, and Monetarists. See, for example, the various studies by Thomas Mayer, Karl Brunner, David Fand, and the contributions in Jerome L. Stein, ed., Monetarism (Amsterdam: North-Holland, 1976).

BIBLIOGRAPHY

Chapter 1

Broaddus, A. "Aggregating the Monetary Aggregates: Concepts and Issues." Economic Review, Federal Bank of Richmond, Virginia, November/December 1975, p. 7.

Friedman, Milton. "Marx and Money." Newsweek, October 27, 1980, p. 95.

____. Studies in the Quantity Theory of Money. Chicago: University of Chicago Press, 1956, p. 4.

Keynes, John Maynard. The General Theory of Employment, Interest and Money. New York: Harcourt, Brace, 1936.

Macesich, George. The International Monetary Economy and the Third World. New York: Praeger, 1981.

____. "The Rate of Change in the Monetary Stock as a Leading Canadian Indicator." Canadian Journal of Economics and Political Science, August 1962, pp. 424-31.

____. "Sources of Monetary Disturbances in the United States, 1834-45." Journal of Economic History, September 1960, pp. 407-34.

____ and Close, F. A. "Comparative Stability of Monetary Velocity and the Investment Multiplier of Austria and Yugoslavia." Florida State University Slavic Papers 3 (1969).

____. "Monetary Velocity and Investment Multiplier Stability Relativity for Norway and Sweden." Statsoknonmisk and Tidsskrift, 1969.

Woytinsky, W. "What Was Wrong in Forecasts of Postwar Depression." Journal of Political Economy 55 (April 1947):142-51.

Chapter 2

Dimitrijević, D. and Macesich, George. Money and Finance in Contemporary Yugoslavia. New York: Praeger, 1973.

Gerhrels, Franz. "Monetary Systems for the Common Market." Journal of Finance, May 1959, pp. 312-21.

Halm, George. "The Case for Greater Exchange-Rate Flexibility in an Interdependent World." In Issues in Banking and Monetary Analysis, edited by G. Pontecorvo, R. P. Shay, and A. G. Hart. New York: Holt, Rinehart, and Winston, 1967.

Hart, Albert G. "Commentary." In Issues in Banking and Monetary Analysis, edited by G. Pontecorvo, R. P. Shay, and A. G. Hart. New York: Holt, Rinehart, and Winston, 1967.

Hayek, F. A. The Constitution of Liberty. Chicago: University of Chicago Press, 1960.

Ingram, J. C. Factors Affecting the United States Balance of Payments. Washington, D.C.: U.S. Government Printing Office, 1962.

Kenen, Peter P. "Toward a Supranational Monetary System." In Issues in Banking and Monetary Analysis, edited by G. Pontecorvo, R. P. Shay, and A. G. Hart. New York: Holt, Rinehart, and Winston, 1967.

Krause, L. B. and Salant, W. S., eds. European Monetary Unification and Its Meaning for the United States. Washington, D.C.: Brookings Institution, 1973.

Macesich, George. Commercial Banking and Regional Development in the United States, 1950-1960. Tallahassee: Florida State University Press, 1965.

_____. "Economic Theory and the Austro-Hungarian Ausgleich." Paper prepared for the International Congress on the Austro-Hungarian Ausgleich of 1967. Proceedings of the Congress.

_____. "Inflation and the Common Market." Review of International Affairs, June 5, 1964.

____. The International Monetary Economy and the Third World. New York: Praeger, 1981.

____. Money and the Canadian Economy. Belgrade: National Bank of Yugoslavia, 1967.

____. Money in a European Common Market Setting. Baden-Baden: Nomos Verlagsgesellschaft, 1972.

____. "Supply and Demand for Money in Canada." In Varieties of Monetary Experience, edited by David Meiselman. Chicago: University of Chicago Press, 1970.

____. "The Theory of Economic Integration and the Experience of the Balkan and Danubian Countries Before 1914." A paper delivered before the First International Congress on Southeast European Studies, Sofia, Bulgaria, August-September 1966. Florida State University Slavic Papers 1 (1967).

____. Yugoslavia: Theory and Practice of Development Planning. Charlottesville: University Press of Virginia, 1964.

McKinnon, Ronald I. "Optimum Currency Areas." American Economic Review, September 1963, pp. 717-25.

Mundell, Robert A. "A Theory of Optimum Currency Areas." American Economic Review, September 1961, pp. 657-64.

Schmidt, Wilson E. "Commentary." In Issues in Banking and Monetary Analysis, edited by G. Pontecorvo, R. P. Shay, and A. G. Hart. New York: Holt, Rinehart, and Winston, 1967.

Wood, J. H. Business Review, Federal Reserve Bank of Philadelphia, September 1972.

Yeager, L. B. "Exchange Rates within a Common Market." Social Research, January 1959, pp. 415-38.

Chapter 3

Bhattacharya, B. B. "Demand and Supply of Money in a Developing Economy: A Structural Analysis for India." Review of Economics and Statistics 56 (1974):502-10.

Brunner, Karl. "A Schema for the Supply Theory of Money." International Economic Review, January 1961, pp. 79-109.

_____ and Meltzer, Allan. "Predicting Velocity: Implications for Theory and Policy." Journal of Finance, May 1963, pp. 319-54.

Burger, Albert E. The Money Supply Process. Belmont, Calif.: Wadsworth, 1971, pp. 24-72.

Evans, Michael K. Macroeconomic Activity. New York: Harper & Row, 1969, pp. 314-15.

Fand, David I. "Some Issues in Monetary Economics." Review Federal Reserve Bank of St. Louis, January 1970.

Friedman, Milton. "The Demand for Money—Some Theoretical and Empirical Results." Journal of Political Economy 67 (June 1959):327-51.

_____. "A Monetary Theory of National Income." Journal of Political Economy 79 (April/May 1971):323-37.

_____. "A Theoretical Framework for Monetary Analysis." Journal of Political Economy 78 (April/May 1970):193-238

Goldfeld, Stephen M. Commercial Banking Behavior and Economic Activity: A Structural Study of Monetary Policy in the Post-war United States. Amsterdam: North-Holland Publishing Co., 1966.

Hein, Scott E. "Dynamic Forecasting and the Demand for Money." Review, Federal Reserve Bank of St. Louis, June-July 1980, pp. 13-23.

Hendershoot, P. H. and De Leeuw, F. "Free Reserves, Interest Rates and Deposits: A Synthesis." Journal of Finance, May 1957, pp. 238-55.

Horwich, George. "Elements of Timing and Response in the Balance Sheet of Banking, 1953-55." Journal of Finance, May 1957, pp. 238-55.

Johnson, Harry G. Macroeconomics and Monetary Theory. London: Gray-Mills, 1971, p. 135.

Journal of Political Economy 78 (April/May 1970):193-238; "A
Monetary Theory of National Income." Journal of Political
Economy 79 (April/May 1971):323-37.

Keynes, John Maynard. The General Theory of Employment,
Interest and Money. New York: Harcourt, Brace, 1936,
p. 194.

____. "Theory of the Rate of Interest." (1937). Reprinted in
Readings in the Theory of Income Distribution, edited by
W. Feller and B. F. Healey. Philadelphia, 1946.

Laidler, D. The Demand for Money: Theories and Evidence.
Scranton, Pa.: International Textbook Co., 1969, pp. 106-
97.

McDonald, Stephen L. "The Internal Drain and Bank Credit
Expansion." Journal of Finance, December 1953, pp. 407-21.

Meigs, A. J. Free Reserves and the Money Supply. Chicago:
University of Chicago Press, 1962.

Meltzer, Allen H. "The Behavior of the French Money Supply:
1938-54." Journal of Political Economy, June 1959, pp. 275-96.

Minsky, H. P. "Central Banking and Money Market Changes."
Quarterly Journal of Economics (May 1957).

"A Monetary Theory of National Income." Journal of Political
Economy 79 (April/May 1971):323-37.

Modigliani, F., Rasche, R. H., and Cooper, J. P. "Central
Bank Policy, The Money Supply and the Short Term Rate of
Interest." Journal of Money, Credit and Banking, May 1970,
pp. 168-218.

Patinkin, Don. Money, Interest, and Prices, 2d ed. New York:
Harper & Row, 1965, pp. 144-45.

Selden, R. "Monetary Velocity in the United States." In Studies
in the Quantity Theory of Money, edited by Milton Friedman.
Chicago: University of Chicago Press, 1956.

Smith, Lawrence B. and Winder, W. L. "Price and Interest Rate
Expectations and the Demand for Money in Canada." Journal
of Finance, June 1971, pp. 671-82.

Smith, P. E. "Money Supply and Demand: A Cobweb?" International Economic Review, February 1967, pp. 1-11.

Teigen, Ronald L. "Demand and Supply Functions for Money
in the United States: Some Structural Estimates." Econometrica, October 1964, pp. 476-509.

Chapter 4

Ball, R. J. "Some Econometric Analysis of the Long-Term Rate
of Interest in the United Kingdom, 1921-1961." Manchester
School of Economic and Social Studies, January 1965.

Baumol, W. J. "The Transactions Demand for Cash: An Inventory
Theoretical Approach." Quarterly Journal of Economics,
November 1952.

Bronfenbrenner, M. and Mayer, T. "Liquidity Functions in
the American Economy." Econometrica, October 1960.

Brunner, K. and Meltzer, A. H. "Predicting Velocity: Implications for Theory and Policy." Journal of Finance, May 1963,
pp. 319-54.

Cagan, Phillip. "The Monetary Dynamics of Hyperinflation."
In Studies in the Quantity Theory of Money, edited by Milton
Friedman. Chicago: University of Chicago Press, 1956.

Chow, G. C. "On the Long-Run and Short-Run Demand for
Money." Journal of Political Economy 74 (April 1966):111-31.

____. Demand for Automobiles in the United States: A Study
in Consumer Behavior. Amsterdam: North-Holland, 1964.

Christ, C. F. "Interest Rates and 'Portfolio Selection' among
Liquid Assets in the United States." In C. F. Christ and
others, Measurement in Economics: Studies in Mathematical
Economics and Econometrics—In Memory of Yehuda Grunfeld.
Stanford, Calif.: Stanford University Press, 1963.

Courchene, T. and Shapiro, H. "The Demand for Money: A
Note from the Time Series." Journal of Political Economy 72
(October 1964):498-503.

Eisner, Robert. "Another Look at Liquidity Preference."
Econometrica 31 (July 1963):532-33.

Friedman, Milton. "The Demand for Money—Some Theoretical
and Empirical Results." Journal of Political Economy 67
(June 1959):327-51.

____. "The Quantity Theory of Money—A Restatement." In
Studies in the Quantity Theory of Money, edited by Milton
Friedman. Chicago: University of Chicago Press, 1956.

Goldsmith, R. W. A Study of Savings in the United States.
Princeton, N.J.: Princeton University Press, 1956.

Gurley, J. and Shaw, E. S. Liquidity and Financial Institutions
in the Post-War Economy. Study Paper 14, Joint Economic
Committee, 86th Cong., 2d sess. Washington, D.C., 1960.

Hamburger, M. J. "The Demand for Money by Households,
Money Substitutes, and Monetary Policy." Journal of Political
Economy 74 (December 1966):600-23.

Harberger, Arnold G. "The Dynamics of Inflation in Chile."
In C. F. Christ et al., Measurement in Economics: Studies
in Mathematical Economics and Econometrics—In Memory of
Yehuda Grunfeld. Stanford, Calif.: Stanford University
Press, 1963.

Heller, H. R. "The Demand for Money: The Evidence from the
Short Run Data." Quarterly Journal of Economics 79 (May
1965):291-303.

Johnson, H. G. "Monetary Theory and Policy." American
Economic Review, June 1962, p. 345.

Khusro, A. M. "Investigation of Liquidity Preference."
Yorkshire Bulletin of Economic and Social Research, January
1952.

Kisselgoff, A. "Liquidity Preference of Large Manufacturing
Corporations." Econometrica, October 1945.

Laidler, David E. The Demand for Money: Theories and Evidence.
Scranton, Pa.: International Textbook Co., 1969, p. 93.

____. "The Rate of Interest and the Demand for Money—Some Empirical Evidence." Journal of Political Economy 74 (December 1966):545-55.

____. "Some Evidence on the Demand for Money." Journal of Political Economy 74 (February 1966):55-68.

Latane, H. A. "Cash Balances and the Interest Rate—A Pragmatic Approach." Review of Economics and Statistics, November 1954.

____. "Income Velocity and Interest Rates: A Pragmatic Approach." Review of Economics and Statistics, November 1960.

Lee, T. H. "Alternative Interest Rates and the Demand for Money: The Empirical Evidence." American Economic Review 57 (December 1967):1168-81.

Lerner, Eugene. "Inflation in the Confederacy 1861-65." In Studies in the Quantity Theory of Money, edited by Milton Friedman. Chicago: University of Chicago Press, 1956.

Meltzer, Allan. "The Demand for Money: The Evidence from the Time Series." Journal of Political Economy 71 (June 1963): 224.

____. "Yet Another Look At The Low Level Liquidity Trap." Econometrica 31 (July 1963):545.

Selden, Richard. "Monetary Velocity in the United States." In Studies in the Quantity Theory of Money, edited by Milton Friedman. Chicago: University of Chicago Press, 1956.

Teigen, R. L. "The Demand for and Supply of Money." In W. L. Smith and R. L. Teigen, Readings in Money, National Income, and Stabilization Policy. Homewood, Ill.: Irwin, 1965, p. 54.

Tobin, James. "Liquidity Preference and Monetary Policy." Review of Economics and Statistics, February 1947.

____. "Liquidity-Preference as Behavior Toward Risk." Review of Economic Studies, February 1958.

Turvey, R. Interest Rates and Assets Prices. London, 1960.

Chapter 5

Bhattacharya, B. B. "Demand and Supply of Money in a Developing Economy: A Structural Analysis for India." Review of Economics and Statistics 56 (1974), pp. 502-10.

Broaddus, Alfred. "Aggregating the Monetary Aggregates: Concepts and Issues." Economic Review, Federal Reserve Bank of Richmond, Virginia, November/December 1975, p. 7.

Brunner, Karl. "A Case Study of U.S. Monetary Policy: The Inflationary Gold Flows of the Middle Thirties." Schweizerische Zietschrift fuer Volkswirtschaft and Statistik 44 (June 1958).

_____. "A Schema for the Supply Theory of Money." International Economic Review 2 (January 1961).

_____. "The Structure of the Monetary System and the Supply Function of Money." Unpublished paper, 1961.

_____ and Meltzer, Allan. "Predicting Velocity: Implications for Theory and Policy." Journal of Finance 18 (May 1963).

_____. "Some Further Investigations of Demand and Supply Functions of Money." Journal of Finance 19 (May 1964).

Cagan, Phillip. Determinants and Effects of Changes in the Stock of Money, 1875-1960. New York: Columbia University Press, 1965.

_____. "The Monetary Dynamics of Hyperinflation." In Studies in the Quarterly Theory of Money, edited by Milton Friedman. Chicago: University of Chicago Press, 27-35.

Fand, David. "Some Implications of Money Supply Analysis." Papers and Proceedings of the American Economic Association 57 (May 1967):380.

Federal Reserve Bank of St. Louis. Working Paper No. 1, "The Three Approaches to Money Stock Analysis," 1967.

_____. Working Paper No. 7, "A Summary of the Brunner-Meltzer Non-Linear Money Supply Hypothesis," 1968.

Friedman, Milton and Schwartz, Anna J. A Monetary History of the United States 1867-1960. Princeton, N.J.: Princeton University Press, 1963.

Haulman, Clyde Austin. "Determinants of the Money Supply in Canada, 1875-1964." Ph.D. Dissertation, Florida State University, 1969.

Liu, Fu-Chi. Essays on Monetary Development in Taiwan. Tapei: China Committee for Publication Aid and Prize Awards, 1970.

Meigs, James A. Free Reserves and the Money Supply. Chicago: University of Chicago Press, 1962.

Meltzer, Allan. "The French Money Supply 1938-1954." Journal of Political Economy 67 (June 1959).

Modigliani, F., Rasche, R. H., and Cooper, J. P. "Central Bank Policy, the Money Supply and the Short Term of Interest." Journal of Money, Credit and Banking 2 (May 1970).

Morrison, George. "Transitional Elements in the Demand for Money." Econometrica 35 (Supplementary Issue, 1967):136.

Phillips, C. A. Bank Credit. New York: Macmillan, 1921.

Polak, J. J. and White, W. H. "The Effects of Income Expansion on the Quantity of Money." IMF Staff Papers 4 (August 1955).

Smith, P. E. "Money Supply and Demand: A Cobweb?" International Economic Review 8 (February 1967):1-11.

Teigen, Ronald L. "Demand and Supply Functions for Money in the United States: Some Structural Estimates." Econometrica 32 (October 1964):476-509.

Chapter 6

Cohen, B. J. "The Euro-Dollar, the Common Market, and Currency Unification." Journal of Finance, December 1963, pp. 605-21.

Commission on Money and Credit. "The Organization of the
Federal Reserve System." In Monetary Economics, edited
by Jonas Prager. New York: Random House, 1971.

"Comparative Features of Central Banks in Selected Foreign
Countries." Joint Economic Committee, 88th Cong. 1st sess.
Washington, D.C.: U.S. Government Printing Office, 1963.

Dimitrijević, D. and Macesich, George. Money and Finance in
Contemporary Yugoslavia. New York: Praeger, 1973.

"Eminger Sees Need for a European 'Fed.'" European Community,
June 1958, p. 18.

European Economic Community. Commission Memorandum of the
Commission on the Action Programme for the Second Stage.
Brussels, October 24, 1962.

Friedman, Milton and Schwartz, Anna J. Monetary History of
the United States. Princeton, N.J.: Princeton University
Press, 1963.

Holbik, Karel, ed. Monetary Policy in Twelve Industrial Countries. Boston: Federal Reserve Bank of Boston, 1973.

Macesich, George. Economic Stability: A Comparative Analysis.
Belgrade: BGZ, 1973.

____. "Major Trends in the Post-War Economy of Yugoslavia."
In Contemporary Yugoslavia: Twenty Years of Socialism,
edited by Wayne S. Vucinich. Berkeley: University of
California Press, 1969.

____. Money in a European Common Market Setting. Baden-
Baden: Nomos Verlagsgesellschaft, 1972.

____, ed. Proceedings and Reports. Tallahassee: Florida State
University Center for Yugoslav-American Studies, Research,
and Exchanges, Florida State University Slavic Papers 1963-
74.

____. "Supply and Demand for Money in Canada." In Varieties
of Monetary Experience, edited by David Meiselman. Chicago:
University of Chicago Press, 1970.

_____. Yugoslavia: Theory and Practice of Development Planning. Charlottesville: The University Press of Virginia, 1964, Chapter 9.

McIvor, R. Craig. Canadian Monetary, Banking, and Fiscal Development. Toronto: The Macmillan Company of Canada, 1958, pp. 236-37.

Monthly Report of the Deutsche Bundesbank. May 1954.

Plescoft, George. "International Liquidity: The Cases of the Common Market." American Economic Review, May 1968, pp. 608-19.

Treaty Establishing the European Economic Community and Connected Documents. Brussels: Publishing Services of the European Communities, 1958.

Trezise, P. H., ed. The European Monetary System: Its Promise and Prospects. Washington, D.C.: Brookings Institution, 1979.

Chapter 7

Chow, Gregory C. "Tests of Equality between Sets of Coefficients in Two Linear Regressions." Econometrica 28 (1960): 591-604.

Fisher, F. M. "The Relative Sensitivity to Specification Error of Different k-Class Estimators." Journal of the American Statistical Association 61 (1966):345-56.

Friedman, Milton. The Optimum Quantity of Money and Other Essays. Chicago: Aldine, 1969.

_____. "The Quantity Theory of Money—A restatement." In Studies in the Quantity Theory of Money, edited by Milton Friedman. Chicago: University of Chicago Press, 1956.

Hafer, R. W. and Hein, Scott E. "The Dynamics of Estimation of Short-Run Money Demand." Review, Federal Reserve Bank of St. Louis, March 1980, pp. 26-35.

Hein, Scott E. "Dynamic Forecasting and the Demand for Money." Review, June/July 1980, p. 30.

International Monetary Fund. International Financial Statistics. Various issues for the year 1951-80. Washington, D.C.: IMF.

Kessel, Reuben A. and Alchian, Armen A. "Effects of Inflation." Journal of Political Economy 70 (1962):521-37.

Kimball, Ralph C. "Wire Transfer and the Demand for Money." New England Economic Review, Federal Reserve Bank of Boston, March/April 1980, p. 14.

Klein, L. R. and Goldberger, A. A. An Econometric Model of the United States, 1929-1952. Amsterdam: North-Holland, 1955.

Kloek, T. and Mennes, L. B. M. "Simultaneous Equation Estimations Based on Principal Components of Predetermined Variables." Econometrica 28 (1960):45-61.

Robertson, D. H. Money, 6th ed. New York: Pitman, 1948, p. 1719.

Theil, Henri. Principles of Econometrics. New York: John Wiley, 1971.

Chapter 8

Cagan, Phillip. "A Commentary on Some Current Issues in the Theory of Monetary Policy." In Patterns of Market Behavior, edited by Michael J. Brennan. Providence: Brown University Press, 1965.

Dewald, W. G. and Johnson, Harry G. "An Objective Analysis of the Objectives of American Monetary Policy." In Banking and Monetary Studies, edited by Deane Carson. Homewood, Ill.: Richard D. Irwin, 1963, pp. 171-89.

Friedman, Milton. "The Role of Monetary Policy." American Economic Review, March 1968, pp. 1-17.

Reuben, G. L. "The Objectives of Canadian Monetary Policy, 1949-1961. Journal of Political Economy, April 1964, pp. 109-32.

Chapter 9

Bailey, Martin J. National Income and the Price Level. New York: McGraw-Hill, 1962, pp. 174-75.

Bank of Canada. Annual Report of the Governor to the Minister of Finance, 1959-65.

Cagan, Phillip. Determinants and Effects of Changes in the Stock of Money, 1875-1960. New York: National Bureau of Economic Research, 1965.

____. "The First Fifty Years of the National Banking System: An Historical Appraisal." Banking and Monetary Studies, edited by Deane Carson. Homewood, Ill.: Richard D. Irwin, 1963.

Canadian Statistical Review, January 1963 and January 1965.

Chambers, Edward J. "Canadian Business Cycles Since 1919: A Progress Report." Canadian Journal of Economics and Political Science, May 1958, p. 172.

____. Late Nineteenth Century Business Cycles in Canada." Canadian Journal of Economics and Political Science, August 1964, pp. 391-412.

Commission on Money and Credit. Stabilization Policies. Englewood Cliffs, N.J.: Prentice-Hall, 1963.

Culbertson, John M. "Reply." Journal of Political Economy 69 (1961).

Dimitrijević, D. and Macesich, George. Money and Finance in Contemporary Yugoslavia. New York: Praeger, 1973, pp. 188ff.

Friedman, Milton. "Note on Lag in Effect of Monetary Policy." American Economic Review, September 1964, p. 760.

____. The Optimum Quantity of Money and Other Essays. Chicago: Aldine, 1969.

____. "The Supply of Money and Changes in Prices and Output." In U.S. Congress, Joint Economic Committee, The Relation

of Prices to Economic Stability and Growth: Compendium
(Doc. No. 23734). Washington, D.C.: U.S. Government
Printing Office, March 31, 1958, pp. 241-56.

____ and Schwartz, Anna J. "The Lag Effect of Monetary Policy."
Journal of Political Economy 69 (1961):452.

____. A Monetary History of the United States 1867-1960.
Princeton: Princeton University Press, 1963.

____. "Money and Business Cycles." Review of Economics and
Statistics 45, no. 1, pt. 2 (February 1963):32-75.

Hay, K. A. J. "Money and Cycles in Post Confederation
Canada." Journal of Political Economy, June 1967, pp. 263-
73.

Keran, Michael W. "Monetary Policy, Balance of Payments and
Business Cycles." Review, Federal Reserve Bank of St.
Louis, November 1967, pp. 7-20.

Macesich, George. Commercial Banking and Regional Development in the United States, 1950-60. Tallahassee: Florida
State University, 1965.

____. "A Monetary Hypothesis and Southern Development."
Revista Internazionale di Scienze Economiche e Commerciali,
February 1966, pp. 128-47.

____. "Sources of Monetary Disturbance in the United States,
1834-45." Journal of Economic History, September 1960,
pp. 407-34.

____. "Supply and Demand for Money in Canada." In Varieties
of Monetary Experience, edited by David Meiselman. Chicago:
University of Chicago Press, 1970.

Mayer, Thomas. "The Inflexibility of Monetary Policy." Review
of Economics and Statistics 40 (1958).

McIvor, R. Craig. Canadian Monetary Banking and Fiscal
Development (Toronto: The Macmillan Company of Canada,
1958.

North, Douglass. Economic Growth of the United States, 1790-
1860. Englewood Cliffs, N.J.: Prentice-Hall, 1961.

Uselton, Gene C. Lags in the Effects of Monetary Policy: A New Parametric Analysis. New York: Marcel Dekker, 1974.

Warburton, Clark. "Variations in Economic Growth and Banking Development in the U.S. from 1835 to 1885." Journal of Economic History, September 1958, pp. 283-97.

White, W. H. "The Flexibility of Anticyclical Monetary Policy." Review of Economics and Statistics 43 (1961).

Chapter 10

Bronfenbrenner, M. "Statistical Tests of Rival Monetary Rules." Journal of Political Economy 69 (1961):7.

_____. "Statistical Tests of Rival Monetary Rules: Quarterly Data Supplement." Journal of Political Economy 69 (1961):621.

Lindbeck, Assar. "Stabilization Policy in Open Economies with Endogenous Politicians." American Economic Review, May 1976, pp. 1-19.

Macesich, George. Geldopolitik in Einem Gemeinsamen Europaischen Markt. Baden-Baden: Nomos Verlagsgesellschaft, 1972.

_____. "Monetary Policy in Common Market Countries: Rules versus Discretion." Weltwirtschaftliches Archiv 108, no. 1 (1972):29-52.

Modigliani, Franco. "Some Empirical Tests of Monetary Management and of Rules versus Discretion." Journal of Political Economy 72 (1964):211.

Simons, Henry. "Rules versus Authorities in Monetary Policy." Journal of Political Economy, February 1936.

Tucker, Donald P. "Bronfenbrenner on Monetary Rules: A Comment." Journal of Political Economy 71 (1963):173.

Chapter 11

Bergsten, Fred C. and Cline, William R. "Increasing International Economic Interdependence: The Implications for

Research." American Economic Review 66, no. 2 (May 1976): 157.

Bilson, John F. O. "The Current Experience with Floating Exchange Rates: An Appraisal of the Monetary Approach." American Economic Review: Papers and Proceedings 68, no. 2 (May 1978):392-97.

Caves, Douglas and Feige, Edgar L. "Efficient Foreign Exchange Markets and the Monetary Approach to Exchange-Rate Determination." American Economic Review 70, no. 1 (March 1980): 120-34.

Dornbusch, Rudiger. Open Economy Macroeconomics. New York: Basic Books, 1980.

_____ and Fisher, Stanley. "Exchange Rates and the Current Account." American Economic Review 70, no. 5 (December 1980):960-71.

Frankel, Jeffrey A. "On the Mark: A Theory of Floating Exchange Rates Based on Real Interest Differentials." American Economic Review 69, no. 4 (September 1979):610-22.

Frenkel, Jacob A. "A Monetary Approach to the Exchange Rate: Doctrinal Aspects and Empirical Evidence." Scandinavian Journal of Economics 78, no. 2 (May 1976):200-24.

_____ and Johnson, Harry G., eds. The Monetary Approach to the Balance of Payments. London: George Allen and Unwin, 1978.

_____. "The Monetary Approach to the Balance of Payments: Essential Concepts and Historical Origins." In The Monetary Approach to the Balance of Payments, edited by Jacob A. Frenkel and Harry G. Johnson. London: George Allen and Unwin, 1978, p. 21.

Friedman, Milton. "The Case for Flexible Exchange Rates." In Essays in Positive Economics, edited by M. Friedman. Chicago: University of Chicago Press, 1953.

Frisch, Helmut. "Inflation Theory 1963-1975: A 'Second Generation Survey.'" Journal of Economic Literature 15, no. 4 (December 1977):1909.

Johnson, Harry G. "Monetary Approach to the Balance of Payments: A Nontechnical Guide." In The Contemporary International Economy: A Reader, edited by John Adams. New York: St. Martin's Press, 1979, p. 205.

Kemp, D. S. "A Monetary View of Balance of Payments." In The Monetary Approach to International Adjustment, edited by Bluford H. Putnam and D. Sykes Wilford. New York: Praeger, 1978.

King, David T., Putnam, Bluford H., and Wilford, D. Sykes. "A Currency Portfolio Approach to Exchange Rate Determination: Exchange Rate Stability and the Independence of Monetary Policy." In The Monetary Approach to International Adjustment, edited by Bluford H. Putnam and D. Sykes Wilford. New York: Praeger, 1978, p. 199.

Laursen, S. and Metzler, L. "Flexible Exchange Rates and the Theory of Employment." Review of Economics and Statistics 32 (1950):251-99.

Macesich, George. The International Monetary Economy and the Third World. New York: Praeger, 1981.

Miles, Marc A. "Currency Substitution: Perspective, Implementations, and Empirical Evidence." In The Monetary Approach to International Adjustment, edited by Bluford H. Putnam and D. Sykes Wilford. New York: Praeger, 1978, 173-74.

Mundell, R. A. International Economics. New York: Macmillan, 1968.

Parkin, N., Richards, I., and Zis, G. "The Determination and Control of the World Money Supply under Fixed Exchange Rates, 1961-71." The Manchester School 43 (September 1975): 293-316.

Putnam, Bluford H. and Wilford, D. Sykes, eds. The Monetary Approach to International Adjustment. New York: Praeger, 1978.

Sohmen, Egon. Flexible Exchange Rates. Chicago: University of Chicago Press, 1969.

Zecher, J. Richard. "Preface" to The Monetary Approach to International Adjustment, edited by Bluford H. Putnam and D. Sykes Wilford. New York: Praeger, 1978, pp. ix-x.

Chapter 12

Brzeski, A. "Forced-Draft Industrialization with Unlimited Supply of Money." In Money and Plan, edited by Gregory Grossman. Berkeley: University of California Press, 1968, p. 28.

Dimitrijević, D. and Macesich, George. Money and Finance in Contemporary Yugoslavia. New York: Praeger, 1973, Chapter 10.

Economist, January 28, 1978, pp. 91-93; November 29, 1980, p. 13; December 6, 1980, pp. 70-71.

Frankel, S. Herbert. Two Philosophies of Money: The Conflict of Trust and Authority. New York: St. Martin's Press, 1977, p. 78.

Frenkel, Jacob and Harry G. Johnson, eds. The Monetary Approach to the Balance of Payments. London: George Allen and Unwin, 1978.

Friedman, Milton. "A Biased Double Standard." Newsweek, January 12, 1981, p. 68.

____. "Marx and Money." Newsweek, October 27, 1980, p. 95.

____. "A Memorandum to the Fed." Wall Street Journal, January 30, 1981, p. 20.

____. "The Role of Monetary Policy." In The Optimum Quantity of Money and Other Essays, edited by Milton Friedman. Chicago: Aldine, 1969, p. 99.

____. Teorija Novca I Monetarna Politika (Theory of Money and Monetary Policy). Belgrade: RAD, 1973.

Grossman, Gregory, ed. Money and Plan. Berkeley: University of California Press, 1968, pp. 10-11.

Heller, Walter W. "What's Right with Economics." American Economic Review, March 1975, p. 5.

International Monetary Fund. The Monetary Approach to the Balance of Payments. Washington, D.C., 1977.

Laidler, David and Rowe, Nicholas. "Georg Simmel's Philosophy of Money: A Review Article for Economists." Journal of Economic Literature, March 1980, pp. 97-105.

Macesich, George. The International Monetary Economy and the Third World. New York: Praeger, 1981.

Robert, Dieter. Makroökonomische Konzeptionen in Meinungsstreit: zur Auseinandersetzung zwischen Monetaristen und Fiskalisten. Baden-Baden: Nomos Verlagsgesellschaft, 1978.

Stein, Jerome L., ed. Monetarism. Amsterdam: North-Holland, 1976.

Szeplaki, L. and Taylor, R. A. "Banking Credit and Monetary Indicators in Reformed Socialist Planning." Journal of Money, Credit, and Banking, August 1972, pp. 572-81.

Wiles, P. J. D. Economic Institutions Compared. New York: John Wiley, 1977, Chapters 12-14.

INDEX

Amsterdam Stock Exchange, 105

Argentina, 1, 209

Austrian school, 198

balance of payments, 12, 23, 134, 142, 159, 160, 167, 190

Bank Act of 1934, 86-87

Bank Act of 1970, 88

bank deposits, 76, 86-87, 89

Bank of Belgium, 104

Bank of Canada and monetary policy, 86-89

Bank of England, 13, 95, 135

Bank of France, 104, 107-08

Bank of Italy, 105, 109-11

Bank of the Netherlands, 105

Bank of Sweden, 93

Bank of Yugoslavia, National, 98-101

bank reserves, 39, 40, 41, 70, 71, 75-76, 86-87, 88

banks, 34-40, 70, 85-86, 89, 90, 93, 95, 97-98, 99, 104-05, 107, 108-11

Belgium, 101, 104, 106, 117-31, 136, 159-60, 169-71

Bhattacharya, B. B., 36, 41, 72, 80, 81

Brazil, 1, 209

Brunner, K., 36, 54, 58, 59, 60, 61, 62, 72, 73, 75, 76, 77, 78, 79, 80, 81

Brzeski, A., 208

Bundesbank, 104-05, 108-09

Cagan, Phillip, 66, 72, 73, 74, 75

Canada, 4, 85-89, 117-31, 135, 150-58, 169, 182

Cantillon, Richard, 11-12

cash balances, 5, 6, 34, 58, 122

chartered banks, 89

Chicago school, 192-93

Chile, 1, 209-10

China, 210

Chow, G. C., 65, 66

Christ, C. F., 45

Cooper, J. P., 36, 72, 79, 80, 81

Courchene, T. J., 64

currency, 37, 38

demand and supply of financial institutions, 15

deposits, 38

Dewald, W. G., 140, 141, 142

Dewald-Johnson Model, 125, 139-48

discretionary authority, 165

Dornbusch, Rudiger, 194

Econometric society, 72

economic system, 1, 85

Eisner, R., 52

elasticities, 117, 120-21, 128, 129

employment, 27, 134

estimates: of money demand function, 117; of money supply function, 125ff.

European Economic Community, 1, 85, 101-11, 137, 159-60, 168, 185

European Federal Reserve System, 103

European Monetary System
(EMS), 102, 103, 166

Fand, David, 72
Federal Republic of Germany,
101, 104-05, 108-09, 117-
31, 159-60, 165, 200, 201
Federal Reserve Act, 90
Federal Reserve Bank, 77
Federal Reserve Board, 90
Federal Reserve System, 20,
90-92, 103, 135, 164; and
banking organization, 90
Fischer, Stanley, 194
financial institutions and
economic development, 4,
16
fiscal policy, 24, 93
fixed exchange rates, 25,
134, 135, 191
flexible exchange rates, 26,
135, 159-60, 190-92
France, 16, 101, 104, 107-08,
117-31, 136, 169, 171, 199,
204
Frankel, Jeffrey A., 192-93
Frenkel, Jacob A., 188, 189
Friedman, Milton, 1, 3, 8,
12, 13, 30, 31, 32, 54, 62,
63, 64, 65, 66, 73, 74, 78,
79, 81, 132, 138, 139, 152,
153, 157, 189, 190, 209-10

Germany (see, Federal
Republic of Germany)
goals, 134
Goldberger, A. S., 116
Goldfeld, S., 36, 80, 81
Goldsmith, R. W., 52
Grossman, Gregory, 208
Gurley, J., 56

Hamburger, M. J., 65
Hansen, A., 80
Harberger, A. G., 66

Hayek, F. A., 13, 14
Heller, H. R., 64
Hicks, J. A., 80
high-powered money, 37, 38,
73-75, 190
Hume, David, 12

ideology, 1, 7, 23, 30, 208,
209-10
income, 8, 46, 47-48; expenditure theory, 2, 3, 4;
velocity of money, 3, 4,
58, 59, 60, 61, 131-32
Industrial Development Bank,
88
Industrial Revolution, 12
inflation, 3, 7, 12, 66
instruments of monetary
policy, 92-101
interest rate, 3, 6, 7, 35, 41,
45, 46, 47, 48, 49-50, 51,
52-53, 57, 64, 192
international Monetary Fund
(IMF), 1, 166, 168, 199,
200
investment, 2, 3
Italy, 101, 117-31, 159-60,
169, 173, 176

Japan, 1, 209
Johnson, Harry, 140, 141,
142, 188, 189

Karaken, John, 151
Kemmerer missions, 22
Keynes, J. M., 2, 12, 13, 31,
33, 34, 45, 47, 52, 61, 62,
139, 165, 189, 190
Keynesians, 45, 47, 51, 59,
60, 64, 138, 189, 192, 193
Khusro, A. M., 47
Kimball, Ralph C., 123
Kisselgoff, A., 45
Klein, L. R., 116
Kloek, T., 116

Laidler, D. , 53, 54, 64
Latane, H. A. , 45, 46, 47, 59
Law, John, 11
Lee, T. H. , 65
Lerner, Eugene, 66
limits to monetary policy, 137-38
liquidity preference, 2, 33, 34, 45, 46, 47, 62, 64; models, 45
liquidity trap, 51, 52
Liu, Fu-Chi, 72
Locke, John, 11
Luxembourg, 101, 117-31, 169

Marx, Karl, 209
Mayer, T. , 47, 48, 49, 50, 51, 52, 53
Mead, James, 188
Meigs, A. J. , 70
Meiselman, David, 3
Meltzer, A. , 36, 51, 53, 54, 55, 56, 57, 58, 59, 60, 61, 62, 64, 72, 73, 75, 76, 77, 78, 79, 80, 81
Mennes, L. B. M. , 116
Mill, John Stuart, 12
Modigliani, F. , 36, 79, 80, 81
monetarism, 188, 190
Monetarists, 31, 207
monetary: arrangements within the European Economic Community, 101; committee, 101; policy, 23, 24, 85, 104, 134-48, 150-60, 164-86, 192, 198; theory, 1, 2, 3, 4, 5-6, 8, 9, 11, 12, 15, 21, 40-41, 159, 164, 207-08
money: creation, 103; demand function, 32, 34, 35, 45, 46, 47, 48, 51, 52, 53, 55, 56, 57, 58, 59, 62, 63, 64, 65, 66, 115-25; effect on interest rates, 6; effect on

output, 5; market, 16-21; supply, 36, 37, 39, 52, 53, 70, 71, 72, 73, 76, 77, 79, 115, 125-31
Morrison, George, 72
multiple currencies under a specie standard and a unified currency system, 24
multiplier, 2, 3
Mundell, Robert, 188

National Bank of Belgium (see, Bank of Belgium)
National Bureau of Economic Research, 151
National Credit Bank, 107
National Pension Insurance Fund (NPIF), 94
Netherlands, 105, 117-31, 137, 169, 176
Netherlands Bank (see, Bank of the Netherlands)
New York Clearing House, 20
nonbank financial intermediaries, 89
nonlinear hypothesis, 77

Parkin, N. , 189
permanent income models, 8, 45, 53, 60, 61, 62-66, 81, 138
Phillips, C. A. , 75
Polak, J. J. , 70, 71
Poland, 208-09
political-administrative system, 165-66
Post Office Giro System, 106, 109
price level, 3, 11-12, 32, 34-35, 65
problems of independent monetary policy in common market countries, 23
Putnam, Bluford H. , 188

quantitative tests for rival
  monetary rules, 164-86,
  199; European experience
  1956-80, 169
quantity theory of money, 4,
  6, 7, 12, 31, 96, 189, 208

Rasche, R. H., 36, 79, 80, 81
rational expectations, 193-94
real bills, 2
Reuben, G. L., 140
Ricardo, David, 12
Richards, I., 189
role of money, 1-2

Schwartz, Anna J., 73, 74,
  78, 79, 152, 153
Selden, Richard, 66
Shapiro, H. T., 64
Shaw, E. S., 56, 58
Smith, P. E., 36, 79, 80
socioeconomic, legal, and
  political systems and monetary behavior, 21-23
Solow, Robert, 151
sovereignty, 103
Soviet Union, 22, 208
statistical tests, 115-17
Sweden, 1, 8, 85, 93-94, 135,
  169, 179

Teigen, R. L., 41, 65, 71,
  72, 78, 79, 80, 81
theoretical framework, 30
Tobin, James, 45, 48, 59, 72

unemployment, 13, 134, 197
United Kingdom, 1, 13, 15,
  85, 95-96, 117-31, 135-36,
  169, 176, 179, 204
United States, 1, 4, 8, 14,
  19, 85, 87, 90-93, 96,
  117-31, 135, 169, 182,
  204, 209

wealth models, 54-56, 58, 60
White, W. H., 70, 71, 151
Wilford, D. Sykes, 188
World War I, 13, 86, 153
World War II, 1, 19, 89, 157,
  166

Yugoslavia, 1, 8, 93, 96-101,
  160 169, 179, 206-07,
  209-10

Zecher, J. Richard, 188, 190
Zis, G., 189

ABOUT THE AUTHORS

GEORGE MACESICH is Professor of Economics and Director of the Center for Yugoslav-American Studies, Research, and Exchanges at Florida State University in Tallahassee. He received his Ph.D. in Economics from the University of Chicago. His books include Commercial Banking and Regional Development in the U.S., Yugoslavia: Theory and Practice of Development, Planning, Money in the European Common Market Setting, Money and Finance in Contemporary Yugoslavia, with D. Dimitrijević; and The International Monetary Economy and the Third World. He is also author of numerous articles in professional journals.

HUI-LIANG TSAI is Research Associate in the Center for Yugoslav-American Studies, Research, and Exchanges at Florida State University, Tallahassee. He received his Ph.D. in Economics from Florida State University. He is a regular contributor to professional journals.